CRITICAL ISSUES IN CURRICULUM

John Willinsky, EDITOR

Gender In/forms Curriculum:
From Enrichment to Transformation
Jane Gaskell and John Willinsky, Editors

Narrative in Teaching, Learning, and Research
Hunter McEwan and Kieran Egan, Editors

Sexuality and the Curriculum:
The Politics and Practices of Sexuality Education
James T. Sears, Editor

Understanding Curriculum as Phenomenological
and Deconstructed Text
William F. Pinar and William M. Reynolds, Editors

Reading and Writing the Self:
Autobiography in Education and the Curriculum
Robert J. Graham

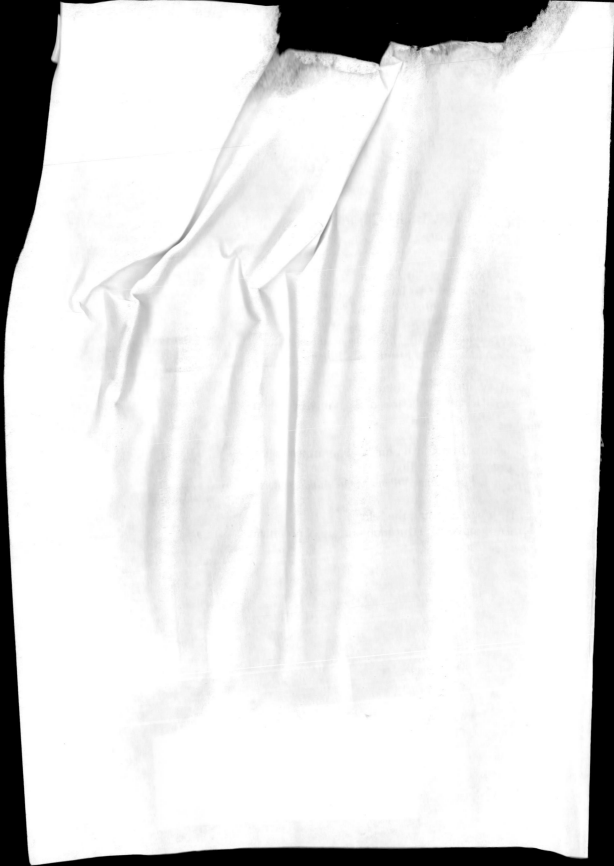

NARRATIVE IN TEACHING, LEARNING, AND RESEARCH

EDITED BY
HUNTER MCEWAN AND KIERAN EGAN

TEACHERS
COLLEGE
PRESS

Teachers College, Columbia University
New York and London

Published by Teachers College Press, 1234 Amsterdam Avenue, New York, NY 10027

Library of Congress Cataloging-in-Publication Data

Narrative in teaching, learning, and research / edited by Hunter
    McEwan and Kieran Egan.
        p.   cm. — (Critical issues in curriculum)
    Includes bibliographical references and index.
    ISBN 0-8077-3400-4. — ISBN 0-8077-3399-7 (pbk.)
    1. Storytelling. 2. Teaching. 3. Learning. 4. Narration
(Rhetoric) 5. Critical pedagogy. I. McEwan, Hunter. II. Egan,
Kieran. III. Series.
LB1042.N34   1995
371.3—dc20   94-33601

ISBN 0-8077-3399-7 (paper)
ISBN 0-8077-3400-4 (cloth)

Printed on acid-free paper

Manufactured in the United States of America

02 01 00 99 98 97 96 95   8 7 6 5 4 3 2 1

Contents

INTRODUCTION   vii
Hunter McEwan and Kieran Egan

Part I: The Place of Narrative in Teaching

CHAPTER 1   3
ON THE PLACE OF NARRATIVE IN TEACHING
Philip W. Jackson

CHAPTER 2   24
THE NARRATIVE NATURE OF PEDAGOGICAL CONTENT KNOWLEDGE
Sigrun Gudmundsdottir

CHAPTER 3   39
NARRATIVE LANDSCAPES AND THE MORAL IMAGINATION:
TAKING THE STORY TO HEART
Carol S. Witherell, with Hoan Tan Tran and John Othus

CHAPTER 4   50
REASON AND STORY IN WISE PRACTICE
Shirley Pendlebury

Part II: The Roles of Narrative in Learning

CHAPTER 5   69
RADICALIZING CHILDHOOD: THE MULTIVOCAL MIND
Brian Sutton-Smith

CHAPTER 6   91
LOOKING FOR MAGPIE: ANOTHER VOICE IN THE CLASSROOM
Vivian Gussin Paley

CHAPTER 7   100
THE ROLE OF NARRATIVE IN INTERPRETIVE DISCUSSION
Sophie Haroutunian-Gordon

CHAPTER 8   116
NARRATIVE AND LEARNING: A VOYAGE OF IMPLICATIONS
Kieran Egan

Part III: Narrative in the Study of Teaching and Learning

CHAPTER 9   127
WORKING WITH LIFE-HISTORY NARRATIVES
Michael Huberman

CHAPTER 10   166
NARRATIVE UNDERSTANDING IN THE STUDY OF TEACHING
Hunter McEwan

CHAPTER 11   184
TELLING TALES
Ivor Goodson and Rob Walker

CHAPTER 12   195
STORIES OF TEACHING AS TRAGEDY AND ROMANCE:
WHEN EXPERIENCE BECOMES TEXT
Robert J. Graham

CHAPTER 13   211
NARRATIVE RATIONALITY IN EDUCATIONAL RESEARCH
Nancy Zeller

ABOUT THE CONTRIBUTORS   227

INDEX   231

Introduction

I

We begin with Barbara Hardy's celebrated observation that we "dream in narrative, daydream in narrative, remember, anticipate, hope, despair, believe, doubt, plan, revise, criticize, construct, gossip, learn, hate and live by narrative" (1977, p. 13). The "turn to narrative" whose dramatic growth we have witnessed recently has been one of the more impressive shifts in the history of educational research. It is as though we are all learning, along with Robert Coles, "a respect for narrative as everyone's rock-bottom capacity, but also as the universal gift" (1989, p. 30). Narrative is a fundamental human capacity, and as such its role in education clearly merits attention.

So what is this narrative endowment that is so pervasive and so basic to our lives? Imagine one of the editors sitting down to work on this introduction (the invitation to imagine something is an inseparable part of the act of telling a story). He looks up from the papers in front of him to see the winter-flowering jasmine bright pink through the bare cherry tree. Closer to the house, the lilac buds are swelling, light green under a dull sky. Spring is coming.

This brief narrative sets a context. It has a subject, an "I" from whose perspective something is experienced and a certain meaning established (a perspective that we are more inclined to associate with the editor in Vancouver than the one in Hawaii). It possesses, albeit in an inchoate form, a structure out of which a more developed pattern may emerge. And, crucially, this pattern of symbols carries an affective force, however slight: one that we associate with the coming of spring. Further, it reflects from this familiar natural event a rhythm on which the affective movement of the narrative is appended. A familiar human emotion is aroused and set in harmony with the rhythm of nature. In narratives, whatever their subject, the rhythms of human feelings are never entirely submerged.

In form, a narrative is basically extended language configured in such a way that its earlier embodiment in life becomes revealed. An extensive list is not a narrative. What distinguishes the narrative is that it takes shape, in however attenuated a form, as a rhythm that ultimately springs from patterns implicit in human life and action. A list merely supplies the parts; a narrative reflects a structural symmetry between its contents and human life. As Paul Ricouer's (1984) work suggests, there is no clear disjunction between art on the one hand and life on the other, or between stories and the events that the stories are supposed to describe.

In Alasdair MacIntyre's words: "It is not just that poems and sagas narrate what happens to men and women, but that in their narrative form poems and sagas capture a form that was already present in the lives which they relate" (1981, p. 117). A narrative, and that particular form of narrative that we call a story, deals not just in facts or ideas or theories, or even dreams, fears, and hopes, but in facts, theories, and dreams from the perspective of someone's life and in the context of someone's emotions. It is helpful to remember that all the knowledge we have has been gained in the context of someone's life, as a product of someone's hopes, fears, and dreams. By focusing on narrative in education we hope to find ways of returning to the content of the curriculum, and to other features of teaching and learning, the human emotions that alone can give them adequate meaning and fulfillment.

As David Lodge observes, "Narrative is one of the fundamental sensemaking operations of the mind, and would appear to be both peculiar to and universal throughout humanity" (1990, p. 141). There is not much that is peculiar to and universal among human beings. This rock-bottom, universal characteristic, therefore, seems a most worthwhile candidate for educationalists' continued attention.

This volume, then, is a result of our invitation to a number of researchers and theorists in the field of education to explore aspects of this turn to narrative as they apply to the study of teaching and learning. Their work represents no unified theory of narrative in education; for, indeed, even if this task were possible, it is clearly too soon to expect such a result. Our purpose has been rather to offer an opportunity for these authors to present their own perspectives on narrative and narrative thought as it applies to an understanding of how teachers teach and learners learn. These essays, therefore, should be read as a series of progress reports that will help, first, to clarify some of the theoretical issues in the study of narrative in teaching and learning, and, second, to identify some of the opportunities and applications that such a study implies for educational practice.

Before we discuss the individual contributions to this volume, however, we would like to provide a brief map of the territory of narrative as it applies to education. We hope that this sketch of the terrain will provide some direction for the reader in what has become a rather disorienting intellectual milieu. The issues that we address, though by no means definitive, may be of use as landmarks or navigational aids to help locate a number of identifiable issues within the study of narrative, and thus help to clarify the concept for the reader and provide a number of perspectives from which to understand the functioning of narrative in teaching and learning.

II

The preceding discussion raised the vital link that exists between narrative form and human action. In addition, we alluded to the fundamental importance of narrative to understanding the way that the human mind works. In this section we wish to explore, more particularly, the interesting coincidence of the story form with educational thought and practices. We have observed that two interrelated kinds of story make an especially important contribution to educational discourse.

First, narrative structure is a feature of accounts of the history of human consciousness as such—the stories by which we relate in general terms the educational journey of the human species and the changes that have marked our development as thinking beings. These are the stories of the growth of knowledge, the discovery of new ideas and the exploratory voyages that culminate in our modern conceptions of science, the arts, and the humanities and their deployment in human projects and practices. Often these stories form subplots within even more all-encompassing sets of stories that philosophers are particularly adept at constructing: the so-called "grand narratives." Hegel's grand narrative of the triumphal march of Reason is an example of such a narrative. And Plato's Allegory of the Cave or Rousseau's Romantic conception of the history of human consciousness can also be read as a sort of parable of the direction and end point of our human strivings to gain knowledge. Sometimes these stories may be told as grand narratives of human progress and perfectibility (Condorcet, Macaulay, Marx, Hegel); and sometimes, of decline and the loss of being (Spengler, Heidegger, Rousseau). More recent versions of the structure of human history (Gellner, 1988) may be viewed as efforts to give expression to a more coherent vision of the patterns that are already present in human thought and action. Gellner views this project of bringing hidden narratives to the surface as an essential task: "those who spurn philosophical history are slaves of defunct thinkers and unexamined theories" (p. 12). Such a narrative study of the structure of human history provides a framework for understanding individual narrative histories through which cultures come into being, flourish, and fade.

Second, at the level of the individual consciousness, the idea of the educated person brings to mind stories of personal growth from infancy, through youth and adulthood, to sagacious old age. This latter group of stories is most frequently represented in literature rather than in the history of ideas. These stories make up the wealth of moral tales: autobiographies, confessions, biographies, case studies, bildungsroman, fables, and any number of other didactic forms within the arts and popular culture.

Often, these stories of individual educational development are framed by or pay tacit tribute to one or other of these "grand narratives." Thus we can read Augustine's *Confessions*, or Rousseau's, not merely as the story of a particular education but as somehow emblematic of the growth of human consciousness as a whole and full of prophetic wisdom about its possibilities.

One influential version of this kind of thinking, in which narrative plays a decisive role, is represented in Dewey's philosophy of education. The central insight of this approach is that each learner must reconstruct the periods, phases, or levels of the growth of human mentality. This is not to say that each learner must rediscover or live through the same invariant sequence of events or narrative history that the originators of these ideas experienced. Such a position represents a naive recapitulationist theory, the subject of Dewey's own devastating criticism (1916/1966, p. 71). A reconstructionist approach, rather, points to the forms of consciousness present in all developed thought and identifies certain patterns as characteristic of a particular epoch in its growth. A parallel sequence is held to apply to different phases in the formal development of individual consciousness. Thus, for example, the forms of consciousness that we identify with oral societies have an important function to play in the growth of literacy in modern society. The later stages of consciousness depend on the earlier ones for their development, not just in the history of the growth of mind but also in the mind of each learner.

Because the story form is enormously important in oral cultures, and to the extent that our modern literate culture retains oral practices, narrative continues to play a vital foundational role in teaching and learning. A primary, undifferentiated narrative quality of thought is common to the beginner as well as to the inhabitants of oral cultures, whose systems of thought retain a multipurpose, multi-stranded quality as opposed to the neat and logical division of labor and functions characteristic of specialized work and instrumental reason (Gellner, 1988, pp. 39–53). As Plato tells us, stories form the natural food of the young. And it is also true that stories form the intellectual and practical nourishment of oral cultures.

One influential account of the role that narrative plays in learning derives from the work of James Britton and other members of the "London School," a group of educational linguists who have tirelessly promoted the vital place that oral language processes play in learning across the curriculum (Britton, 1970; Rosen, 1985). In the view of this group, narrative is immanent in ordinary speech and expressive discourse. It represents a primary or privileged form. In Barbara Hardy's definition: "Narrative . . . is not to be regarded as an aesthetic invention used by artists to control, manipulate, and order experience, but as a primary act of mind transferred to art from life" (1977, p. 12). Narrative discourse, which is expressive, exploratory, and conducted in the idiom of informal conversation, is not just a manner of speaking but foundational to learning as a whole. Thus, the capacity to narrate is a condition of learning the more developed forms of thought and writing. We cannot learn these specialized genres, such as the formal essay or scientific report, if we do not first engage the subject through narrative. And it is through informal narrative discussions that the qualities inherent in narrative discourse find employment. Informal talk is not just idle chatter but a vitally important stage in developing our understanding of topics that are new to us. It allows us to put ideas into our own words. Our capacity to tell a story, then, is not something that we wish to lose. It is more than just a feature of our childhood because it plays a vital role in adult consciousness and is most active when we begin to learn something new. To put it as simply and straightforwardly as possible, we begin to learn something new with a story in mind.

It may, of course, seem strange to write about narrative and story as features of informal speech, especially considering the emphasis that our discussion has placed on formal or structural considerations. But to define story and narrative in a purely formal way places unreasonable limits on our understanding of these terms. Function also matters. And it is the similarity in function between narrative and informal discourse that Britton identifies as important. Jerome Bruner employs the metaphor of a landscape in a helpful way to explain how speech and story share narrative functions. "Story," he writes, "must construct two landscapes simultaneously" (1986, p. 14)—the outer landscape of action and the inner one of thought and intention. Although we can make this distinction between an inner and outer landscape, each part is in fact always present in narrative. Narrative language allows us to delve beneath the outward show of human behavior to explore the thoughts, feelings, and intentions of agents. Narrative is "thick description" in the sense that Clifford Geertz (1973) uses the phrase. And as Alasdair MacIntyre writes: "Narrative history of a certain kind turns out to be the basic and essential genre for the characterization of human actions" (1981, p. 208). The gifted novelist takes to a sublime level of structural sophistication the capacity inherent in ordinary speech to portray human actions, thoughts, feelings, and intentions. We share with the great storytellers, even at the less exalted level of informal talk, the rock-bottom gift of narrative.

The importance of the above arguments to the current debate about the study of teaching and learning is that they provide a rationale for the "turn to narrative" in education. Walter Benjamin (1968) in his celebrated essay on Nikolai Leskow, "The Storyteller," observed somewhat sadly the decline of the storyteller as a present force in the modern world. "He has become something remote from us and something that is getting even more distant" (p. 83). For Benjamin, as well as for many other recent critics of the modern world's haste to reduce everything to technique and machinelike systematicity, the storyteller is a victim of an age that values nonnarrative discourse as a measure of sophistication in rationality, as opposed to the mere "entertainment value" that stories possess. Truth, for the tireless promoters of modernity and technical rationality, is measured in terms of standard procedures that demand an icy, critical stare at the object of study. In contrast, the story form invites the listener or reader to suspend skepticism and embrace the narrative flow of events as an authentic exploration of experience from a particular perspective. The decline of the storyteller, or narrator, may be read as a symptom of the desire for a certain kind of objectivity, the application of a neutral, unbiased point of view from which to gauge the veracity of knowledge claims. Art, religion, morals, and even philosophy are suspected of not measuring up to the dictates of such thoroughgoing positivism. But in forging ahead with this program, we forget the power of narrative to inform and instruct. In an unforgettable phrase, Milan Kundera (1988) describes one effect of this neglect of narrative as "the depreciated legacy of Cervantes." We have forgotten how magnificently the great novelists have contributed to our understanding of ourselves, and of the complex nature of our humanity. Narrative, it seems, both as a way of knowing and as a way of organizing and communicating experience, has become, if not lost, at least of less importance than it ought to be. The return to narrative suggests that we reconsider the value of the form and function of stories in all areas of human life, but especially in education, where a pervasive nonnarrative and behaviorist chill has prevailed. Perhaps the turn to narrative signals a reversal of this decline. In the past few years, we have been witness to a resurgence of professional and semiprofessional storytellers, which may be a reason for hope, and an indication that things are changing for the better.

But though the story form contributes to our self-understanding, it may just as easily contribute to self-deception. There is a dark side to the functioning of narrative, as our proneness to the seductive power of myths and ideologies suggests. Thus, the question of narrative content arises as a problematic dimension in any discussion of narrative in education, especially when they are used to distort or conceal other perspectives and to promote or legitimate one point of view to the detriment of others. Critical theorists and poststructuralists have been especially persuasive in demonstrating this power of narratives to shape our consciousness and direct the operations of our educational institutions.

In a less critical vein, recent attempts to construct a narrative study of education have an encouragingly multidisciplinary, multicultural ring to them. Feminist scholars, for example, have been amongst the foremost adherents of accounts of narrative rationality and have argued persuasively against the suppression of narrative as a way of knowing. They have identified narrative as an important expression of distinctively feminine values that form connections rather than make divisions, and work collaboratively rather than in hierarchically ordered systems and organizations. Philosophers, too, like Alasdair MacIntyre (1981), Charles Taylor (1989), and Paul Ricouer (1984) have made narrative thought and story an essential part of our cognitive and affective life; one that is firmly connected to ethics and practical affairs. Indeed, if we follow recent scholarship in this matter, it becomes clear that narrative is essential to the purpose of communicating who we are, what we do, how we feel, and why we ought to follow some course of action rather than another. Taylor (1989) has argued that to a large degree, and especially in the resolution of disagreement, practical reasoning is narrative in form. And finally, postmodern analyses of our educational processes and institutions have brought to the surface the implicit narratives that underlie them and provide legitimacy for their operations.

These conclusions cannot fail to resonate with educational researchers and policy makers who are interested in studying teaching and learning, and implementing informed educational change. Stories, it would seem, have a vital role to play in helping us to understand the curriculum, the practices of teachers, the processes of learning, the rational resolution of educational issues, and the matter of practicing how to teach in informed and sensitive ways.

To summarize, narratives form a framework within which our discourses about human thought and possibility evolve, and they provide the structure and functional backbone for very specific explanations of this or that educational practice. They contribute to our capacity to deliberate about educational issues and problems. In addition, since the function of narrative is to make our actions intelligible to ourselves as well as to others, narrative discourse is essential to our efforts to understand teaching and learning. We need to learn more about narrative and the role of stories in education, not less.

III

The following essays, we believe, will offer some needed material on narrative for those who wish to discover its value and applications in teaching and learning. We have divided the set of essays into three parts. The first looks at the roles of narrative in the practice of teaching. This topic recurs in essays in other sections, as might be expected, but in this first part a set of implications for the practice of teaching are explored. That teachers use narrative as fundamental to their ordering and communication of content suggests that a better understanding of narrative may give us clues to better teaching practice. It is not coincidental that we most commonly recognize good teaching in the imaginative hold the narratively-ordered content has over students' attention. The essays in this first section consider the use of story structures in organizing teaching and curriculum content, and also consider moral and affective features of teaching that are brought to the fore when narrative is the focus. Throughout the essays in the book the affective and the moral find a more prominent place than has been common in research that has focused on a relatively narrow range of cognitive skills. As that kind of research very largely set the agenda in the past, the narrative turn is significant in bringing back toward the center of our attention features of human life that have been somewhat neglected in educational research.

The second section considers some implications of narrative for our view of the learner. If the mind is, to quote another contributor, a "narrative concern," and if, as Britton (1970, p. 165) asserts, "narrative speech constitutes an important stage in learning to write," then a renewed concern with narrative brings to the fore features of children's thinking and learning that have also tended to be somewhat neglected in more traditional research. These features of children's thinking are, the essays show, very significant. These explorations open up a range of children's narrative capacities that points to little-attended-to learning principles with significant implications for both teaching practice and the curriculum. They lead us beyond simplistic characterizations of children as "concrete" thinkers whose cognition is radically different from that of adults, and they give us clues about engaging the imaginations of children from underprivileged backgrounds in educational activities usually inaccessible to them. Focus on narrative tends to expose learning processes often ignored when we are encouraged to research a relatively narrow range of cognitive skills.

The final section details the rich array of possibilities that narrative has opened up for the study of teaching, and the direct implications this research yields to teaching practice. The essays explore the use of narrative as a means of empowering teachers to reflect on, enlarge upon, and, at the same time, enrich their understanding of their own practice. They explain the role of narrative in helping researchers gain a more complex understanding of teaching. They describe in detail the power of the story form and other rhetorical strategies to elaborate on the meaning of teaching experience and communicate it more richly to others. Various essays elaborate methods for realizing the value of oral and written narratives for reconstructing pedagogic experience and for making it accessible to reflection.

And finally, these essays enable us to understand the complex mental life of the teacher, not bound within the narrow confines of instrumental conceptions of thought and action, but conceived more fruitfully in comparison with the storyteller and artist, in whose lives imagination and creative energy play an important part.

In sum, these essays suggest a rich array of directions in which narrative is helping us to gain a better understanding of teaching, opening up new avenues of research, and pointing towards new prescriptions for improved practice. The topic of narrative in teaching and learning is of widespread current concern in educational research as is readily apparent from the international representation of authors in this volume. And, as several of our contributors demonstrate, it is beginning to have an impact on the practice of teaching.

REFERENCES

Benjamin, W. (1968). The storyteller. In H. Arendt (Ed.), *Illuminations* (pp. 83–109). New York: Harcourt, Brace & World.

Britton, J. (1970). *Language and learning*. Harmondsworth, UK: Penguin.

Bruner, J. (1986). *Actual minds, possible worlds*. Cambridge, MA: Harvard University Press.

Coles, R. (1989). *The call of stories: Teaching and the moral imagination*. Boston: Houghton Mifflin.

Dewey, J. (1916/1966). *Democracy and education*. New York: Free Press.

Geertz, C. (1973). Thick description: Towards an interpretive theory of culture. In *The interpretation of cultures* (pp. 3–30). New York: Basic Books.

Gellner, E. (1988). *Plough, book, and sword: The structure of human history*. London: Collins Harvill.

Hardy, B. (1977). Narrative as a primary act of mind. In M. Meek, A. Warlow, & G. Barton (Eds.), *The cool web* (pp. 12–33). London: Bodley Head.

Kundera, M. (1988). *The art of the novel*. New York: Grove Press.

Lodge, D. (1990). Narration with words. In H. Barlow, C. Blakemore, & M. Weston-Smith (Eds.), *Images and understanding* (pp. 141–153). Cambridge, UK: Cambridge University Press.

MacIntryre, A. (1981). *After virtue* (2nd ed.). Notre Dame, IN: University of Notre Dame Press.

Ricouer, P. (1984). *Time and narrative* (K. McLaughlin & D. Pellauer, Trans.). Chicago: University of Chicago Press.

Rosen, H. (1985). *Stories and meaning*. Sheffield, UK: National Association for the Teaching of English.

Taylor, C. (1989). *Sources of the self: The making of the modern identity*. Cambridge, MA: Harvard University Press.

PART I

THE PLACE OF NARRATIVE IN TEACHING

CHAPTER 1

On the Place of Narrative in Teaching

Philip W. Jackson

Students of all ages spend a lot of time listening to stories in school. Except for the very youngest and the most severely retarded, they also spend a lot of time reading stories on their own, sometimes voluntarily but more often because they are required to do so. Moreover, these listening and reading activities are frequently but the beginning phases of a class's encounter with a particular narrative. Next come discussions in which teacher and students scrutinize the story more carefully, dispelling ambiguities, analyzing plot and character, evaluating the story's worth, and so forth. Quizzes sometimes follow, as do writing assignments designed to find out how well the students understood and remembered what they heard or read.

In what school subjects do these formal encounters with stories take place? Foremost in history and literature, certainly, subjects whose content is essentially narrative in structure. But stories are prominent elsewhere in the curriculum as well. Teachers of reading, which would include those who teach the reading of foreign languages, rely upon them, as do teachers of social studies, the sciences, and the arts. In fact there is probably not a single school subject in which stories play no part at all. For even when the material being taught is not itself a story, the lesson usually includes a number of narrative segments all the same. These take the form of jokes, recollections, testimony, anecdotes, illustrations, examples, and more. Indeed, it is hard to imagine a lesson totally devoid of narrative in one form or another.

This state of affairs should not surprise us, given the prominence of stories in our lives. Indeed, it would be strange were it otherwise. "Man lives surrounded by his stories and the stories of others," Sartre tells us, "he sees everything that happens to him through them, and he tries to live his

An earlier version of this essay, using the same title, appeared in *Talks to teachers: A festschrift for N. L. Gage*, D. C. Berliner & B. V. Rosenshine, Eds. (New York: Random House, 1987).

life as if he were recounting it" (Sartre, 1965, p. 61). What this means is that we rarely can get through a day, hardly even an hour, without either hearing or reading a story in whole or part or telling one to someone else. This condition of being surrounded by stories no matter where we turn may make their prominence in school affairs seem rather unnoteworthy. What changes that is the presumption of their educational value. Unlike many of the stories we meet elsewhere, those we read and hear in school are usually designed to do us good. The assumption is that we will be better off for having heard or read them, changed in ways that are both beneficial and enduring. We seldom expect the same of most of the stories that we casually encounter elsewhere. What we usually insist upon instead is that they be entertaining. The latter is certainly true of most of the stories on television, for example, and the same holds for the other mass media, including the popular press. Of course, the stories studied in school can be entertaining as well as educational—many obviously are—but, as a general rule, the primary reason for requiring students to study them is the presumption of their contributing to some lasting good.

How do stories educate? What "lasting good" do we credit them with helping to produce? Historically, educators have offered two quite different answers to those questions. One answer says that the educative function of stories is chiefly to equip students with knowledge that will later prove to be useful. The other posits the possibility of using them to achieve deeper and more profound educational goals, ones having little to do with the acquisition of knowledge per se.

What might these deeper educational purposes of storytelling and storyreading be said to be? The answer to that question is not easy to give, but one thing seems certain—it has to do with *what we want students to be like as human beings*, that is, the attributes we expect them to possess when they finish school, above and beyond what we want them to *know*. These attributes would include the values we want them to hold, the characteristic traits we want them to exhibit, the views of the world and of themselves we want them to cultivate, and so forth.

Of those two dominant reasons for our paying so much attention to stories in school, the first requires little in the way of explication, for it accords well with the popular view of school as a place where one acquires many forms of useful knowledge. Yet, though it may be quite conventional, this view is by no means free of controversy, as we shall presently see. The second answer poses more problems than the first, not because it is any less understandable in an abstract sense, but simply because it deals with educational goals that are themselves hard to pin down, as are the criteria for their attainment and the procedures by which they are most effectively attained.

These two views of the educational value of stories comprise the bulk of the exposition to follow. After examining each view in some detail, I shall introduce a concrete example of a teacher making use of a story in a manner that looks as though he is trying to effect some kind of a change in the attitude or character of those present. The teacher is Socrates as depicted in the closing scene of Plato's *Gorgias* (1960). His introduction of narration in that episode is instructive in several ways. It prompts us to think about the uncertainty associated with the educational use of stories, particularly when they are employed for what might be thought of as moral or ethical purposes. It also raises questions about how purposeful a teacher's use of stories must actually be.

THE EPISTEMOLOGICAL FUNCTION OF STORIES

By far the most obvious reason for requiring students of all ages to study stories of one kind or another in school is because so many of those stories contain knowledge that is readily put to use in the world outside. Indeed, in many instances the stories do not simply *contain* knowledge, *they are themselves the knowledge we want students to possess.* As a shorthand way of referring to this use of stories, let us call it their "epistemological function." "To be a participant in a culture," the philosopher Richard Kuhns asserts, "is, by definition, to have experience of the community established by literary statements" (Kuhns, 1974, p. 5). What Kuhns seemingly means is that our sense of being part of a community is established, at least in part, by our shared *knowledge* of a set of well-known stories. Lacking that knowledge, a person is unable to participate fully in the social community to which he or she belongs.

As a crude test of Kuhns's claim, all we need do is to name two or three of the best known stories within our own culture, either fictional or true, and then try to imagine what it would be like for a person to be without that knowledge in today's world. Would an American man who knew nothing, say, of the story of Adam and Eve, the story of Lincoln's life and assassination, and the story of World War II be in any way handicapped by his ignorance? I find it hard to imagine him not being at least inconvenienced by such a deficiency. To begin with, he presumably would not know what people were talking about when they referred to those events, either directly or indirectly. How often might that happen? There is no way of telling, of course, for the answer would obviously depend on the person, his line of work, his social acquaintances, and so forth. However, the canonical preeminence of each of these stories within the culture at large allows us to predict that no one could manage to escape them for long.

More importantly, however, a person who was completely without knowledge of those three stories would also lack the understanding each of them gives to related events and to the more broadly encompassing stories in which each is embedded. For example, one who knows nothing of Adam and Eve likely knows nothing of the Bible as a whole. Someone who has never heard of Abraham Lincoln is certain to have a very incomplete knowledge of the Civil War, if he or she knows anything about it at all. A person lacking knowledge of World War II would certainly have difficulty understanding the state of the world today. And so it would go. Other untoward consequences of such calamitous ignorance are easily imagined.

How many stories are like that? How many must we know on penalty of suffering severe social discomfort of one kind or another? "Scores," would be a reasonable guess. "Hundreds," might be closer to the mark. What portion of that number are first encountered in schools and perhaps only there? No one can say for sure, but the percentage has to be large. Where else but in school do most people first hear of such well-known characters as Columbus, Goldilocks and the Three Bears, Huck Finn, Hamlet, Hitler, Snow White, and Omar Khayyam—each embedded in its own story? And what of the stories of how the earth was formed, how the midwest was settled, how the atom bomb came to be dropped, and how the nation of Israel came into being? These too are tales first heard by most of us during our early years of schooling.

As commonsensical as it might appear, the epistemological function of stories provides plenty of room for argument. One source of disagreement arises over which stories should be taught. Should every school child in America be introduced to the story of Abraham Lincoln? What of Adam and Eve? And how about the stories of Shakespeare? Though all three of those selections may sound conventional enough and, therefore, quite suitable to most Americans, the likelihood of them arousing controversy is by no means absent. Schools in certain sections of the country might not look as kindly on the story of Lincoln as would schools elsewhere. Some people might object to the story of Adam and Eve on religious grounds. Even the stories of Shakespeare might be objected to on utilitarian grounds, the argument being that only students who are going on to college need be familiar with them.

Controversy over which stories to include in the curriculum and which to leave out is but one form of uncertainty associated with the epistemological function of narration. When the broader question of what knowledge is of most worth is raised, stories, even ones as well-known as those that have been mentioned, do not always fare well. The person unable to read or write or figure, or who lacks what today are sometimes called "marketable skills," is looked upon by many as being far worse off from the standpoint of getting by in our society than is one whose only deficiency is lack of knowledge of our country's history, let's say, or of the plot of this or that Shakespearean play.

What this means, as teachers of the humanities in many of our colleges and universities have known for some time and as teachers within our public schools are lately coming to find out, is that those school subjects in which narratives predominate are looked upon by some people, perhaps even the majority of our citizens, as less essential and hence less important than are some of the more skill-oriented subjects. Indeed, in many of our inner city schools—especially those whose teachers and administrators have espoused the so-called "back-to-basics" movement—humanistically-oriented studies, which rely heavily on narration, are consciously de-emphasized if not totally ignored. As the Report of the Commission on Humanities pointed out some years back, "wherever basic education concentrates exclusively on the three R's, or whenever academic achievement is reduced to what can be measured by standardized testing, the humanities are likely to be misunderstood as expendable frills" (Report, 1980, p. 28).

The Report's point about standardized testing brings us to yet a third difficulty confronting the defense of stories as knowledge. This one has to do with the amount of detail in which the stories taught in school are to be presented and remembered. One or two brief examples should suffice to convey a sense of the problem. Suppose all a person knew of the biblical story of Adam and Eve was that the Bible presents them as being the first man and woman, that Eve was tempted by the serpent to eat of the forbidden fruit of the Tree of Knowledge, which she also gave to Adam, and that the two of them were expelled by God from the Garden of Eden. Would that not be enough to get by in most of life's situations in which knowledge of that famous tale is called for? Or, take as another example, the story of Lincoln and his assassination. Suppose one knew that Lincoln was a boy of the plains who became president and led the northern states in a civil war against slavery before he was assassinated while attending a theatrical performance. What more does one need to know in order to earn at least a passing grade on whatever "tests" about Lincoln might come up in the course of a lifetime?

Though not themselves conclusive, these two brief examples are certainly suggestive. They hint at a conclusion whose pedagogical consequences are enough to make most educators shudder. For the truth seems to be that from a purely epistemological point of view we can commonly make do with very skimpy knowledge indeed of even the most widely propagated stories. The bare bones of plot and character are all we usually need to know. From there it is only a step to the question: Why teach any more than the bare bones to start with?

To this point we have examined three objections to arguments on behalf of the epistemological function of the stories taught in school. These are: (1) the possibility of disagreement over which stories are important enough to be taught and which are not; (2) the insistence that other educational objectives have a higher priority than those requiring students to hear and read stories; and (3) the observation that from a purely utilitarian point of view most of us probably do not need to remember much about the stories we have been taught, which raises the question of whether we needed to know more than that to start with. How badly do these three objections damage the case for the defense?

To begin, they do not affect the initial assertion on behalf of including stories within the curriculum, namely, that a person who lacked knowledge of a fair number of such stories would be seriously handicapped for life. The fact that there may be disagreement over which stories are important and which are not does nothing to weaken the claim that most of us need to possess at least a rudimentary knowledge of such tales in order to be considered "culturally literate." It also does nothing to contradict the assertion that school is where most of us are introduced to such knowledge.

The contention that there are more important things to learn in school than stories—the Three R's, for instance—does constitute an attack upon the educational worth of narration in general. The assault, however, is indirect and somewhat ineffectual. Unless accompanied by a claim that the so-called "basics" are *all* that should be learned in school, a position which few defenders of the back-to-basics movement are willing to support, it leaves open the possibility of finding room for stories within the curriculum, perhaps even ample room, once the basics have been taken care of.

The assertion that plot summaries and outlines are all one needs to know about most stories may sound reasonable enough so long as we stick with the epistemological function of narration and do not ask what else stories might do besides provide us with useful knowledge. But even here there are difficulties. What's wrong with such a *Reader's Digest* point of view? For one thing, it is by no means obvious that people actually do make use of no more than fragmentary knowledge of the stories they have heard and studied. The claim that they do so may make sense as a hypothesis but it lacks empirical verification. Furthermore, there are a variety of reasons why students may need to study material in greater detail than they will be called upon to recall at some later date. Perhaps we more easily retain the key points of stories that we have heard or read in full. Perhaps hearing or reading the whole story contributes crucially to the motivation required to undertake the task of remembering. Other possibilities of this kind would have to be investigated before we could say for certain that the study of detailed and complete stories seems totally unnecessary from a purely epistemological point of view.

However, when it comes to defending the place of stories in the school curriculum there are other considerations as well. Chief among them are arguments having to do with what stories do for us *beyond* providing information that might later prove to be useful. What other purpose might stories have from an educational point of view? A preliminary answer to that question has already been given. Stories, we noted, are often credited with changing us in ways that have relatively little to do with knowledge per se. They leave us with altered states of consciousness, new perspectives, changed outlooks, and more. They help to create new appetites and interests. They gladden and sadden, inspire and instruct. They acquaint us with aspects of life that had been previously unknown. In short, they *transform* us, alter us as individuals. Some of the forms these alterations may take and the dynamics of their accomplishment are the topics to which we now turn.

THE TRANSFORMATIVE FUNCTION OF STORIES

The most rudimentary of all stories designed to *transform*, as opposed to *inform*, must surely be the fable. Consider, for example, the ancient stories of the "Tortoise and the Hare" or the "Fox and the Grapes," each with its tacked-on moral. Why introduce either one to a classroom full of 10-year-olds? The answer is obvious. The chief reason for doing so is to suggest to the youthful listeners that one way of behaving is more prudent than another. The fable, in other words, resembles a fancy piece of embroidery whose ornamental stitching embellishes a simple moral message. The hope is that the message will not simply be heard and understood but will be taken to heart. At the other extreme of complexity among stories intended to transform us are religious narratives, which purport to convey not simply an isolated moral message but something more akin to a tradition, a total way of life. Here is how one modern theologian addresses the centrality of narrative within Christianity:

> The nature of Christian ethics is determined by the fact that Christian convictions take the form of a story, or perhaps better, a set of stories that constitutes a tradition, which in turn creates and forms a community. Christian ethics does not begin by emphasizing rules or principles, but by calling our attention to a narrative that tells of God's dealing with creation. . . . My contention is that the narrative mode is neither incidental nor accidental to Christian belief. There is no more fundamental way to talk of God than in a story. (Hauerwas, 1983, pp. 24–25)

Whether or not we accept Hauerwas' claim about the essential nature of narration within Christianity, we hardly can deny that most religions do indeed have one or more sacred texts whose narrative content is thought to be both morally and intellectually enlightening. The way those stories are to be taken, whether as literally true or as fictive constructions—albeit divinely inspired, perhaps—varies considerably from one religious group to another and even, where permitted, from one member of the congregation to another. However, insofar as their transformative power is concerned, what is important about them has less to do with their literal truth than with their capacity to arouse allegiance and commitment among those whose religious views they shape.

Hauerwas tells us that the set of stories within Christianity "constitutes a tradition, which in turn creates and forms a community." How does that happen? How does a set of stories constitute a tradition? It does so, one might imagine, by being passed along from generation to generation, by being pored over word by word and studied with loving care, often to the point of memorization. It does so by becoming so firmly embedded in the collective consciousness and the way of life of a group of people that, as Hauerwas says, it actually creates and forms them into a community. In short, religions and their stories transform us by becoming "ours" and we, by subscribing to what they tell us, become "theirs."

If an isolated Aesop fable stands for the simplest example of a story being employed for transformative ends, and an entire religious text—such as the Koran or the Hebrew or Greek Bible—stands for the most complex, what lies between? A complete answer would have to take in all the different forms of narration that convey a moral of any kind. The latter would include most myths, fairy tales, and biographies, certainly. They would also include stories that might have a corrupting influence on those who read or listen to them. For nothing about the transformative power of narration limits it to being positive in its effect. Other narrative forms, such as histories and political treatises, may be powerfully transformative as well. Consider, as an instance, the testimony of William H. McNeill, an historian, describing his own encounter, some 45 years earlier, with the writings of fellow historian, Arnold J. Toynbee:

> Only two or three times in my life have I been transported by reading a work of intellectual discourse. It often happens that imaginative literature can do this by inviting the reader to identify himself with characters in a poem, play or novel. My reading of Toynbee was that kind of experience. But on this occasion I identified with another person's ideas, expressed abstractly and without the mediation of imaginary human characters. Nevertheless, for a while his thoughts were my thoughts—or so it seemed. Afterward, letdown; more mundane experience flowed in; differences of outlook and sensibility obtruded; questions arose for me that Toynbee had not touched on. But the moment of transport left its mark, as rapture always does. Older ideas required readjustment in my mind to make room for Toynbee, and conversely, Toyn-

bee's ideas had to be twisted about so as to fit in with what I already knew and believed. (McNeill, 1985, p. 24)

Here we have another instance of a story or something akin to a story achieving transformative ends, but ones quite different from those having to do with either the fable or the religious conversion. McNeill certainly sounds as though he has been changed irreversibly by the experience. Let us look a little more closely at his testimony. He says that for a time Toynbee's thoughts were his thoughts—"or so it seemed." It was as though he had replaced his own way of thinking with that of someone else. But the replacement was only temporary, for "Afterward, letdown; more mundane experience flowed in; differences of outlook and sensibility obtruded; questions arose for me that Toynbee had not touched on." So the magic of transformation was only momentary. Yet, "the moment of transport left its mark," McNeill reports, adding almost incidentally, "as rapture always does" (p. 24). The language he uses to describe what happened call to mind Piaget's notions of *assimilation* and *accommodation*. "Older ideas required readjustment in my mind to make room for Toynbee," he tells us, "and conversely, Toynbee's ideas had to be twisted about so as to fit with what I already knew and believed" (p. 24).

Yet a third conception of how narrative operates to render the kind of transformations we have been speaking of is provided by Arthur C. Danto. His observations, which were part of his presidential address to the American Philosophical Association, are ostensibly concerned with the difference between literature and philosophy, but his thoughts inevitably turn to the question of what literary works do to us. Literature, he explains, "is about each reader who experiences it. . . . The work finds its subject only when read" (Danto, 1985, p. 79). He then proceeds to make use of a well-known metaphor, " . . . it is natural to think . . . of literature as a kind of mirror," Danto tells us,

> not simply in the sense of rendering up an external reality, but as giving me to myself for each self peering into it, showing each of us something inaccessible without mirrors, namely that each has an external aspect and what that external aspect is. . . . It is a mirror less in passively returning an image than in transforming the self-consciousness of the reader who in virtue of identifying with the image recognizes what he is. Literature is in this sense transfigurative, and in a way which cuts across the distinction between fiction and truth. (Danto, 1985, pp. 78–79)

The exact meaning of Danto's observations is hard to fathom; more so, of course, when all we have to work with is a snippet taken from a longer address. However, even this brief fragment suffices to convey the general direction of Danto's thoughts. What he seems to be saying is that through identifying ourselves with characters in texts (and perhaps with more than just the characters, perhaps with the constellation of meanings embodied in the text as a whole) we somehow become ourselves. Our encounters with texts change us, all right, but according to Danto they do more than that. In his view, the stories we read and study—at least some of them—*actually make us what we are.* They are constitutive of our person-hood. Danto's description of the process sounds akin to what McNeill experienced upon reading Toynbee, though broader in scope perhaps. In relation to our two extreme examples—fables and religious texts—it appears to fall somewhere in-between; far beyond what one might expect to be the outcome of reading the "Fox and the Grapes," let us say, yet not nearly as all-encompassing as the transformations thought to accompany our acceptance of a religious "story" as our own.

Transformed and transfigured by stories. Transported by them. The examples and the testimony we have drawn upon leave little doubt that narratives of various kinds can indeed be powerful in their effect. But how common are such events? How many stories have that kind of an impact on us? Not very many, it would seem. For the kind of experience McNeill relates is surely rare, as are the sorts of transformations that Hauerwas and Danto discuss.

But if such moments are rare, what does that say about the place of narration in our schools? If teachers cannot rely upon the transformative impact of stories, if such miraculous events occur only once in a blue moon, shouldn't teachers give them up as goals and concentrate instead on the epistemological function of stories, that is, the kinds of benefits that we have already discussed? Perhaps any more profound and enduring changes should simply be left to chance rather than being incorporated as plat of a teacher's plans or aspirations. In short, why should teachers seek to achieve transformative goals at all if the chances of doing so are either remote or unpredictable?

To examine that question within the context of a particular teaching situation, we turn now to a famous Socratic dialogue: Plato's *Gorgias.* In that dramatic narrative, Socrates relates a mythical tale in the presence of his companions. He does so with what appears to be a transformative goal in mind. In preparation for our asking what the episode tells us, if anything, about the place of narration in schools and about other risky ventures on the part of ordinary teachers, let us see how the situation comes about and what comes of it.

THE TRANSFORMATIVE FUNCTION IN PLATO'S GORGIAS

With his four companions—Chaerephon, Polus, Gorgias, and Callicles—Socrates has been discussing the merits of oratory. This discussion has led to the question of whether it is better to suffer wrong or to do wrong, with Socrates taking the position that a wrongdoer is in the worst position possible. On this point he manages to convince or silence all but Callicles, who remains adamant in his conviction that a tyrant who does wrong is better off than the persons who suffer under his rule. Perhaps realizing that he has reached the limits of Callicles's understanding, or at least of his willingness to continue with the discussion, Socrates introduces a story as though to put a kind of finishing touch on his argument. He does so with these words: "Give ear then, as they say, to a very fine story, which will, I suppose, seem fiction to you but is fact to me; what I am going to tell you I tell you as the truth" (Plato, 1960, p. 142).

Socrates then proceeds to relate a tale about man's fate after death. It seems that in the time of Cronus there was a law which ordained that when righteous men died they would depart to the Isle of the Blessed, whereas wicked men and those who were godless would instead be imprisoned in a place of retribution and punishment called Tartarus. However, at that time men had foreknowledge of the date of their death and they also appeared before living judges who decreed their ultimate destination on the very day on which they were fated to die. "This led to perversion of justice," Socrates relates,

> so Pluto and the overseers of the Isles of the Blessed came to Zeus and complained that men were arriving at both destinations contrary to their deserts. Then Zeus said: 'I will put an end to this. The cause of this miscarriage of justice is that men, being tried in their life-time are tried in their clothes. Many whose souls are wicked are dressed in the trappings of physical beauty and high birth and riches, and when their trial takes place they are supported by a crowd of witnesses, who come to testify to the righteousness of their lives. This causes confusion to the judges, who are also hampered by being clothed themselves, so that their soul's vision is clouded by the physical veil of eyes and ears and the rest of the body, and their own vesture as well as the accused's constitutes an obstacle between them and the truth. Our first task, then,' said Zeus, 'is to take from men the foreknowledge of the hour of their death which they at present enjoy. I have charged Prometheus to bring this to an end. Next, they must all be tried naked, that is, when they are dead, and to ensure complete justice the judge too must be naked and dead himself, viewing with bare soul the bare soul of every man as soon as he is dead, when he has no kinsmen to aid him and has left behind on earth all his former glory.' (Plato, 1960, pp. 142–143)

To this end, Zeus appointed three of his own sons—Minos, Rhadamanthus, and Aeacus—to become judges upon their deaths, thus assuring "that men's ultimate destiny is decided in accordance with perfect justice" (Plato, 1960, p. 144).

After relating this story in only slightly greater detail than is presented here, Socrates reiterates his belief in its truth. "This, Callicles, is what I have heard and believe to be true," he says (Plato, 1960, p. 144). He then goes on to draw a set of conclusions that seem to him to follow from the account he has given. These epitomize the line of argument that led up to his telling of the story. In essence, they highlight the importance of leading a good life and reaffirm the value of punishment for those who are wrong-doers. He concludes by urging Callicles to join him in the practice of virtue; his final words deliver a stinging judgment of the view of life the latter has sought to defend. " . . . it is quite worthless, Callicles," Socrates solemnly intones, and on that sober note the dialogue comes to a close (Plato, 1960, p. 149).

In employing the fable as he does, Socrates certainly seems to be using it to achieve a transformative end, the goal being that of getting Callicles to "see the light," so to speak. Moreover, what Socrates looks as though he is trying to accomplish with his telling of the tale calls to mind Arthur Danto's remarks about how literature seems to work. In fact, Danto's exact words fit the situation quite well. Socrates seems to be using the fable "as a kind of mirror" for Callicles, "not simply in the sense of rendering up an external reality" but for showing him an aspect of himself that he "would not know was [his] without benefit of that mirror." The goal seems to be that of "transforming the self-consciousness of [Callicles] who in virtue of identify-ing with the image [of the man who after death is judged to be a wrong-doer]" will recognize what he is and what fate awaits him. Even Danto's description of literature as being "transfigurative in a way that cuts across the distinction between fiction and truth" is echoed in Socrates's insistence that the tale he is about to tell is "fact" and "the truth" as he himself sees it, though it might seem like fiction to Callicles. Does Socrates believe in the literal truth of the story he tells? He certainly calls the story "true," as we have already seen, and he follows that by saying, "Personally, Callicles, I put faith in this story. . . . " (Plato, 1960, p. 147). Yet the dialogue leaves room for other interpretations. One possibility is that Socrates is supremely confident of the moral truths embodied in the myth—that to do wrong is far worse than to suffer it and that there is no happiness for the wrong-doer—and means nothing more than that by his profession of faith. Here is the way one exegete of the dialogue puts it:

> When Socrates says, 'Personally, I put faith in this story', we must remember the connection between belief and will here. 'I put faith in this story' means 'I hope that nothing will get me to depart from the path of justice, and nothing will ever persuade me to put considerations of justice and decency second.' (Dilman, 1979, p. 174)

Further along in his argument the same critic observes,

> Yet Socrates' faith in [the story's] truth does not rest on the kind of evidence with which one would support an ordinary prophesy. His desire to live a good life, his preferring to suffer rather than inflict wrong on others, is not conditional to what will happen to him in the future in the hands of his judges. (Dilman, 1979, p. 176)

Whatever we might believe about Socrates' acceptance or rejection of the literal truth of the story he tells, he clearly is deeply committed to the moral message it contains and remains so throughout the dialogue. Indeed, the depth of his commitment calls to mind the kind of attachment to religious narratives that we have already discussed.

We asked earlier whether terms like "transforming," "transfiguring," and so on might not be a bit hyperbolic when applied to what a teacher was trying to do when he introduced a story or fable into his teaching. The episode from the *Gorgias* was offered as evidence that Socrates seems to have had just such a goal in mind when he closed his conversation with Callicles by telling the "judgment day" story. From that one might infer that if it is legitimate for Socrates to use a story in that way, so might it be for other teachers as well.

There is a difficulty, however, with using the *Gorgias* to legitimize a teacher's use of narration for transformative ends. The problem is that the dialogue, like many others involving Socrates, comes to an indecisive close. The reader is left to guess what Callicles' reaction might be to both Socrates' story and the conclusions he or she draws from it. Did the tale work? Did Callicles come to his senses at last? Was he undergoing a change of heart even as Socrates spoke? We are denied the answers to those questions in the dialogue itself and cannot look for them elsewhere, for it is generally supposed that Callicles, unlike the others who appear in *Gorgias,* is himself a work of fiction. However, the fact that such questions can be asked at all leaves the door open to the possibility that Socrates might not have accomplished much of anything by telling the tale to Callicles. Perhaps he was just wasting his time. That possibility is disturbing, as we have already seen, for what it says is that stories may or may not "work" as intended, which in turn raises the question of whether they are sufficiently reliable as instruments of transformative change to warrant their widespread use in classrooms.

We return, then, to the conclusion we reached before, which was that such stories do not always have the effects teachers wish them to have and that sometimes they may seem to have no effect at all. What shall we make of that undeniable fact? One answer would seem to be that if such efforts proved to be highly unreliable in their effects, teachers should discontinue using them. But how unreliable must they become before teachers should give them up? Perhaps we should take an empirical tack in trying to answer such questions. Perhaps someone should develop "before" and "after" tests of transformative ends in order to find out whether the educational benefits of telling stories to students were sufficiently reliable to warrant continuing such a practice. Are such tests feasible? Is that the approach we would recommend to a modern day Socrates? To see why the empirical tack is probably the wrong one to take, we need to return to the puzzle created by Callicles' utter silence during the closing moments of the dialogue and by the absence of any response from him when Socrates' impromptu tale had ended.

We first must ask, how reasonable is it to expect a character like Callicles to experience a change of heart in response to a story whose narration could not have taken more than a few minutes? The answer is easy. Even without knowing anything about Callicles, we can safely guess that the success of such a brief effort would be highly unlikely. When told that Callicles is a person who is very set in his ways, so much so that he makes use of abusive language in his exchanges with Socrates, the answer becomes even easier to discern. A single story, even when told by Socrates, is insufficient to make such a person change his mind. And, indeed, that is what we find in the dialogue itself. Callicles stays in character to the bitter end. His brooding silence in response to Socrates' entreaties leaves little doubt that his defensive armor remains impenetrable. But why, then, did Socrates bother? Why, in particular, did he finally resort to telling a story to such a recalcitrant and headstrong companion? Shouldn't he have known better?

Not necessarily, I would say. He may have had his reasons. I can think of two lines of defense for his actions from a pedagogical point of view. One is that he was not thinking so much of Callicles when it came time to tell the story as he was of the other three characters—Chaerephon, Polus, and Gorgias—who were obviously within earshot of what was being said and were therefore in a position to be influenced by the story. Perhaps Socrates told it as much for their sakes as for Callicles' alone. The fact that Callicles' three companions also remain silent in the end still leaves us in the dark with respect to how well the story worked for *them*. However, the reasonable manner that Polus and Gorgias earlier adopt in their conversations with Socrates makes it at least plausible to imagine them being influenced by a well-told tale.

(Incidentally, if we shift the target of the question from Socrates to Plato by asking Plato why he included the story in the dialogue, assuming the whole construction to be his creation, a similar line of reasoning would seem to hold, only in that case it would be *Plato* who included the story in order to influence someone other than Callicles, i.e., the dialogue's readers.)

A second way of explaining Socrates' decision to proceed with his story, even, perhaps, while harboring serious misgivings about its effectiveness, calls for a rather different slant on teaching than is customary these days. It asks us to think of teachers not simply as individuals acting purposefully, that is, as persons in charge of helping students attain a standard set of educational goals, but, instead, as individuals engaged in what the philosopher Justus Buchler once referred to as a kind of "methodic groping, . . . a kind of comradeship with chance." Buchler went on to describe this relationship as "a conditional alliance" (Buchler, 1961, p. 84). To maintain that alliance, he explained,

> the methodic agent requires only alertness and strength of perception. In a sense, the profoundest of methods, those of the sciences, the arts, and philosophy, depend upon the alliance most heavily. . . . Each instance of practice contains an element of contingency and obscurity which only a desire for new insight can surmount. This element of contingency is a trait of the method, and not merely of the method's particular conditions.
>
> No inventive process can be said to obviate groping on the part of those who engage in it. For every direction is vague in some degree when it starts with the prospect of uniqueness and unknown value in the product. (Buchler, 1961, p. 85)

Teachers are certainly no less in the dark than are the scientists, artists, and philosophers that Buchler mentions, even though the darkness they experience as they go about their work may have its unique patternings. They too, however, must maintain "a kind of comradeship with chance—a conditional alliance." For them, no less than the others, "[e]ach instance of practice contains an element of contingency and obscurity" which only desire combined with effort can surmount.

What does such an alliance with chance entail? For teachers, and perhaps for all others as well, it obviously means doing what *feels* right from time to time, even when you can't say for sure why you are doing it. When the teacher is someone like Socrates, it also seems to mean being true to one's ethical principles and acting in their light when all other guides fail, even when doing so promises to yield no benefit whatsoever insofar as a specific "learning outcome" is concerned. As applied to what went on with the *Gorgias*, this explanation would say that Socrates told the story as he did simply because he felt like doing so. It seemed the right thing to do under the circumstances, right in a variety of ways, perhaps in more ways than either Socrates or Plato themselves clearly understood.

Adopting this point of view, we might picture Socrates as recollecting the story at some point during the discussion—perhaps only milliseconds before telling it, one might imagine—immediately sensing its relatedness to all that he had been saying to that point, and finally deciding to use it as a capstone for his argument. He tells it not solely or even primarily because of the effect it likely will have on Callicles or anyone else. Instead, he does so for what might be called intuitive reasons. It simply feels right. It fits.

Something like the same line of reasoning would again seem to apply to Plato's decision to include the story in the dialogue. As author of the work—hence himself a storyteller—Plato too was probably feeling his way much of the time as he tried to figure out how best to portray Socrates in action, while perhaps hoping to accomplish a variety of additional goals as well, some pedagogical and others not. Why, then, did he add the myth at the end? Because here was a story that fit both the rhetorical and the dramatic requirements of the dialogue better than anything else he could think of at the time. It also happened to embody the fundamental moral truth that Socrates is portrayed as seeking to affirm, namely that the virtuous life is the only one worth living. What better reasons could he have had for such an ending?

This view of the intuitive element in teaching is doubtless discomforting to those who hope for the day when teaching will be a science or something akin to it. It seems to give teachers too much license perhaps, the freedom to tell stories in class or assign them to be read outside of school simply because it feels like the right thing to do, without worrying too much about what exactly will be accomplished by such an exercise. "Such freedom *might* work if all teachers were as talented as Plato or Socrates," the critics of such a policy might concede, "But, as we all know," they might add, "most teachers are not that talented, which is why the ordinary teacher's rationale for the use of stories ought to be spelled out in considerable detail and should include a clear description of the goals he or she is trying to reach."

There is something reasonable about the critics' admonition, but something unsettling as well. What seems reasonable about it is the tacit expectation that teachers should take their work seriously. This means, among other things, careful deliberation and choice when it comes to the materials they use and the assignments they make. The trouble with that advice when put into practice is that the rationality it advocates often turns out to be of a particular kind, one that seeks to tie teachers' actions to observable outcomes of instruction and little else, thereby grossly constricting the range of reasons that might legitimately guide what a teacher does.

What seems needed, if we are to leave room for teachers not only to introduce stories when the occasion seems to call for it but also to do so in a spontaneous and natural way, is a view of both teaching and narration that allows the complexity of each to become more fully understood and appreciated than either seems to be at present. Two aspects of that complexity merit special mention. One has mostly to do with teachers, the other with texts.

Like most other people, teachers sometimes behave enigmatically. They do things for reasons that are not immediately apparent. They give conflicting signals about what they think of their students and what they expect of them. They can be all smiles one minute and all frowns the next. They occasionally are contradictory and inconsistent in what they say and do. In short, they behave in ways that are downright puzzling at times.

Again, like most people, teachers are sometimes puzzling not only to their students and others who might be watching them but also to themselves. They too may wonder why they behave this way toward one student and that way toward another. They also may wonder why they teach as they do, preferring one set of activities or one pedagogical style to another. Of course, to say that they *may* wonder about such things is not to say that they invariably do so, nor is it to say that they wonder about the same aspects of their behavior that are puzzling to others. They could quite possibly have no good explanation for why they behave in a certain way yet not be particularly curious about their actions. Moreover, the fact that teachers (and the rest of us) sometimes behave in puzzling ways does not mean that all such puzzles are necessarily solved by either the teacher or those with whom he or she interacts. Some puzzles remain puzzles for a very long time. Others are never solved. We just learn to live with them.

Texts can be as puzzling as people at times, some even more so, perhaps. We all know what it's like not to be able to understand a text. We often find them disappointing in their lack of clarity. They get us mixed up. We have difficulty following them. When the texts present portrayals of people, as stories commonly do, we sometimes find their actions more inexplicable than those of people in real life.

Now when stories are told to us or assigned to us to be read, the kinds of complexities unique to texts and those that pertain solely to our understanding of others have a way of becoming entangled with one another. It is then that special questions occur to us, such as: Why is he telling this story? Why was this assigned? What does she expect me to get out of it? These add to whatever complexity we might encounter within the text alone. At such moments texts and teachers join together to produce a puzzle that is doubly enigmatic.

Angela S. Moger offers a tracing of the relationship between teachers and texts that is sufficiently provocative to make it worth quoting at length. Both pedagogy and narrative, she contends,

are coincident in their reliance on the mechanism of desire as a modus ope-
randi. Teaching and telling exist, endure, function, by means of perpetually
renewed postponement of fulfillment. If desire comes into being and is sustained as a result of inaccessibility or otherness of the object which one would
like, in principle to tame or consume, can't we rightly contend that narrative
operations and didactic operations intersect in their implicit intention to refrain
from closing the gap which is the goal of their explicit pretensions? Once the
object of desire has been appropriated, it loses its status as desirable. Now,
meaning is to narrative as fulfillment is to desire; possession means death.
Stories work by going through the motions of imparting information which
they only promise but never really deliver. A story is a question to be pursued;
if there is no enigma, no space to be traversed, there is no story.

Teaching is another such "optical" illusion; it functions by a similar
sleight of hand. The pedagogical stance is a pretext that there is something
substantive to be deciphered and appropriated. But wisdom, like love and the
story, is not found in nature; it has no empirical status. Like the beloved or
the narrative, it exists only in the eye of the beholder; I am a teacher only
in the mind of one who thinks I might teach him something he does not know.
But since I do not possess the knowledge he desires, to teach is only to continue
to generate the desire for wisdom. Pedagogy, like narrative, functions by means
of withholding rather than by means of transmission. . . . If the immediate
goal of teaching is the satisfaction of the quest for knowledge, it can also be
said that its fundamental goal is the denial of that satisfaction in favor of the
renewal of questing itself. (Moger, 1982, pp. 135–136)

Stories always leave you with Q's.

What shall we make of Moger's contentions? What light, if any, do
they shed on the problems associated with a teacher's use of stories? In
order to answer that question, let us first summarize her two main points.

Stories, we are told, work by promising to impart information that
is never really delivered. They arouse desire but perpetually postpone its
fulfillment. Similarly, to teach, Moger insists, is to continue to generate the
desire for wisdom, to deny satisfaction in favor of the renewal of questing
itself. It would seem to follow, then, that when teachers use stories in their
teaching their students are being doubly tantalized by the promise of goods
that are never delivered.

Is there any truth in all that? Do both stories and teaching arouse and
sustain desires that are never fully satisfied? There is more than one sense in
which they seem to do so. Some stories certainly end before we want them
to. They leave us wishing we could know more about the characters and
events within them. Others, which may include many of the first type,
awaken a hunger for more of the same but not necessarily the same book or
the same characters. They increase our appetite for more books by the same
author, perhaps, or more within the same literary genre—detective stories
or historical novels, for instance. Teachers have been known to have similar

effects on their students. Some teachers make us wish the class or course would never end. A few, like Socrates, leave us hungering for more knowledge in general.

But, as we all know, our encounters with both stories and teachers can be richly satisfying and fulfilling as well. At the finish of some stories we remain buried in thought. We then want nothing to disturb our lingering enjoyment of the experience we have just had. After a time our intellectual appetite revives and we once more seek the kind of enjoyment that only a fresh story can give. However, feelings of satisfaction and satiety remain very much a part of our exposure to narrative accounts. And so it is, or so we might suppose, with the best of teaching as well. There too we commonly experience a sense of completion and fulfillment when a class or a course has finished. Yet, as with stories, we sooner or later start hungering for more.

This must be what Moger means when she claims that teaching proceeds by continually renewing the desire for wisdom. But her assertion that "to teach is *only* [italics added] to continue to generate the desire for wisdom" seems a bit extreme. Though many teachers may generate a desire for wisdom among their students—and may even do so without conscious intent—there is surely more to teaching than that. There is, for example, the common expectation that teachers will *teach* us something, that they will leave us more knowledgeable than before and, further, that we will find that new knowledge satisfying in and of itself and not simply as a prelude to our hankering for more.

Moger's view that "[p]edagogy, like narrative, functions by means of withholding rather than by means of transmission. . . . " might be called her "double tease" theory of what happens when teachers become storytellers, and seems to be only partially true, at best. It remains helpful, all the same, by reminding us that within almost any teaching encounter one may come upon layers of significance and meaning about which none of the participants, including the teacher, are fully aware. This reminder is helpful because we often seem to forget that such discoveries require a kind of reflection that can only occur *after* we have acted rather than *before*. The significance of this fact for teaching deserves comment.

When we ordinarily think about what teachers do, we imagine them first making plans and then carrying them out. During the planning period—the pre-teaching phase of the process, one might call it—teachers are pictured as making decisions about goals and objectives as well as about their proposed means of reaching them. Only with those well-formed plans in hand, we commonly assume, are teachers prepared to act respon~'' '
But what of the way teachers actually work? Is it necessary, or ɩ
able, for them to proceed in this neat, two-step fashion?

Moger's remarks about teachers promising more than they deliver can be read as a kind of Freudian assault on the rationality implicit in any plans-into-action model of teaching. They imply, first of all, that there is far more going on in most teaching situations than one might guess (as in the world of human action in general) and they then proceed to suggest that at least some of those unconscious "goings on" may have a dark side to them, one that many teachers would prefer not to acknowledge. However, there is also a bright side to that way of thinking, one that Moger herself skips over. It is that many teachers actually *deliver* more than they *promise*, which is the exact opposite of what Moger's Freudian analysis would lead us to anticipate. They do so by delivering lessons that are far richer in content and fuller of wisdom than a perusal of their planbooks or a conversation with them ahead of time would ever reveal. They seize upon opportunities that open up while their lessons are in progress. They come to discover the worth of what they are doing in the process of doing it. Such "extras" may not occur daily, of course, but anyone who has ever looked at a teacher's planbook and then watched that teacher in action knows that there is no comparison between the bare bones of the plans and the richness of what actually happens in classrooms.

Does something similar happen with the stories teachers read or assign in school? Do we find that there too what gets delivered often turns out to be more than what was promised? I suspect so. My guess is that many teachers make use of stories as we imagined Socrates doing in the *Gorgias*. They read them or assign them in the hope that something good will come of such effort, yet they would be hard-pressed to say exactly what that good might be. They further cannot bank upon its occurrence.

What shall we make of this kind of uncertainty in teaching? Should it be encouraged or discouraged? Should we insist that teachers only rely upon the use of stories when they know exactly what they are doing, that is, when they are using them for purely epistemological ends, or should we allow for the introduction of narratives whose function is unclear and whose outcomes remain unmeasurable? And who is the "we" who might be doing the insisting and allowing? Is it teacher educators? School administrators? The public-at-large? Might it be teachers themselves? Not only the future of modern teaching practice but the future of education itself may depend upon the answers all of us give to such questions.

REFERENCES

Buchler, J. (1961). *The concept of method*. New York: Columbia University Press.
Danto, A. C. (1985). Philosophy as/and/of literature. In J. Rajchman & C. West (Eds.), *Post-analytic philosophy* (pp. 63–83). New York: Columbia University Press.

Dilman, I. (1979). *Morality and the inner life*. New York: Harper & Row.

Hauerwas, S. (1983). *The peaceable kingdom*. Notre Dame, IN: University of Notre Dame Press.

Kuhns, R. (1974). *Structures of experience*. New York: Harper & Row.

McNeill, W. H. (1985, December 29). Encounters with Toynbee, *New York Times Book Review*, pp. 1, 24.

Moger, A. S. (1982). That obscure object of narrative. In The pedagogical imperative: Teaching as a literary genre. *Yale French Studies, 63*, 129–138.

Plato. (1960). *Gorgias*. New York: Penguin.

Report of the Commission on the Humanities. (1980). *The humanities in American life*. Berkeley: University of California Press.

Sartre, J-P. (1965). *Nausea*. Harmondsworth, UK: Penguin.

CHAPTER 2

The Narrative Nature
of Pedagogical Content Knowledge

Sigrun Gudmundsdottir

Interest in narrative as a way of knowing is a prominent feature of research in a number of disciplines, such as literary criticism, semiotics, philosophy, anthropology, linguistics, cognitive psychology, and history. While only partial, the list does provide a sense of the widespread interest in narrative, especially among a number of the disciplines that the educational community traditionally draws upon to inform its own research. Correspondingly, we begin to see a dawning sense of the importance of narrative as a means of informing educational research and practice. But, how is the educational researcher to make sense of these various definitions and approaches to narrative? I wish to review some of this work with the aim of informing our understanding of the ways that teachers *present* knowledge. In short, I wish to explore the question of the nature of pedagogic content knowledge as it is related to narrative ways of knowing.

DEFINITIONS OF NARRATIVE

The words "narrative," "narration," and "narrate" have Latin roots that suggest a close connection with knowledge and expert or skillful practice (Whyte, 1981). The present uses and definitions of the word "narrative" retain some sense of its Latin roots. Regardless of the discipline or scholarly tradition, narrative refers to the structure, knowledge, and skill required to construct a story. Story and narrative, in everyday language, are taken to refer to the same thing: accounts of action usually involving humans or humanized animals. A story has characters; a beginning, a middle and an end; and is held together by a series of organized events, called plots. Fry (1984), for example, considers the story form to represent a collection of relational models by which what would otherwise be nothing more than a series of mechanically connected events can now be connected substantially and morally. Other specialists have developed various definitions to inform related concepts such as *discourse* and *inquiry*. The different approaches can be grouped into two separate traditions.

Structuralist literary theorists make a clear distinction between narrative, story, and discourse (Culler, 1975). A narrative has two parts: story and discourse (Chatman, 1978). The story includes the events, characters, settings and so on that constitute the content of a narrative. The discourse is the telling, expression, presentation, or narration of the story. The discourse can be spoken, written, or acted out in drama, motion picture, mime, or dance. The end product is a narrative, an organized text (Chatman, 1981). In this view, a story is considered to have well-marked beginning, middle, and end phases (Scholes, 1981; Whyte, 1981). Whyte (1981) takes narratives to incorporate a point of view that imposes "a certain number of exclusions and restrictive conditions" (p. 3). On the other hand, Scholes (1981) focuses on the structural and communicative aspects of narratives and maintains that a narrative is a "text that refers, or seems to refer, to some set of events outside of itself" (p. 205).

Other scholars entertain a much looser distinction between story and narrative. This looser distinction is more flexible and, consequently, more useful to researchers in the social sciences who wish to apply it to the analysis of a wide range of social phenomena. Herrenstein-Smith (1981), for example, finds the structural definition of narrative too limiting. It prevents us from using it "fruitfully" in the analysis of "language, behavior and culture." She proposes an alternative definition that is based on the idea that narrative is more than simply a structural feature of texts. It is something, rather, that is embedded in human action (p. 227). Narrative, in this account, is a series of verbal, symbolic, or behavioral *acts* sequenced for the purpose of "telling someone else that something happened" (p. 228). Thus, the social context in which a narrative is related, the narrator's reason for telling it, the narrator's narrative competence, and the nature of the audience, are all important elements in developing an understanding of narrative (see also the chapter by Shirley Pendlebury in this volume).

This approach to defining story and narrative has been adopted by many education researchers and scholars who wish to study narrative within its social and educational contexts (Ben-Peretz, 1990; Carter, 1992; Connelly & Clandinin, 1988; Elbaz 1983, 1990, 1991). Narratives have found their practical application in two areas in the field of education, both concerned with "telling someone else that something happened." The first area is in teaching content (see the chapter by Jackson in this volume). Narrative seems an obvious choice as an organizing structure. Talented teachers, such as Leimar (1974), Marshall (1963), Paley (1990), and Warner (1963) have described how they use stories to engage their children. Educational philosophers, such as Egan (1988), have advocated that teachers should use narrative as a means of structuring the curriculum. Egan's alternative model organizes the curriculum on the basis of binary opposites, which represent the "main structural lines along which [a] story moves forward" (p. 27). A study of experienced teachers has shown that they intuitively use narratives to bring order to what they consider a disjointed curriculum (Gudmundsdottir, 1991). Narrative structure is also what novice teachers seem to use when they try to make sense of the curriculum both for themselves and their students (Carter, 1991; Gudmundsdottir, 1990a). Narrative structure also characterizes the ways in which veteran teachers organize what they know about teaching. "Hanna," a retired teacher, communicates her important professional knowledge by means of stories of past events and people she knew decades before, and (perhaps) thanks to the narrative form, she still vividly remembers the details (Ben-Peretz, 1990). When Hanna and her fellow practitioners, young and old, have to transform "knowing into telling" (Whyte, 1981), narrative becomes their natural choice.

The second area within education where narratives have found a useful application is in educational research. Elbaz (1990) identifies the story as one of the main themes in research on teaching. She makes the observation that "the story is the very stuff of teaching, the landscape within which we live as teachers, researchers and within which the work of teachers can be seen as making sense (Elbaz, 1990, p. 31). Elbaz is referring to three types of narratives: the narrative in the curriculum, the narrative in the teachers' lives, and the researchers' narrative about the other two. Elbaz recognizes that narratives are becoming quickly established in educational research. Increasingly, they represent the object of the researcher's interests, their method of inquiry, and the form that they chose to structure their own writings, as in the case study and ethnography (see Chapter 13 by Zeller in this volume).

Clandinin and Connelly (1990) call their work, and other related research, "stories of experience and narrative inquiry," that is, they tell stories of practitioners and conduct narrative inquiry. Narrative, to them, means both the "phenomenon and the method" (Clandinin & Connelly, 1990, p. 2). It is clear that many good researchers on teaching use narratives both in the inquiry process and in the reporting of research results. As Spence (1984) noted "there seems no doubt but that a well constructed story possesses a kind of narrative truth that is real and immediate" (p. 21). Researchers' narratives of individual teachers, student teachers, or small groups of these, show that the narrative seems like a natural mediator between a particular student and teacher in a particular classroom and students and teachers in classrooms all over the Western world. The stories of the "Lads" (Willis, 1977), "Sarah" (Elbaz, 1983), "Bruce" (Clandinin & Connelly, 1986), "Stephanie" (Clandinin, 1986), "Colleen" (Grossman, 1987), "Nancy" (Gudmundsdottir, 1988, 1991), and "Benny" (Erwanger, 1973) play well in Scandinavia too.

One of the reasons why these stories are accepted on the other side of the Atlantic Ocean is because there is something basically human about narratives. Whyte (1981) suggests that the study of narratives involves "reflection on the very nature of culture and possibly even on the nature of humanity itself" (p. 1). Stories, like culture and language, have been constant traveling companions to human beings, always and everywhere. For example, we see this in the cave drawings in France and Spain. The drawings may be read as narratives describing a hunt, and in considering these vivid and dramatic paintings, we gain an insight into the culture and values of the people who drew them. Today, different cultures maintain their stock of narratives to communicate and conserve shared meanings. To participate in a culture is to know and use a range of accumulated and shared meanings. These shared meanings, however, are not static but are in constant revision. It is this idea of shared meanings that underlies Bruner's (1986) claim that we, as individuals, express only a "variant of the culture's canonical forms" (p. 15). His words are echoed by McIntyre (1985), who goes as far as to say that if children are deprived of stories "you leave them unscripted, anxious stutters in their actions as in their words" (p. 216).

PEDAGOGICAL CONTENT KNOWLEDGE:
A NARRATIVE WAY OF KNOWING

Ever since Lee Shulman (1987) introduced the concept *pedagogical content knowledge*, increasing numbers of researchers and teachers have come to recognize that it represents an important element in teachers' knowledge base. The concept refers to the teachers' ways of knowing and understanding their subject matter that is "unique for teachers and teaching" (Shulman, 1987). It makes intuitive sense that experienced teachers should know their subject matter differently than those who are not engaged in teaching. Moreover, this concept and the model that Shulman (1987) has developed portray teaching as an interpretative and reflective activity, where teachers imbue the curriculum and the texts they teach with their values and meaning (Gudmundsdottir, 1990a). This image of teaching as a narrative concern is further illuminated by the work of Ben-Peretz (1990), Carter (1992), Connelly and Clandinin (1988), Doyle (1992), Egan (1988), Elbaz (1991), and Jackson (1986), as well as by the contributors to this volume.

Even though Shulman's concept has captured the imagination of many teachers and researchers, the concept, and the knowledge it stands for, remains diffuse. Researchers have described how this way of knowing develops among novices (Carter, 1991; Grossman, 1987; Grossman & Gudmundsdottir, 1987; Gudmundsdottir, 1990b; Reynolds, 1987; and Wineburg, 1987); and research focusing on experienced teachers demonstrates that this group of teachers know their subject matter differently than their less experienced colleagues (Grant, 1988; Gudmundsdottir, 1988; Hashweh, 1987; Leinhardt & Smith, 1985). Their knowledge is practical, it has developed over the years through accumulated "wisdom of practice" (Shulman, 1987). It is characterized by its narrative qualities.

What is implied in pedagogical content knowledge is that teachers' content knowledge has been transformed into something different from what it was before, a form that has practical application in teaching. Subsequent discussions of the concept have focused on this transformed content knowledge. Wilson, Shulman, and Richert (1987) have described some of the initial phases of this transformation. One of their informants, Frank, a student teacher, realized that the approach to the subject matter he had learned as an undergraduate in college did not lend itself to his high school classroom. Frank figured that if he were to teach his subject properly and effectively he would have to "handle 150 different approaches to biology." Frank is not complaining that he does not know enough biology, but rather he has discovered that the way he knows biology is not appropriate for teaching high school students.

The components of content knowledge that make it more pedagogical have been described by Grossman, Wilson, and Shulman (1989). They identify basically two components that facilitate the process, one that Dewey refers to as "psychologizing" the subject matter. First, they describe "dimensions of subject matter for teaching." These dimensions are overlapping and partly integrated. The first of these is "content knowledge for teaching," which is defined as "'the stuff' of the discipline: factual information, organizing principles, central concepts" (p. 27). They note that student teachers with a specialization in a narrow area often have the wrong sort of content knowledge for teaching. The second dimension is "substantive knowledge for teaching." This way of knowing the subject matter refers to Schwab's (1978) "substantive structures of the discipline." These are the theoretical frameworks that combine, organize, and give meaning to knowledge within disciplines. The third dimension is "syntactic knowledge for teaching." And again, they draw on Schwab's powerful ideas. This way of knowing the discipline describes the structures that guide inquiry in a discipline. It is fundamental to the way in which content knowledge later develops and is transformed pedagogically.

Second, Grossman and colleagues (1989) describe a component they call "beliefs about subject matter." They claim that teachers' beliefs about the subject matter combined with their beliefs about students, schools, learning, and the nature of teaching "powerfully affect their teaching" (p. 31). Two types of beliefs are identified. One is concerned with subject matter and the priorities teachers assign to topics. The second type of belief is related to teachers' orientation to the subject matter. These beliefs, also called values (Gudmundsdottir, 1990b), shape the kind of history, literature, math, or science teachers feel is important for students to know. It also legitimates or excludes a range of pedagogical strategies that teachers feel are appropriate or inappropriate for teaching their subject matter to a given group of students.

It is this belief in the value-laden nature of subject matter, teaching, learning, and school practices that provides the foundation for understanding the narrative nature of pedagogical content knowledge. Values and narratives are inexorably intertwined. Together they have one fundamental principle in common, a principle that is basic to the narrative nature of pedagogical content knowledge. This basic principle is that narratives help us interpret the world. Values and narratives are interpretative tools that constitute a practical, but also highly selective, perspective with which we look at the world around us. We use narratives to make sense of facts, whether they are various kinds of text or curriculum or instructional practices, from the moment we first walk into a school. This aspect of narrative as an organizer of experience is vividly exemplified in Carter's (1991) study of "well remembered events" among student teachers.

In spite of the popularity of Shulman's ideas, they have not gone without criticism. McEwan and Bull (1991), while remaining sympathetic to the idea that knowledge is pedagogic, have argued that there can be no content knowledge without a pedagogic dimension because the understanding and communication of an idea is itself a pedagogic act. They go on to say that "to understand a new idea is not merely to add to the existing stock; it is also to grasp hold of its heuristic power—its power to teach. Explanations are not only of something; they are also always for someone" (p. 332). This is not a criticism that disposes of Shulman's ideas; it clarifies them. Thus, by viewing content knowledge as possessing both pedagogic and narrative qualities, we can more easily understand its "heuristic power." Narrative functioning always involves interpretation and reinterpretation, the structuring of experience, and the act of telling someone something. It involves, in short, the transformation of "knowing into telling" (Whyte, 1981), a process that I will explain in the next section.

EXPERIENCE NARRATIZED

Pedagogical content knowledge is a practical way of knowing the subject matter. It is learned mostly on the job from trying things out and observing, talking, and working with other teachers. Tradition provides the narrative models to draw upon to understand and construct the present, and it is maintained by the sense of accumulated practice that is also shared by others. The narratives told within a tradition are "packages of situated knowledge" (Jordan, 1989). Practitioners well versed in their tradition know what stories to tell, when, to whom, and for what purpose (Orr, 1987).

Teachers live in stories. They use them in order to tell their students about some of the things they know. When researchers offer themselves to teachers as sympathetic listeners, they can learn from teachers about who they are, what they know, and their world in the classroom. As researchers probe and guide with their questions, the teachers' stories inevitably become a joint production. This process is a dynamic one. Past experiences are not buried in the ground like archeological treasures waiting to be recovered and studied. Rather, the past is recreated through telling (Gudmundsdottir, 1992). It is through this narrative dialogue of reflection and interpretation that experience is transformed into pedagogical content knowledge.

The study of teachers' stories and narratives brings us right to the heart of pedagogical content knowledge, in all its variety and richness. Such a study should focus on the four dimensions of narratives within *pedagogical content knowledge*: practical experience, interpretation, reflection, and transformation (Shulman, 1987).

Practical Experience

Practitioners who work with people usually encode their experiences in narrative form. Often they use case histories and narrative explanations, as is exemplified in Schon's (1983) work. The practitioners he studied were architects, engineers, and psychotherapists, but only the latter group dealt with people, and they characteristically offered stories to explain and justify their thinking and actions. Similarly, the world of the teacher is one filled with human activity and cares. At times it is chaotic, unpredictable and multidimensional (Doyle, 1977), but by representing events through narratives teachers achieve a certain order over this chaos and derive a level of practical knowledge that informs their actions. The research studies of Elbaz (1983), Connelly and Clandinin (1988), Grant (1988), and Gudmundsdottir (1988) describe the different ways in which experienced practitioners structure their practical knowledge. Elbaz along with Connelly and Clandinin (1988) have identified a body of knowledge they describe as "practical knowledge." It is a "complex practically oriented set of understandings which teachers actively use to shape and direct the work of teaching" (p. 19). Elbaz (1983) identifies five categories of teachers' practical knowledge: of self, of the milieu of teaching, of subject matter, of curriculum development, and of instruction.

Those who study what experienced teachers know about teaching and the world of classroom inevitably find themselves listening to stories that teachers tell to explain the essence of what they know. "Bruce" (Clandinin & Connelly, 1986) told a story about one of his former students to explain and morally justify the way he used language in the classroom. There are many such stories to be found in the studies of Elbaz (1983), Clandinin (1986), and others who have studied what experienced teachers know about their work. Research into experienced teachers' knowledge and practice also demonstrates that they are concerned explicitly or implicitly with values and other moral issues in their practice. Huberman (1983) observes that studies on values among teachers has "consistently shown [them] to be highly altruistic and socially oriented" (p. 501). Huberman reports that teachers scored high on the Allport-Vernon-Lindzey scale, "slightly below theologians but well above doctors, lawyers, pharmacists, and engineers" (p. 501). Morals and narratives seem like natural partners in the life of teachers.

By using narrative form we assign meaning to events and invest them with coherence, integrity, fullness, and closure. When we place events drawn from our experiences within an order provided by narrative, we also invest them with a moral significance. Whyte (1981) claims that by placing events in a narrative sequence, every story becomes a kind of allegory endowed with moral significance. Telling a story is accordingly "intimately related to, if not a function of, the impulse to moralize reality, that is to identify it with the social system that is the source of any morality we can imagine" (p. 14). Studies on student teachers show that they are also concerned with moral values, especially those teachers who are interested in their subject matter (Grossman, 1987; Gudmundsdottir, 1987). Yet, at the same time, they seem unable to fully integrate their pedagogic values with their developing knowledge of how to teach the subject. Experienced teachers, on the other hand, have thoroughly integrated their values with their subject matter, goals, and views of students and teaching (Gudmundsdottir, 1990b). It seems that their values have become a scaffolding for their *pedagogical content knowledge*.

The narration of practical experience comes naturally, like learning a language. Mandler (1984) considers the story schema to be parallel to learning a grammar. It is a natural way to recount experience, and a solution to a fundamental problem in life—creating a reasonable order out of experience. Order is achieved along several cognitive dimensions (Robinson & Hawpe, 1986): *economy*, *selectivity*, and *familiarity*. *Economy* means that narrative order can be applied to almost all aspects of our lives—past, present, and future. *Selectivity* is vital since we cannot pay equal attention to all our experiences. The narrative schema classifies and assigns significance to information and places it in the narrative. *Familiarity* is achieved by repetition and the creation of similar accounts of typical events. This makes stories told within a tradition more familiar and easier to understand than if the setting is strange and foreign to the students' experience.

Interpretation

In the construction and telling of a narrative there is always someone who is an interpreter, situated, as Barthes says, between our experiences and our efforts to make sense of them and describe them. Narratives are never straight copies of the world like photographic images. They are interpretations. To engage in interpretation, according to Palmer (1969), is to stand in the place of an author. In the teachers' case, they have their minds fixed on their audience (the student) and they engage in what McEwan (1987) calls "pedagogical interpretation," producing something I want to call a "pedagogical text." As Barthes reminds us, an author is not the one who invents the most fantastic stories or poems, but the one who achieves the greatest mastery over a particular culture's narrative codes.

To interpret in this way requires that teachers learn to look and comprehend texts, practices, and classrooms pedagogically. There are, however, many ways one can look at the world. Fish (1980) told his class that a list of names on the blackboard was a "poem." As soon as his students were told that this text was a poem, they began looking at it "with poetry-seeking-eyes." Thus, the students had activated their previous set of experiences with poetry and had engaged a set of expectations about what poems can do. Their definition of "poetry" functioned like a "recipe" of what to look for, and in the process they produced meanings for the text. The text itself is like a skeleton waiting to be brought alive in various ways with different readers looking at it with "poetry-seeking-eyes" or, for that matter, "pedagogically-seeking-eyes."

The texts used in teaching, such as textbooks and other curriculum materials, require that teachers look at them with "pedagogically-seeking-eyes." Understanding, according to classical hermeneutics (Palmer, 1969), requires that the reader reconstruct the text. The interpreter must know the texts, be intimate with the texts and the subject matter they represent, and immerse himself or herself in this world of texts and subject matter. Only then can a pedagogically meaningful interpretation take place. To create a new text, a pedagogical text, certain aspects of the text must first be selected (Polkinghorne, 1988). For example, when "Nancy" and "Naomi" teach Huck Finn each of them selects specific episodes in Twain's novel (Gudmundsdottir, 1988). "Snorre," a Norwegian social studies teacher, selects facts, figures, and pictures out of his textbooks and adds to them other materials he has in his private curriculum collection (Gudmundsdottir, study in progress). Second-order referents are created by establishing a causal pattern that integrates all the first-order referents into a meaningful whole, a narrative. This narrative is an interpretation of the text, which in turn is an interpretation of an earlier text. Interpretations are always inevitably interpretations of interpretations. "Snorre" created a new history "text," one he thought was more "pedagogical." The two American teachers, "Nancy" and "Naomi," each created a new "text" from the first-order referents they selected from Huck Finn, a narrative that each felt communicated what she saw in the novel. The 10 experienced teachers I have worked with on both sides of the Atlantic Ocean are different in many ways, but they have each acquired a pair of "pedagogically-seeking-eyes" that they use to study texts and construct new "pedagogical interpretations" (McEwan, 1987).

Reflection

It is an achievement to learn to look at texts in this way, and a measure of the complex nature of experienced teaching. A sound basis for this achievement probably arises in college as a student begins to study the subject matter. But the most important lessons in pedagogical interpretation take place on the job in a cycle of practical application and reflection. Reflection involves thoughtful explanation of past events. Mere moments and happenings have no systematic cognitive connection. They stand behind one another in a temporal sequence and it is only through reflection that they begin to take on the form of a story and acquire meaning. Such a match, according to Robinson and Hawpe (1986), is a natural way to recount experience. They believe that this naturalness is evidence for the ubiquity of narrative thinking in everyday life, especially among practitioners who deal with people.

Pendlebury (Chapter 4, this volume) describes how reflection can create a delicate but important balance between two "states of character": "reflective equilibrium" and "perceptive spontaneity." The former is typical of teachers who teach by the rule book; the latter is characteristic of teachers who seem unreflective and prone to whimsical decision making. Pendlebury maintains that balance is achieved when teachers learn to reflect on concrete and real situations.

Transformation

Narratives are a valuable *transformative* tool. They allow us to understand the world in new ways and help us to communicate new ideas to others (see Jackson, Chapter 1, this volume). We can make worlds in many new ways (Goodman, 1978). Narratives allow us to discover new meanings by assimilating experiences into a narrative schema. For example, in experiments involving subjects observing moving geometric figures, it was shown that participants confidently composed elaborate stories to account for the simplest of these configurations (Michotte, 1963)—a clear demonstration that people have a natural and strong urge to tell a story in order to give their experiences meaning. The experiment with the geometric figures involved progressing from something almost meaningless to a form endowed with meaning. In most cases, transformation involves progressing from a incomplete story to one that is more complete and compelling. We do this by establishing first the connectedness or coherence that moves the storyline along through time. Next comes the direction of the story, the goal or point of it all. With the goal established, events are selected, rejected, or transformed and take on a significance that they would not have otherwise possessed. Good stories are interpretive, memorable, functional, and entertaining. These characteristics help us remember them, and a clear narrative form ensures that they are generalizable and applicable to a wide range of situations.

Experienced teachers are masters at transforming their curriculum (Gudmundsdottir, 1991). They have a large supply of well-organized curriculum units that are constantly renarratized, or put into a larger narrative structure in the curriculum, not unlike the "tale chunks" of the Xhosa tribe in Africa (Gough, 1990). These are coherent stretches of narratives that are combined in different ways to create a larger narrative. The Xhosa narrator is free, within limits, to put these tale chunks together in novel ways.

Drawing on their pedagogical content knowledge, experienced teachers are constantly revising old narrative units in their curriculum and constructing alternatives as they try to figure out new ways to make something interesting to their students. For example, "Torolf" and "Hallgerd," who teach literature in a high school in Norway, are required to teach poems by a sixteenth-century poet whose language students find extremely difficult to understand. Both teachers are constantly figuring ways to make it easier for students to be interested in the poet and understand his poetry. They approach this task by constructing an elaborate curriculum unit that has a clear narrative structure, presenting the poet, his poems, and his sixteenth-century world. The motive behind these changes is not just that the students should understand this literature, but also that it is valuable for them to understand it. This suggests a second sense of transformation, the sense that Jackson discusses in an earlier chapter, that teachers' narratives are not intended just to *in*form the students but to *trans*form them, as well.

CONCLUSION

As a body of knowledge developed mostly through practice, pedagogical content knowledge retains some of the elements that characterize the knowledge of those who work with people in the practical domain. Pedagogical content knowledge is mostly "home made," developed on the job by working with texts, subject matter, and students in different contexts year after year, and in the case of some experienced teachers, for decades. Narratives and stories are the tools practitioners frequently use to make sense of experience and organize it into a body of practical knowledge. The theory of textual interpretation suggests that understanding a story involves a re-construction — new text is created out of old text. Teachers are in a unique position because they also have to interpret these texts pedagogically, that is, with a mind to the understanding of their students. It is pedagogical interpretation that I believe is at the heart of pedagogical content knowledge. Good teachers do this and have done so since the dawn of human-kind. I think it is time we begin to consider teaching what it is, a "timeless text," a continuing tradition of stories told and retold with the express purpose of engaging students.

REFERENCES

Ben-Peretz, M. (1990, April). *Scenes from the past: Professional episodes remembered by retired teachers*. Paper presented at the International Conference on Teacher Thinking, Ben-Gurion University, Beer-Sheva, Israel.

Bruner, J. (1986). *Actual minds: Possible worlds*. Cambridge, MA: Harvard University Press.

Carter, C. (1992). The place of story in research on teaching. *Educational Researcher, 22*(1), 5–12.

Carter, K. (1991). *Well remembered events*. Paper presented at the annual meeting of the American Educational Research Association, Chicago.

Chatman, S. (1978). *Story and discourse: Narrative structure in fiction and film*. Ithaca, NY: Cornell University Press.

Chatman, S. (1981). What novels can do that films can't (and vice versa). In W. Mitchell (Ed.), *On narrative* (pp. 117–136). Chicago: University of Chicago Press.

Clandinin, D. J. (1986). *Classroom practice: Teacher images in action*. London: Falmer Press.

Clandinin, D. J., & Connelly, F. M. (1986). On the narrative method, personal philosophy, and narrative units in the story of teaching. *Journal of Research in Science Teaching, 23*(4), 293–310.

Clandinin, D. J., & Connelly, F. M. (1990). Story of experience and narrative inquiry. *Educational Researcher, 19*(5), 2–14.

Connelly, F. M., & Clandinin, D. J. (1988). *Curriculum planners: Narratives of experience*. New York: Teachers College Press.

Culler, J. (1975). *Structuralist poetics: Structuralism, linguistics, and the study of literature*. Ithaca, NY: Cornell University Press.

Doyle, W. (1977). Learning the classroom environment: An ecological analysis. *Journal of Teacher Education, 28*(6), 51–55.

Doyle, W. (1992). Curriculum and pedagogy. In P. Jackson (Ed.), *Handbook of research on curriculum* (pp. 486–515), New York: Macmillan.

Egan, K. (1988). *Teaching as storytelling: An alternative approach to teaching and curriculum in the elementary school*. London, Ontario: Althouse Press.

Elbaz, F. (1983). *Teacher thinking: A study of practical knowledge*. London: Croom Helm.

Elbaz, F. (1990). Knowledge and discourse: The evolution of research on teacher thinking. In C. Day, P. Denicolo, & M. Pope (Eds.), *Insights into teachers' thinking and practice* (pp. 15–42). London: Falmer Press.

Elbaz, F. (1991, September). *Hope, attentativeness and caring for difference: The moral voice in teaching*. Paper presented at the International Study Association of Teacher Thinking (ISATT5), University of Surrey, Guildford, UK.

Erwanger, S. (1973). Benny's conception of rules and answers in IPI mathematics. *Journal of Childrens' Mathematical Behaviour, 1*(2), 7–26.

Fish, S. (1980). *Is there a text in this class? The authority of interpretive communities*. Cambridge, MA: Harvard University Press.

Fry, N. (1984). *Fables of identity*. New York: Harcourt Brace Jovanovich.

Goodman, N. (1978). *Ways of worldmaking*. Indianapolis, IN: Hackett.

Gough, P. B. (1990). The principle of relevance and the production of discourse: Evidence from Xhosa folk narratives. In B. K. Britton & A. D. Pellegrini (Eds.), *Narrative thought and narrative language* (pp. 199–218). London: Lawrence Erlbaum.

Grant, G. (1988). *Teaching critical thinking*. New York: Praeger.

Grossman, P. L. (1987). A passion for language: A case study of Colleen, a beginning English teacher. In *Knowledge growth in a profession publication series*. Stanford, CA: Stanford University, School of Education.

Grossman, P. L., & Gudmundsdottir, S. (1987, April). *Teachers and texts: An expert/novice comparison in English*. Paper presented at the annual meeting of the American Educational Research Association, Washington, DC.

Grossman, P. L., Wilson, S., & Shulman, L. S. (1989). Teachers of substance:

Subject matter knowledge for teaching. In M. C. Reynolds (Ed.), *Knowledge base for the beginning teacher* (pp. 23–36). Oxford: Pergamon Press.

Gudmundsdottir, S. (1987, April). *Learning to teach social studies: Case studies of Cathy and Chris*. Paper presented at the annual meeting of the American Educational Research Association, Washington, DC.

Gudmundsdottir, S. (1988). *Knowledge use among experienced teachers: Four case studies of high school teaching*. Unpublished doctoral dissertation, Stanford University, Stanford, CA.

Gudmundsdottir, S. (1990a). Curriculum stories. In C. Day, P. Denicolo, & M. Pope (Eds.), *Insights into teachers' thinking and practice* (pp. 107–118). London: Falmer Press.

Gudmundsdottir, S. (1990b). Values in pedagogical content knowledge. *Journal of Teacher Education, 41*(3), 44–53.

Gudmundsdottir, S. (1991). Story-maker, story-teller: Narrative structures in curriculum. *Journal of Curriculum Studies, 23*(3), 207–218.

Gudmundsdottir, S. (1992, April). *The research interview as a joint construction of reality*. Paper presented at the annual meeting of the American Educational Research Association, San Francisco.

Gudmundsdottir, S., & Shulman, L. S. (1987). Pedagogical content knowledge in social studies. *Scandinavian Journal of Educational Research, 31*(2), 59–70.

Hashweh, M. (1987). Effect on subject matter knowledge in teaching of biology and physics. *Teaching and Teacher Education, 3*(2), 109–120.

Herrenstein-Smith, B. (1981). Narrative versions, narrative theories. In W. Mitchell (Ed.), *On narrative* (pp. 209–232). Chicago: University of Chicago Press.

Huberman, M. (1983). Recipes for busy kitchens: A situational analysis of routine knowledge use in school. *Knowledge: Creation, Diffusion, Utilization, 4*(4), 478–510.

Jackson, P. (1986). *The practice of teaching*. New York: Teachers College Press.

Jordan, B. (1989). Cosmopolitan obstetrics: Some insights from the training of traditional midwives. *Social Science Medicine, 28*(9), 925–944.

Landau, M. (1986). Trespassing in scientific narrative: Grafton Elliot Smith and the Temple of Doom. In T. Sarbin (Ed.), *Narrative psychology: The storied nature of human conduct* (pp. 45–64). New York: Praeger.

Leimar, U. (1974). *LTG metoden*. Copenhagen: Gyldendals Pëdagogiske Bibliotek.

Leinhardt, G., & Smith, D. (1985). Expertise in mathematics instruction: Subject matter knowledge. *Journal of Educational Psychology, 77*(3), 247–271.

Mandler, J. (1984). *Stories, scripts, and scenes: Aspects of schema theory*. Hillsdale, NJ: Lawrence Erlbaum.

Marshall, S. (1963). *An experiment in education*. Cambridge, UK: Cambridge University Press.

McEwan, H. (1987). *Interpreting the subject domains for students: Towards a rhetorical theory of teaching*. Unpublished doctoral dissertation, University of Washington, Seattle.

McEwan, H., & Bull, B. (1991). The pedagogic nature of subject matter knowledge. *American Edcucational Research Journal, 28*(2), 316–334.

McIntyre, A. (1985). *After virtue*. Notre Dame, IN: University of Notre Dame Press.

Michotte, A. (1963). *The perception of causality*. London: Methuen.

Orr, J. (1987). Narratives at work. *Field Service Manager: The Journal of Association of Field Service Managers International*, 47–60. Palo Alto, CA: Intelligent Systems Laboratory.

Paley, V. G. (1990). *The boy who would be a helicopter*. Cambridge, MA: Harvard University Press.

Palmer, R. (1969). *Hermeneutics*. Evanston, IL: Northwestern University Press.

Polkinghorne, D. (1988). *Narrative knowing and the human sciences*. New York: State University of New York Press.

Reynolds, A. (1987). Everyone is invited to the party: A case study of Catherine, a beginning English teacher. *Knowledge Growth in a Profession Publication Series*, Stanford University, School of Education.

Robinson, J., & Hawpe, L. (1986). Narrative thinking as a heuristic process. In T. Sarbin (Ed.), *Narrative psychology: The storied nature of human conduct* (pp. 111–125). New York: Praeger.

Scholes, R. (1981). Language, narrative, and anti-narrative. In W. Mitchell (Ed.), *On narrative* (pp. 200–208). Chicago: University of Chicago Press.

Schon, D. (1983). *The reflective practitioner: How professionals think in action*. New York: Basic Books.

Schwab, J. (1978). Education and the structure of the disciplines. In I. Westbury & N. Wilkof (Eds.), *Science, curriculum and liberal education* (pp. 229–272). Chicago: University of Chicago Press. (Originally published in 1958)

Shulman, L. S. (1987). Knowledge and teaching: Foundations of the new reform. *Harvard Educational Review, 57*(1), 1–22.

Spence, D. (1984). *Narrative truth and historical truth*. New York: W. W. Norton.

Warner, S. A. (1963). *Teacher*. New York: Touchstone.

Whyte, H. (1981). The value of narrativity in the representation of reality. In W. Mitchell (Ed.), *On narrative* (pp. 1–24). Chicago: University of Chicago Press.

Willis, P. (1977). *Learning to labour*. London: Gower.

Wilson, S. M., Shulman, L. S., & Richert, A. E. (1987). "150 different ways" of knowing: Representations of knowledge in teaching. In J. Calderhead (Ed.), *Exploring teachers' thinking* (pp. 104–124). London: Cassell.

Wineburg, S. (1987). From fieldwork to classwork: A case study of Cathy, a beginning social studies teacher. *Knowledge Growth in a Profession Publication Series*, Stanford University, School of Education.

ERRATUM: Page 39 should read as it appears below:

CHAPTER 3

Narrative Landscapes and the Moral Imagination

TAKING THE STORY TO HEART

Carol S. Witherell

with Hoan Tan Tran and John Othus

> What do stories do?
> Affect us,
> Nothing else.
> —Primus St. John, *Dreamer*

Other contributors to this volume have explored the power of narrative to communicate cultural meaning, to lead to self-understanding, to join with reason and imagination to shape practical wisdom, to recover romance, and to transform our experience into texts whose interpretations are at the heart of teaching and learning. This chapter explores the power of story and narrative as tools of the moral imagination. Through both written and oral narrative we can feel profoundly with another, imagining a larger world than the one we inhabit. Such leaps of empathy and imagination can bind us in deeper and wider relationships, provide bridges across cultures, and enable us to "look into the heart of wisdom." Samples of students' writing and thinking in courses where narrative is used as a primary tool for self-reflection illustrate this power. The telling, receiving, and shaping of stories can be, in the words of one student, "redemptive, healing, and transformative."

INTRODUCTION: IMAGINATION AND THE MORAL CALL OF STORIES

In *Crow and Weasel,* Barry Lopez offers an epic tale of a journey of two young men into northern territory beyond where any of their people have traveled before. The two travelers, Crow and Weasel, meet many strangers along the way from whom they learn profound lessons. One of the strangers, Badger, offers them this counsel:

> I would ask you to remember only this one thing. . . . The stories people tell have a way of taking care of them. If stories come to you, care for them. And learn to give them away where they are needed. Sometimes a person needs a story more than food to stay alive. That is why we put these stories in each other's memory. This is how people care for themselves. One day you will be good storytellers. Never forget these obligations. (Lopez, 1990, p. 49)

Stories invite us to come to know the world and our place in it. Whether narratives of history, present experience, or the imagination, stories call us to consider what we know, what we hope for, who we are, and what and whom we care about. Stories have a certain engaging power—a ring of truth; they enable us to "become the friends of one another's minds" in ever-increasing circles of inclusion (Greene, 1991, p. xi).

Crow and Weasel discover this power as they overcome both terrors of the landscape and fear of strangers by learning from and receiving the gifts of the strangers they encounter. In the case of Grizzly Bear, they receive the gift of life itself—he enables them to survive. Their journey is about more than survival, however; it is about the ways that humans imagine their lives and their dreams. And it is a journey of redemption—an illustration that "the community can be redeemed by the stranger who presents himself in all his otherness and asks by his presence to be met" (Shabatay, 1991, p. 137).

Narrative can also serve as an interpretive lens for reflecting the storied nature of human lives, for understanding the moral complexities of the human condition, and for enabling classrooms to expand their borders as interpretive communities. A good story engages and enlarges the moral imagination, illuminating possibilities for human thought, feeling, and action in ways that can bridge the gulf between different times, places, cultures, and beliefs. These functions of narrative are explored in the works by Robert Coles, Annie Dillard, Kieran Egan, Barry Lopez, Alasdair MacIntyre, and Terry Tempest Williams cited in this chapter's bibliography. Coles and Egan explore the power of story and imagination in teaching and learning. Dillard, Lopez, and Williams capture the power of narrative to nurture and heal. MacIntyre examines the narrative nature of moral identities—both individual and cultural. In *Refuge*, Williams offers a personal and family chronicle that links narratives of love and loss with narratives of place and wildlife—in this case, the death of her mother and the birds of Utah's Bear River Migratory Bird Refuge.

Narrative allows us to enter empathically into another's life and being—to join a living conversation. In this sense, it serves as a means of inclusion, inviting the reader, listener, writer, or teller as a companion along on another's journey. In the process we may find ourselves wiser, more receptive, more understanding, nurtured, and sometimes even healed.

Stories enable us to imagine and feel the experience of the other, to "leap into the other," in Cynthia Ozick's words:

> Through metaphor, the past has the capacity to imagine us, and we it. . . . Those who have no pain can imagine those who suffer. Those at the center can imagine what it is to be outside. The strong can imagine what it is to be weak. Illuminated lives can imagine the borders of stellar fire. We strangers can imagine the familiar hearts of strangers. (1986, p. 65)

Through stories we can envision, with our students, new possibilities for human action and feeling, new horizons of knowing and understanding, new landscapes of engagement and even enchantment. "At 20, I've yet to forget about my experience from the ages of 6–9 in Vietnam," wrote one of my students, and the story of a child's terror and the collapse of a culture unfolded.

In rare moments, we may sense that we have entered a profound, even sacred, place. Barry Lopez captures this in his essay, "Children in the Woods," when he recounts the discovery by two children, through the piecing together of the elements of a story, that a jawbone they found in the woods is that of a raccoon:

> Children know that nearly everyone can learn the names of things; the impression made on them at this level is fleeting. What takes a lifetime to learn, they comprehend, is the existence and substance of myriad relationships; it is these relationships, not the things themselves, that ultimately hold the human imagination. (1989, p. 149)

The "other," that entity into which a story draws us to enter, may be another person, or it may be another place, culture, time, or event. The leap, once made, often offers a feeling of pervasive harmony or connection with the world imagined and with oneself. The connection may be one of joy or of despair, but the connection feels true to the core: it gives meaning to one's place in the world. What is affirmed is the sense that we are inextricably intertwined with other lives and with our natural world. Again, Barry Lopez illuminates this feeling and its lesson in the following passage:

> The most moving look I ever saw from a child in the woods was on a mud bar by the footprints of a heron. We were on our knees, making handprints beside the footprints. You could feel the creek vibrating in the silt and sand. The sun

beat down heavily on our hair. Our shoes were soaking wet. The look said: I
did not know until now that I needed someone much older to confirm this, the
feeling I have of life here. I can now grow older, knowing it need never be lost.
(1989, p. 149)

Most of us have known moments like this one in our teaching and in
our learning, moments that are characterized by a deep knowing, by a sense
of the transcendently affirmative in life, by a sense of "how wonderfully all
this fits together, to indicate what a long fierce peace can derive from this
knowledge" (Lopez, 1989, p. 151). This "fierce peace" is drawn from the
intimacy of the story—an intimacy that evokes a harmony between ourselves and our world, between what Lopez labels our interior and exterior
landscapes.

It is such moments of connection, of truthfulness, of wonderful fit, of
"a long fierce peace," that stories can provide, attaching us more deeply to
our surroundings, to others, to our own history and future possibility.
Perhaps these moments are the real texts of teaching and learning.

TEACHING THROUGH NARRATIVE: ON BECOMING
"THE FRIENDS OF ONE ANOTHER'S MINDS"

In my 20 years of teaching I have found that we can create rich opportunities for genuine dialogue through inviting students to read, receive, and
write narratives from oral and written traditions. The dialogue takes many
forms: it occurs between student and student, between student and teacher,
and between student and author. It also takes place within each participant
(students and teacher alike) as we write in our journals and papers at
different points in time during the course. All of these forms of dialogue are
taken seriously as texts in the course, as seriously as the texts that are
required or recommended in the course syllabus. I encourage students to
experiment in their journal writing and in their response papers with many
forms of dialogue: prose, poetry, letters, formal essays, selecting the mode
of writing that best serves their purposes. Students share excerpts from their
writing each day in class, sometimes with a single partner or small group,
sometimes with the whole class; they are encouraged to ask their audience
to respond to particular features or elements of their writing or ideas. This
sharing of texts created by class participants serves to locate the writers in
particular communities and narrative histories in ways that enable us to
receive and respond to each other as we struggle to create a possible world,
a shared future that is larger and more sustaining than that which we
currently inhabit. In the process of creating and sharing these stories and

reflections, we find ourselves addressing such questions as: From what stories and traditions have I come? How have they shaped who I am and what I might become? What kind of world do I wish to live in? How ought we to live? What is the right action to take? How do I care for others? For the planet? For myself? What values and commitments are most important to me and why? To others? What do I do when I see things very differently from my neighbor? What can I learn from their stories and visions? What kind of world, then, can we imagine?

Sometimes the texts created are painful ones, such as the sharing of a painful part of one's past history. One of my students in a college seminar in "Moral Development, Ethics, and Education," after reading Elie Wiesel's *Night* (a recounting of the author's experiences in Auschwitz and Buchenwald as a young boy), decided to share with her classmates her experience as a young girl living with her family under siege in Vietnam in the mid-1970s. Following a classmate's statement that she found it very difficult to relate to Wiesel's *Night* because the death camps were so alien to her own experience, Hoan read aloud from her journal, offering a bridge between two worlds:

> At 20 I've yet to forget about my experience from the ages of 6–9. But being in a new world, new society, new culture, I once thought those 3 years were just something in the past! Yet, to read about someone else's story that is many times more "torturing" than my own made me realize everything is worth remembering and telling. For in not sharing our experiences, everything is too foreign for us to grasp.

Hoan went on to describe her family's suffering and abuse while held captive by Vietnamese soldiers in the labor camp, suggesting that perhaps hearing her story could help some of her classmates make Wiesel's story more real, more compelling. She also expressed her hope that it would help others come to know her, since the events of those 3 years evoke such poignant memories. Hoan's reading aloud from her journal entry provided a bridge for another student to walk with author Elie Wiesel through his journey of terror in *Night*. The story did not just bridge the two worlds (Wiesel's and the student writer's); it asked us to *confront* another world. Robert Brown reminds us that the power of such a pairing of stories is not in their juxtaposition, but in suggesting "that the world in which we are comfortable, with which we are familiar, may not even . . . be the 'real' world any longer" (Brown, 1983, p. 43). The sharing of this and other childhood stories helped shape a vital moral community in this class, one that was characterized by a deep respect for the power of truth and personal narrative in understanding the moral fabric of human lives. While Hoan did not use these terms, I sensed the kind of peace that Lopez speaks of when she felt the impact of her story on other students: it evoked in them a profound empathy and receptiveness toward her. I also sensed in several of her fellow students a deeper and more expansive understanding of Wiesel's story portrayed in *Night:* It was an example of Lopez's "long fierce peace" — an epiphany, some might say — drawn from the sense of one-heartedness that such stories can weave.

I have found that students of all ages — primary grades through post-graduate years — respond energetically to activities such as writing work-shop and reader response groups as ways to discover, construct, and imag-ine their worlds and themselves. Events once considered strange and persons once considered strangers are met as wise teachers and companions once the barriers are traversed. At the end of Crow and Weasel's journey, Badger says to Weasel of his storytelling:

> You make me marvel at the strangeness of the world. That strangeness, the intriguing life of another people, it is a crucial thing to know. (Lopez, 1990, p. 47)

These acts of wonder, Weasel offers later, are the way that we "look into the heart of wisdom." It is a wisdom of one-heartedness, of cocreation of our world, and it is within our reach as teachers and learners.

Maxine Greene has suggested that perhaps education can only take place "when we can be the friends of one another's minds" (1991, p. xi). With my colleague Ruth Hubbard, I designed and co-teach a course titled, "Narrative and Voice: Themes of Gender and Culture Throughout the Life Span." Following Maxine Greene's maxim, drawn from her reading of Toni Morrison's *Beloved,* we selected texts for this course from a variety of literary genres and films that depict the lives and voices of women and men from diverse cultures and age groups.

We start out reading Michael Dorris' *Yellow Raft in Blue Water*, a story told through the voices of three generations: Rayona, a young woman of Native-American and African-American descent; her mother, Christine; and Aunt Ida, Rayona's grandmother. We also read Toni Morrison's *Beloved*, a story of an African-American family during the slavery and post-Civil War eras, and Robert Coles' *The Call of Stories: Teaching and the Moral Imagination*, an autobiographical account of a psychiatrist's use of stories in his practice, his teaching, and his own education. We view several film and video productions: *My Name is Zora*, an American Playhouse dramatization of the life and work of Zora Neale Hurston, arranged and produced by Ruby Dee; Tillie Olsen's *Tell Me a Riddle*, the story of a husband and wife who confront their alienation from each other and their family during their elder years; *Jury of Her Peers*, a story of a woman who faced charges for the murder of her husband during the early part of the century; and interviews with authors Toni Morrison, Michael Dorris, and Louise Erdrich.

In our reading of firsthand and fictional first-voice narratives from many cultures, we find that stereotypes of cultural groups are challenged, judgments of individuals who choose differently than we might imagine ourselves choosing are mitigated, and empathy for those who have suffered and for those who seem strange to us is enhanced. Stories long suppressed are sometimes recovered; voices silenced or unclaimed are often found. Toni Morrison's description of her mission in writing *Beloved* comes to mind:

> If writing is thinking and discovery and selection and order and meaning, it is also awe and reverence and mystery and magic. I suppose I could dispense with the last four if I were not so deadly serious about fidelity to the milieu out of which I write and in which my ancestors actually lived. Infidelity to that milieu—the absence of the interior life, the deliberate excising from the records that the slaves themselves told—is precisely the problem in the discourse that proceeded without us. How I gain access to that interior life is what drives me. . . . (Morrison, 1987b, p. 111)

All class participants, students and instructors alike, write in a reflective journal daily. We write in response to the readings, to class discussions, to other participants' writing, and to our own (earlier) entries in the journal. We reserve time during each class to read from our journal writings in pairs or in response groups, responding to each reader, either in writing or orally.

For their final group papers and presentations, students are required to read one additional book of their own selection that addresses the themes of the course. Groups are formed out of common interests or themes that are identified once individuals have selected their additional book. We recommend authors such as Andre Chedid, Kate Chopin, Carolyn Heilbrun, John Neihardt, and Maxine Hong Kingston.

Class participants use narrative as an interpretive method for making meaning from the predicaments and possibilities that compose a human life. Gender and culture are explored as meaning systems that affect individual responses in the cognitive, social, and moral realms. Students who enroll in the course represent five graduate professional programs that serve teachers, counselors, psychologists, and administrators. The course was designed to deepen our understanding of the ways that patterns and meanings of culture shape our lives. We view "culture" broadly as the ways of knowing and being that are taken for granted as shared understandings within a particular community or group of individuals. Human cultures, then, are the habitats in which our identities are forged: "those 'homes' in which our lives come to be shaped and endowed with meaning" (Alexander, 1992, p. 95).

We explore the meanings and patterns of a culture's ways of knowing and being within cultural contexts such as gender, generation, family, race, ethnicity, region, religion, and locale. Our explorations bring us into the thick of both the continuities and the conflicts that come with living in multiple and diverse cultures. Rather than retreating from the conflicts through the cultivation of a "master narrative" as critics such as Allan Bloom and E. D. Hirsch might urge, we use diverse narratives to explore the creative tensions at the core of these conflicts in order to grasp their meaning and function within their interpretive communities. In the process, we find ourselves both participants in and creators of unfinished narratives of worlds both actual and possible (the historical and the imaginative). As Martha Nussbaum has illustrated in *The Fragility of Goodness,* it is our connectedness with each other and with the world that defines us as ethical beings, and good ethical character requires an emotional, imaginative, and moral grasp of the fragility, but also the necessity, of these connections. Stories such as Hoan's, Elie Wiesel's *Night,* Toni Morrison's *Beloved,* and Lynda Barry's *The Good Times are Killing Me* help to enlarge this grasp. Such understanding, we propose, is crucial to our competence and sensitivity as educators and human service professionals.

The writing of John Othus, one of our students in this class, stands out as an example of the moral necessity of this understanding. A man in his late 30s, John was struggling to come to terms with the racial prejudice he discovered in the newspaper columns written by his great-grandmother in 1906. He begins his final paper, "Voices of Beloved: The Sisyphean Task," as follows:

> When I read *Black Elk Speaks,* a particular voice which connects me however remotely with the events the Sioux holy man describes echoes again in my mind. Today its sound is 126 years old, but for a time I knew that voice in the flesh as my great grandmother. I was 13 when she died. To better understand that voice I have read and reread Dee Brown's *Bury My Heart at Wounded Knee* many times in the last eighteen years. It was an obsession. I have read both volumes of *Son of the Morning Star,* Connell's highly detailed and balanced view of the many events and personalities leading to the infamous battle at the Little Big Horn, and even listened to the complete "Books on Tape" version several times. It was a pilgrimage. I have read *Prophetic Worlds: Indians and Whites on the Columbia Plateau* by Christopher Miller,

an historian who did most of his research at Lewis & Clark College in the early 1980's, outlining the peculiar temporal alignment of beliefs that led to the deadly clash to two completely different religious cultures. It was a release. I have read *Winterkill, River Song, Talking Leaves,* and now *Yellow Raft in Blue Water,* and I have attended many seminars on Native American literature and story telling. I have seen hours and hours of the Nez Perce dances at Wallowa Lake where my family joined with other whites and Nez Perce in their circle dance. It was healing.

Each time I come into contact with Native American views of their culture and the causes of its destruction, even those views which seek some middle ground, I am confronted by that voice and a vision of my own flesh and blood which rises from scattered heaps of childhood memories in the form of an old white woman, a pioneer and my great grandmother. She is a kind of "Beloved" I must deal with because she stood, as a woman of her times, for the unspoken destruction or subjugation of all non-white races. Every time I read Native American viewpoints, I feel that I am murdering some part of her in me. It is this feeling that keeps me searching, reading, seeking some understanding of her times, the context that might help me preserve what I love in her, what I'm proud of in her, being of her flesh and blood. Like Rayona and Christine in *Yellow Raft,* my great grandmother is my "Aunt Ida": a mystery of the blood one is compelled to endlessly search out, and condemned never to understand. It is a Sisyphean task; her voice is my rock. *Black Elk Speaks* has released that rock again.

I offer this lengthy excerpt from John's paper because it illustrates the power of narrative to create bridges between worlds, to force us to confront worlds other than our own, to see ourselves and those we are close to in the stories of others, to address injustices, and to find ourselves changed. The worlds John bridged included those of his own family, the Nez Perce at Wallowa Lake, the Oglala Sioux in John Niehardt's *Black Elk Speaks,* the three generations of women in Michael Dorris' novel *Yellow Raft in Blue Water,* and the slave families in Toni Morrison's *Beloved.* In the remainder of his paper, John imagines, after considerable family and historical research, the cultural and gender influences that might have shaped his great-grandmother's views:

Why do I feel this compulsion? Is it the only way to feed the tremendous sorrow I feel as I read Black Elk's words? Am I seeking to defend my great-grandmother and her generation of whites? Does it seem so ridiculous to feel guilt for actions I could not possibly control? How can such remote family threads and diluted blood lines feel so connecting? — so binding? It is a mystery I can not yet fully explain.

It was a journey not of vindication or even explanation, but of understanding and of personal confrontation — "a demystifying of [one woman's] voice and its place, however painful, in my story."

Both Hoan and John found in the telling of a story the tools to bridge two worlds, to transcend the barriers between generations, cultures, and worldviews. They shared their stories in ways that led to an expanded intercultural understanding of the human condition, enhancing our sense of the fragility of human goodness and the spaciousness of the moral imagination. Through these and other narratives we became, for even this brief period, a community: "a shared project of human care" (Alexander, 1992, p. 105). Along the way, Hoan and John each found a part of themselves that sought a clearer vision, perhaps also a welcome healing. I sensed once again, with Barry Lopez, "what a long fierce peace could derive from this knowledge."

REFERENCES

Alexander, T. (1992). The moral imagination and the aesthetics of human existence. In M. Mitias (Ed.), *Moral education and the liberal arts* (pp. 93–111). Westport, CT: Greenwood Press.

Barry, L. (1988). *The good times are killing me*. New York: Harper & Row.

Bloom, A. (1987). *The closing of the American mind*. New York: Simon & Schuster.

Brown, D. (1991). *Bury my heart at Wounded Knee: An Indian history of the American West*. New York: H. Holt and Co. (Published originally in 1971)

Brown, R. M. (1983). *Elie Wiesel: Messenger to all humanity*. Notre Dame, IN: University of Notre Dame Press.

Coles, R. (1989). *The call of stories: Teaching and the moral imagination*. Boston: Houghton Mifflin.

Connell, E. (1984). *Son of the Morning Star: Custer and the Little Bighorn*. Berkeley: North Point Press.

Dillard, A. (1989). *The writing life*. New York: Harper & Row.

Dorris, M. (1987). *Yellow raft in blue water*. New York: Warner.

Egan, K. (1986). *Teaching as story telling*. Chicago: University of Chicago Press.

Egan, K. (1992). *Imagination in teaching and learning: The middle school years*. Chicago: University of Chicago Press.

Egan, K., & Nadaner, D. (1988). *Imagination and education*. New York: Teachers College Press.

Greene, M. (1991). Foreword. In C. Witherell & N. Noddings (Eds.), *Stories lives tell: Narrative and dialogue in education* (pp. ix–xi). New York: Teachers College Press.

Hirsch, E. D. (1987). *Cultural literacy.* Boston: Houghton Mifflin.

Lesley, C. (1984). *Winterkill.* New York: Dell.

Lesley, C. (1989). *River song.* Boston: Houghton Mifflin.

Lesley, C. (1991). *Talking leaves: Contemporary Native American stories.* New York: Dell.

Lopez, B. (1989). *Crossing open ground.* New York: Vintage.

Lopez, B. (1990). *Crow and Weasel.* San Francisco: North Point Press.

MacIntyre, A. (1981). *After virtue.* Notre Dame, IN: University of Notre Dame Press.

Miller, C. (1985). *Prophetic worlds: Indians and whites on the Columbia Plateau.* New Brunswick, NJ: Rutgers University Press.

Morrison, T. (1987a). *Beloved.* New York: Alfred A. Knopf.

Morrison, T. (1987b). The site of memory. In William Zinsser (Ed.), *Inventing the truth: The art and craft of memoir* (pp. 101–124). Boston: Houghton Mifflin.

Neihardt, J. (1979). *Black Elk speaks.* Lincoln: University of Nebraska Press. (Originally published in 1932)

Nussbaum, M. (1986). *The fragility of goodness.* Cambridge: Cambridge University Press.

Olsen, T. (1961). *Tell me a riddle.* New York: Dell.

Ozick, C. (1986, May). The moral necessity of metaphor. *Harper's Magazine,* p. 65.

St. John, P. (1990). *Dreamer.* Pittsburgh, PA: Carnegie Mellon University Press.

Shabatay, V. (1991). The stranger: Who calls and who answers? In C. Witherell & N. Noddings (Eds.), *Stories lives tell: Narrative and dialogue in education* (pp. 136–152). New York: Teachers College Press.

Thorton, L. (1988). *Imagining Argentina.* New York: Bantam.

Wiesel, E. (1982). *Night.* New York: Bantam. (Originally published in 1959)

Williams, T. T. (1991). *Refuge: An unnatural history of family and place.* New York: Pantheon.

CHAPTER 4

Reason and Story in Wise Practice

Shirley Pendlebury

Practical wisdom is the sovereign virtue of a good teacher—a virtue whose realization in teaching requires a subtle interplay between several binary oppositions: reason and imagination, experience and innocence, cleanness of argument and richness of story, respect for principles and attunement to particulars. A central task and challenge for teacher education is to develop the capacity for such interplay. These are the claims I shall defend and elaborate in this chapter. Unlike Sigrun Gudmundsdottir in Chapter 2, my concern is not with content of teaching but with its contexts, characters, and moral complexities, and with the ways of seeing and acting in teaching. Like Carol Witherell in Chapter 3, I am interested in the relationship between narrative and the moral imagination, with this difference: Witherell focuses on narrative as a teaching medium, whereas I focus on narrative as a medium of understanding in teaching.

I begin with two sketches: one of some recent research on practical wisdom in teaching, the other of a teacher at work. The two sketches are closely related. Barbara Morgan, the teacher in question, was a research participant in Gary Fenstermacher and Virginia Richardson's project on teachers' practical arguments (Fenstermacher & Richardson, 1993; Morgan, 1993). The conflict she experienced between her role as a teacher and her role as a researcher may be interpreted as illustrating two contrasting conceptions of practical wisdom. One conception confirms the interplay between reason and imagination, argument and story, principles and particulars; the other rejects the second member of each pair as the enemy of sound practice.

PRACTICAL WISDOM IN CONTEMPORARY PROJECTS ON TEACHING

The concepts of practical wisdom and practical reasoning play a significant if sometimes confused part in a number of recent projects concerned with teaching, teacher education, and professionalism. Gary Fenstermacher and Virginia Richardson's work on practical arguments (Fenstermacher, 1987a, 1987b; Fenstermacher & Richardson, 1993), Lee Shulman's wisdom-of-practice studies (Shulman, 1987), and Hugh Sockett's proposals for an epistemology of teaching practice (Sockett, 1987, 1989) all assume that practical wisdom is central to good practice. But none, I think, goes far enough in providing an account of practical reasoning in teaching. Sockett rejects instrumental accounts, but offers little more than hints by way of an acceptable alternative; Shulman outlines a model of pedagogical reasoning that fails to capture the complex ways in which reason and action are related in teaching; and, as I have argued elsewhere (Pendlebury, 1993), Fenstermacher and Richardson pay rather too much attention to the formal elements of good practical arguments and too little to the conditions and characteristics of good practical reasoning. These criticisms are not to decry the worth or fruitfulness of the projects. Rather they suggest where more work needs to be done for the different projects to respond richly, vigorously, and sensitively to the competing demands and values inherent in the practice of teaching.

Gary Fenstermacher, in collaboration with Virginia Richardson, has been largely responsible for placing the notion of practical arguments on the agenda for educational research and debate. Recently they have put some of their ideas to work in a project for improving teachers' practical reasoning (Fenstermacher & Richardson, 1993).

Their procedure for improving teachers' practical reasoning depends crucially on the part played by a "dialogical other"—a suitably qualified person who, in sympathetic conversation with a teacher, elicits the practical arguments which underlie some aspect of the teacher's practice. A practical argument consists of a set of premises or statements about the teacher's aims, the class or students concerned, and the conditions and methods for accomplishing the aims. The conclusion to a practical argument is the adoption of a particular course of action. Once the argument has been recorded in a form which the teacher acknowledges as an accurate reflection of her reasons for doing what she does, the "other" takes on a more critical role. Now, applying systematically a set of argument appraisal standards, the task of the "other" is to get the teacher to see where his or her argument is deficient, if indeed it is deficient. Finally, again through conversation, the "other" facilitates the teacher's construction of a better argument.

Fenstermacher and Richardson (1993) specify five argument appraisal standards: four concerning the appropriate grounding for four different kinds of premises that typify pedagogical reasoning and the fifth concerning the logical coherence of the argument as a whole. The four types of premises, they claim, are: (1) value or moral premises, (2) stipulative premises,

(3) empirical premises, and (4) situational premises. Value premises are appraised for their grounding in a coherent moral theory; stipulative premises for their grounding in an understanding of the learner, the subject matter, and the form of instruction; empirical premises for their grounding in observable and proven fact; and situational premises for their accurate judgment of the situation calling for action. In short, the appraisal standards proposed by Fenstermacher and Richardson are none other than the familiar and universally applicable standards for cogent arguments which appear in every textbook on critical thinking.

Fenstermacher and Richardson's procedure of argument elicitation, evaluation, and reconstruction is premised on the assumption that good teaching depends upon sound practical reasoning and that an improvement in teachers' practical *arguments* results in better practical *reasoning*. While the first part of the assumption is probably true (depending on what account is given of practical reasoning), the second is questionable. Sound practical reasoning requires, as I shall argue, situational appreciation (Pendlebury, 1990; Wiggins, 1980), a way of seeing which is better nurtured by stories than by formal arguments.

A TEACHER AT ODDS WITH HERSELF

My sketch of Barbara Morgan at work has its source in her own record of the tensions between the role of teacher and the role of "dialogical other" when these are played by one and the same person—in this case herself (Morgan, 1991; Morgan, 1993). The sketch is an interpretation, not a copy, of its source. To render Morgan's case perspicuous for an account of practical wisdom in teaching, I have taken a degree of license, emphasizing some facets and downplaying or ignoring others.

In an earlier account, Morgan is strikingly alert to the risks of playing "dialogical other" to herself. "Can one go through this procedure and still teach," she wonders, "or would I find myself so busy investigating my thinking about actions that I could no longer act?" (Morgan, 1991, p. 2). As an experienced teacher, she knows that in normal circumstances competent practice is fluent practice. The overly self-conscious teacher becomes hesitant and bumbling, and practice is thoroughly undermined where too many of its taken-for-granted grounds are challenged simultaneously.

Morgan is sensitive, too, to the significance of conflict for genuine self-investigation. For the procedure to be meaningful, she sees that she must be at odds with herself: " . . . I looked for practices about which I felt some conflict (to be my own dialogic partner I needed to be of at least two minds)" (Morgan, 1991, p. 2). Ultimately, the conflicts are deeper than she anticipates.

As I shall characterize them, the deep conflicts are generated by Morgan acting from two opposing *agency postures*: a posture of *reflective equilibrium* and a posture of *perceptive equilibrium*. The main features of the two postures—whose names I have borrowed, again with some license, from the work of John Rawls (1971) and Martha Nussbaum (1990a, 1990b)—will emerge in my account of Barbara Morgan's story and in more detail in the next section of this chapter. For the moment, let me offer a very rough characterization of each. *Reflective equilibrium*, as I shall use the term, is characterized by rational deliberation undertaken from the vantage point of situational distance and guided by principles that are general in form and universal in application. *Perceptive equilibrium*, on the other hand, is characterized by deliberation undertaken from a vantage point of situational immersion and guided by imaginative discernment of the salient particulars of the situation. I contrast these agency postures with a third that I shall call *perceptive spontaneity*, a posture in which a fascination for the particulars overwhelms deliberation. While both reflective equilibrium and perceptive equilibrium result in reflective practice, I shall argue that only perceptive equilibrium results in wise practice in teaching and that perceptive spontaneity results in practice that is neither reflective nor wise. Although I refer to the three positions as agency postures, in cases where they concern a person's enduring traits, they are more aptly called *states of character*.

Let us return now to Barbara Morgan's attempt at self-investigation. After careful consideration of the risks and challenges of the investigative task she has undertaken as part of the Fenstermacher-Richardson project, Morgan chooses to investigate her practice of giving detention to children who fail to complete their weekly book reports (Morgan, 1991; Morgan, 1993). In conversation with herself, she casts her reasons for this practice in the form of a practical argument and then evaluates the argument according to the appraisal standards specified by Fenstermacher and Richardson.

Most of the premises, she concludes, are sound: An appreciation of reading is undoubtedly a worthwhile educational aim; on the evidence of pedagogical experience and research on reading, there are good grounds for believing that such appreciation cannot be cultivated except by the activity of reading itself; teachers' lore and personal experience testify that many children do not read unless reading is a set task to be accomplished by a due date; book reports are indeed both public proof of a completed task and a way of developing interpretive skills; and detention does ensure that quiet time is available for children to complete the task and, in addition, marks it as a task not to be taken lightly.

Sound though the premises may be, Morgan realizes upon reflection that detention is a punitive measure and is thus likely to undermine the very end she is striving for—an appreciation and enjoyment of reading. In short, the means are inconsistent with the end. With so important an end at stake, she concludes that a nonpunitive way must be found to ensure that her students read regularly. She discusses the problem with her class of 9- and 10-year-olds to find out why many of them do not complete (or in some cases, even begin) their book reports. A major cause seems to be a shortage of quiet reading time, so she sets an additional half-hour of nonpunitive reading time at the end of each school day. After a few hiccoughs, the strategy works for all but two children. Bill and Marie are simply not reading.

To this point, Morgan has acted from an agency posture of reflective equilibrium. Following a rational procedure, she has evaluated her approach to pupils' reading and revised it to ensure consistency between means and end. The principles guiding her deliberations (i.e., the argument appraisal standards) are public, general in form, and universal in application. She does not simply impose her views and decisions on the pupils but discusses the matter with them, thus acknowledging their coagency in the educational process and demonstrating her concern with the class as a learning community. Nonetheless, her deliberation, undertaken from a vantage point of *situational distance*, is thoroughly objective: emotion and imagination remain dutifully in the background and the pupils' personal narratives do not impinge in any significant way upon on her decisions.

Marie and Bill call forth a very different quality of response. Through imaginative questions, sympathetic observation, and an openness to their personal narratives, Morgan comes to a rich appreciation of the situation of each child. From a vantage point of *situational immersion,* she discards the easy categories into which other teachers have slotted them. She discards, too, the listing of superficial situational premises that Morgan-as-other insists upon as part of practical argument construction, for example, "It is lunch time on the day after the book reports are due" (Morgan, 1993). Instead, she moves to the language of storytelling and emotionally attuned description: Marie is not willfully disobedient or a reluctant reader but a child who needs time to grieve, a child "so sad she looked boneless" (Morgan, 1993, p. 120); Bill is a "silent child whose laughter doesn't even come out" (Morgan, 1993, p. 121).

In her responses to Marie and Bill, Morgan acts from a position of perceptive equilibrium. She discerns—with clarity, imagination, and a resonance sustained by emotional involvement—the salient particulars of Bill's and Marie's situations. Her discernment makes her part of their personal narratives and them part of hers. Yet she does not simply abandon or bypass her standing commitments as a teacher. The commitment to cultivating an appreciation of reading in all her pupils remains. But in the case of Marie and Bill, she sees, it is a commitment that should wait until other things are in place. In short, Morgan's decisions regarding these two children are the result of a lively interplay between her respect for principles and her attunement to situational particulars.

Morgan-as-other declares her unease about this shift in position, demanding "cleaner arguments less packed in story"; Morgan-as-teacher insists on some of the complications which are "inconvenient but true" (Morgan, 1993, p. 121). And so she should. Practical reasoning at its best is sensitive to all the inconvenient complications, to the particulars of human stories, and to the competing demands of practice. Above all, it depends upon situational appreciation, or what Aristotle called *perception*.

This does not mean that anything goes, nor does it mean that general principles, coherent arguments, or standing commitments are irrelevant. In teaching, as in daily living, the basis for wise action is—to paraphrase Martha Nussbaum's (1990b) remarks in "Literature and the Moral Imagination"—a loving dialogue between principles and particulars, responsibility and perception. It is through such dialogue that perceptive equilibrium is accomplished.

Perceptive equilibrium is to be distinguished from a third agency posture, one that I shall call *perceptive spontaneity*. The spontaneously perceptive agent responds richly to the booming buzzing confusion of the world, taking fine-tuned perception to "a dangerously rootless extreme," delighting in complex particulars for their own sake, "without sufficiently feeling the pull of moral obligation to any" (Nussbaum, 1990b, p. 158). Seductive as such spontaneity may be, it cannot form the basis of wise practice in teaching. Wise practice requires responsible vision, that is, fine-tuned perception or situational appreciation which takes proper account of the standing commitments, principles, and internal goods of the practice.

STANDING COMMITMENTS AND NARRATIVE IN WISE PRACTICE

Let us leave Barbara Morgan's case now and move on to a more detailed consideration of the three agency postures and their bearing on wise practice in teaching.

Earlier in the chapter, I claimed that while both reflective and perceptive equilibrium are appropriate postures for reflective practice, wise practice in teaching is possible only from a posture of perceptive equilibrium. In addition, I claimed that perceptive spontaneity results in practice which is neither reflective nor wise. I have also hinted at the importance of narrative understanding for practical wisdom. A defense and elaboration of these claims involves three related considerations: (1) the role and status of standing commitments and general principles in each of the three agency postures, (2) the proper weighing procedure for accomplishing either of the two postures of equilibrium, and (3) the nature and importance of narrative understanding in teaching. In this section I deal with the first consideration, and continue in the next section with the second. The third consideration is a common strand to be woven through both sections.

Standing Commitments

From a position of perceptive spontaneity, standing commitments are either peripheral or irrelevant. The spontaneously perceptive teacher is the one who, if his or her attention is caught today by an exciting new book, will abandon yesterday's commitment to spend extra time working through difficult calculations with fractions. This is the teacher for whom the exhilaration of trips to the park to write poems about tulips in bloom obscures the value of less flamboyant educational pursuits, like charting the daily progress of slowly sprouting avocado pips in bottles on the classroom windowsill. This is the teacher who is mesmerized by Jason's adolescent angst or Medea's awakening passion for history and leaves the students to flounder. In short, this is the teacher who pushes aside disciplined work in favor of new, exciting, or more immediately absorbing activities and affairs.

Drawn from observations of teachers I have known, and from my own early history as an exuberant but haphazard and sometimes irresponsible teacher, these examples indicate some of the ways in which the perceptively spontaneous teacher is blind to the obligations of practice. Trips to the park in spring, reading a story instead of working through calculations with fractions, caring about the angst of individual pupils—none of these is despicable in itself. Under appropriate conditions all might be praiseworthy. Of course, we want teachers who are alive to the possibilities of the moment, who are able to see freshly and vividly, who are not slaves to regulation. But where a teacher's spontaneity is driven by an habitual blindness to or dismissal of the standing commitments and internal goods of teaching, he or she fails in her responsibility to both her pupils and her subject. A failure in both dimensions of responsibility is a failure that thoroughly undermines the practice of teaching. Unless a teacher feels the pressure of these responsibilities, there is a sense in which we can question whether he or she is teaching at all. Certainly this teacher cannot be a competent, a reflective, or a wise practitioner.

John Gardner's (1985) work on fiction provides a useful conceptual tool for describing the outcome of habitual blindness to obligation and principle. Typically, a story ends in one of two ways: in resolution or in logical exhaustion. A story has exhausted itself when we realize we've reached the stage of infinite repetition; any further events which might follow will all express the same thing: for example, a character whose every action is driven by an overwhelming bitterness or one who is trapped in an endless series of empty rituals. For the teacher who, as a matter of character rather than occasional posture, acts from perceptive spontaneity, there is only one possible narrative end: logical exhaustion. For without attention to the standing commitments and principles of practice, this teacher is not in a position even to recognize typical pedagogical conflicts and problems, let alone resolve them.

Finding Equilibrium

By contrast, the postures of reflective and perceptive equilibrium must both result in resolution. This is precisely what is suggested by the term *equilibrium*. The two postures of equilibrium differ not because the first heeds standing commitments and general principles whereas the second dismisses them, but rather because of the way in which standing commitments, principles, and particulars are related and because of what is brought into equilibrium in each. I have already hinted at the two different sets of relationships in my discussion of the conflict between Morgan-as-other and Morgan-as-teacher. A fuller description calls for a brief conceptual history of reflective and perceptive equilibrium, and some further examples and analysis.

The history begins with Aristotle. The Aristotelian questions "How should I live?" or "What constitutes the good life?" may be posed more narrowly as questions about how best to engage in the practices to which we have committed ourselves. For instance: "How should I teach?" or "What constitutes good teaching?" Like the larger question about the good life, these and similar questions about human practices are concerned with the nature of excellence, in the sense of how to make the best of what we are, what we do, and what we can become. And, like the larger question, they may be addressed by a procedure first described by Aristotle, and elaborated and applied in our times in rather different ways by philosophers like John Rawls (1971) and Martha Nussbaum (1990a).

The procedure has three main steps. First, we try to give a perspicuous description of major alternative views of the good life (or, in our case, of good teaching), holding them up against one another and against our own experiences and intuitions. Second, we describe the tensions and conflicts among the different views. Finally, we revise the overall picture to bring it into harmony with itself, trying to preserve what seems deepest and least optional. A guiding question for this final step is: "What are the costs of eliminating or modifying different elements?" We aim to save those elements that seem most crucial to the good life (or to good practice). Our answers to these questions are guided by a sense of what it means to live a life, as well as by a commitment to consistency and community—consistency because it is basic to rational practice, community because neither the good life nor good practice can be accomplished in isolation.

The successful outcome of the procedure is a temporary equilibrium: "we bring the picture into harmony with itself." John Rawls (1971, pp. 172–175) calls it reflective equilibrium and adds some specifications about which of our judgments to trust and accept in the procedure and which to mistrust and reject. Although he offers his specifications as if they were uncontroversial, Martha Nussbaum (1990a, p. 175) argues that they distort Aristotle's view of practical reasoning.

According to Rawls, judgments to be mistrusted are those made hesitantly or out of fear and other kinds of emotional upset. Also to be mistrusted are judgments from which we stand to gain in some way. Impartiality, certainty, situational distance, and emotional neutrality are presented as the marks of sound deliberation. Rawls also sets five criteria that must be met for an ethical theory to be worth serious consideration: its principles should be public, be universal in application, be general in form, impose a general ordering on conflicting claims, and be decisive as court of last appeal for practical reasoning.

This is very like the procedure followed by Barbara Morgan in analyzing and evaluating her practice of giving detention to students who fail to complete their book reports. Rather than pursuing Morgan's case further here, it may be illuminating to stray for a moment beyond the bounds of fact into the world of narrative fiction, where we find some of the most richly textured illustrations of reflective equilibrium as a state of character rather than an occasional agency posture.

Nussbaum (1990a, pp. 176–185) suggests that Mrs. Newsome, in Henry James' novel *The Ambassadors*, is a comic portrait of a character who consistently acts from a state of reflective equilibrium. A woman of fine cold thought and fixed moral purpose, she lives according to rules of right unsoftened by the light of individual cases or special circumstances. Because she is a "noble and autonomous moral agent" for whom nature has "no power to jolt or surprise," she is able to triumph over life and avoid becoming its victim (p. 178). But that's just it—Mrs. Newsome triumphs over life, she doesn't live it. Her principles and the standing commitments set by her moral purpose impede her response to the complex ebb and flow of human lives and situations. Yet we can admire her for steadfastness, principled action, rationality, and, above all, for the equal respect and dignity she accords everyone regardless of nature or station. At the same time, we find Mrs. Newsome terrifying for her blindness to special circumstances and for the coldness of her equal treatment of others, suggesting that she cares more about principles than about people.

Like Mrs. Newsome, a teacher acting consistently from a state of reflective equilibrium is one who is never overwhelmed by practice. Guided by a steadfast commitment to publicly accepted pedagogical and professional principles, he or she proceeds surely, confidently, and calmly. This teacher's classroom is characterized by a sense of order and quiet dignity. From the outset, his or her pupils understand what is required of them in word and deed. This need not mean that the teacher's approach is dull or trapped in routine. With the thoroughness of one who takes his or her professional commitments seriously, this teacher updates teaching materials regularly and keeps abreast of research on new theories and effective methods. New methods and theories are accepted not from an allegiance to fashion but are weighed and, if necessary, modified according to the rational procedures for reflective equilibrium.

What, we may ask, is wrong with a teacher who is steadfast, responsible, trustworthy, and rational? Nothing, except where such qualities spring from a state of character that cannot but be blind to the deep conflicts—the hard cases—of practice. I have already claimed that a teacher who habitually acts from a position of perceptive spontaneity is blind to standing commitments and general moral principles. Now I want to argue that a teacher who habitually acts from a position of reflective equilibrium is also blind, in another way and for different reasons.

The argument rests on an Aristotelian view of practice (see Nussbaum, 1986, 1990c; Pendlebury, 1990; Wiggins, 1980). In this view, the world of practice has three central, related features which together present a cluster of cognitive uncertainties that make practical deliberation inaccessible to a system of general rules: mutability, indeterminacy, and particularity. Drawing from my earlier work (Pendlebury, 1990), let me outline each of these features with respect to teaching.

Practice is mutable because it changes over time, presenting us with new configurations which cannot be ignored if our deliberations are to be sound. On a large timescale, the practice of teaching is mutable in that it changes with the institutions that contain and support it. As a practice, teaching is also mutable on a smaller time-scale. To give just one of many examples: pupils change not only with age but also with the state of their physical and emotional well-being. A child who is responsive to teaching and eager to learn may become sullen, resentful, and closed for any number of reasons, many of which can only be understood in the light of the child's personal narrative.

The world of practice is indeterminate because practical questions arise within particular contexts. Appropriate choices of action are thus contextually relative. A teacher in a well-equipped suburban school with a strongly established academic culture, for example, has very different choices open to him or her than a teacher in an ill-equipped, overcrowded ghetto school where the culture of learning has been thoroughly undermined by poverty and political disenchantment.

The particularity of teaching is neatly captured by Jere Confrey (1987) in her critical response to some of Fenstermacher's work:

> When I enter a classroom, I know I am going to subject myself to certain constraints; time pressures and group demands are two of the most salient. I carry into this my planned agenda with varying levels of explicitness, and as a result of my interpretation of the cues I allow, promote, ignore, understand or misunderstand. We call this a "practice", and its defining characteristics are its unrelenting pace, its human interactions, its normative dimensions, its competing goals, and its activity (p. 386).

In negotiating his or her planned agenda in action, a teacher reads the particular cues (restlessness, puzzled or desperate looks, whispered questions between pupils) which suggest that a change in pace is required or that he or she backtrack a bit or allow time for discussion or a break. A good teacher is alert to the salient features of each teaching situation and ready to change his or her course of action to meet special circumstances.

But the salient features of a situation do not jump to the eye ready labeled for easy identification. It is up to the teacher to pick them out. This involves what Aristotle calls perception or situational appreciation. Sound practical reasoning is not possible without it. If a teacher is wrong in his or her interpretation of a situation, the result will be inappropriate or misguided action, regardless of the internal coherence of the argument the teacher may give to support his or her actions or of the strength of the teacher's standing commitments and moral principles.

For Aristotle, the initiating or major premise of a practical argument is concerned with the good, whereas the secondary or minor premise is concerned with the possible. I suggest that a wise practitioner is one who has a rich understanding of the goods and ends of the practice and a realistic, clear-sighted, and sensitive perception of what is possible and apt under different circumstances. The second requirement cannot be met by one who is blind to particulars.

I have argued that both perceptive spontaneity and reflective equilibrium are inadequate for wise practice. The first is blind to the principles, definitive ends, and standing commitments of teaching; the second is blind to the fine-grained particulars of practice. Somewhat too neatly and too simply, we can say that each of the two agency postures attends to only one side of the oppositional pairs listed in the opening paragraph to this chapter. What is attractive about the spontaneously perceptive teacher is a liveliness of imagination and a fresh, almost innocent responsiveness to new experiences; what is attractive about the reflectively balanced teacher is a rigor of argument and a deep commitment to principled action. But whatever their attractions, each is a deeply flawed practitioner; the first more deeply than the second because without some attention to the definitive ends and standing commitments of a practice, it is hardly possible for the practice to get off the ground.

To conclude this section, I return briefly to the conceptual history of reflective and perceptive equilibrium. Although the notion of reflective equilibrium is rooted in Aristotle, Rawls' account belongs to a tradition of moral thinking that assumes the epistemological and moral priority of general, universal principles untainted by emotion or particular considerations. In contrast to this tradition, Aristotle's emphasis on perception or situational appreciation indicates the ethical crudeness of moralities based exclusively on general rules. A similar point can be made about the crudeness of teaching based exclusively on general rules.

A "morality of perception," to use Nussbaum's (1990c) term for Aristotle's position, is one in which general principles still have enormous action-guiding significance, but actions are not derived from or dictated by general principles. Right action is not simply a matter of rationality or following moral rules. In *The Fabric of Character*, her illuminating study of Aristotle's *Ethics*, Nancy Sherman argues that emotions as well as reason ground the moral response, for emotions are themselves modes of response that determine what is morally relevant in different situations (Sherman, 1989, p. 2). To act rightly, she claims, is to be emotionally engaged.

I would add that to act rightly is also to be narratively engaged, for it is in the context of human stories that we are best able to see the salient features of different human situations, as is illustrated in Barbara Morgan's response to her pupils Bill and Marie. Narrative understanding plays an important part, too, in the substance we give to the definitive ends and standing commitments of a practice. Logically speaking, the intention of teaching is to bring about learning. A teacher who never acts upon this intention is simply not teaching even although he or she goes through all the motions. But this conceptual claim about the relationship between teaching and learning is a formal claim which must be given substance in different ways for different students in different contexts. How we act on the teaching intention and how we interpret various teaching principles depends partly on the constraints and possibilities set by local conditions and by students' learning histories. It depends, too, on how we conceive of the pedagogical quest and which conflicts we take to be central in our drive for resolution. The decisions we take can turn our students' narratives in a new direction, either opening up new possibilities or impeding future progress in deep and subtle ways.

NARRATIVE AND STRONG EVALUATION IN TEACHING

In both reflective and perceptive equilibrium, some sort of balance or harmony is reached. What is brought into balance in each and by what means?

To ask and answer these questions takes us right to the heart of several related debates in moral philosophy, in decision theory, and in theories about reasoning in teaching. At the risk of setting up some straw positions, but in the interests of not complicating matters unnecessarily, we can say that the central issue is between two opposing conceptions of practical deliberation: *strong evaluation* and *simple weighing* (Nussbaum, 1990c; Taylor, 1985a, 1985b). Strong evaluation is central to wise practice.

According to Charles Taylor (1985a), we engage in strong evaluation when we are concerned with the qualitative worth of our goals or desires. In strong evaluation, as opposed to simple weighing, the fact that I desire something is not sufficient for it to be good or worthwhile. Its being good has to do with its worth in a particular sort of life or for a particular sort of person; within the life of an artist, a teacher, a mother, or a political activist, for instance, or for a person who is committed to fairness and civility in all his or her dealings with others. Although Morgan-as-other desires cleaner arguments, Morgan-as-teacher sees that a sensitive and responsible teacher cannot simply brush aside the unwelcome complications of practice. To do so would be insensitive and irresponsible. As Morgan's response suggests, the judgments of worth in strong evaluation are made in what Taylor (1985a, p. 24) calls a language of qualitative contrast; in terms of fidelity and betrayal, courage and cowardice, honesty and duplicity, and the like—terms which are most at home and have their most telling exemplars in narrative. This surely is one of the reasons why the classic fairy tales have so powerful a grip on our imagination, as Kieran Egan reminds us in chapter 8.

In order to bring the salient features of our concerns into explicit awareness, we need to articulate practical issues in terms of these qualitative contrasts. A rich language of qualitative contrast is thus an important feature of situational appreciation and an enabling condition for wise practice. However, such a language, together with finely tuned attention to particulars, may also bring conflicting and often incommensurable values out into the open, thus making practical deliberation more and not less difficult.

The idea of simple weighing offers a more reliable method of deliberation by reducing practical reason to calculation. Martha Nussbaum identifies four constituent claims in the idea of simple weighing: the claim of singleness, the claim of metricity, the claim of consequentialism, and the claim of maximization (Nussbaum, 1990c). A basic assumption is that in any situation calling for choice there is some single value at stake. A rational chooser weighs the alternative courses of action against some measure of the relevant value and chooses the course which will produce the best consequences by maximizing the relevant value at minimum cost. What we have here is an instrumentalist view of practical rationality, in which deliberation is concerned with finding the most effective and efficient means to an end.

Simple weighing cannot serve as a basis for wise practice in teaching. In the first place, the hard cases in teaching are precisely those in which there is no single value or aim to be pursued but several competing and often conflicting concerns. In the second place, there is uncertainty about how best to specify the ends we wish to accomplish. Characteristically, in nontechnical cases of practical reasoning, a teacher has only a vague description of what he or she wants to accomplish: to engender an appreciation of art, to develop open-mindedness, to be a better teacher. The difficulty is not so much a matter of what would be causally effective in achieving these aims as to see what constitutes an appreciation of art or open-mindedness or being a better teacher. In these cases, the sort of reasoning required is not means-to-end reasoning but what I have called elsewhere constituents-of-end reasoning (Pendlebury, 1990). In the third place, the consequentialist claim of simple weighing implies that in choosing his or her means or methods a teacher need attend only to their effectiveness in bringing about the desired ends. This ignores the fact that the most effective means may also be morally abhorrent or stylistically crass. Finally, the ends of teaching are often not the sort that are accomplished in an hour, a day, a week, or even a year. They are part of an ongoing quest.

Neither reflective nor perceptive equilibrium is to be achieved through simple weighing. As we saw in Barbara Morgan's case, both require judgments of worth and the capacity to articulate concerns in terms of qualitative contrasts. Both are reached through a strong evaluation of the elements to be brought into equilibrium.

A teacher acting from a position of reflective equilibrium has already brought into balance, through strong evaluation, a coherent set of principles which constitute a theory of teaching. This teacher's pedagogical choices are derived from the theory. A teacher acting from a position of perceptive equilibrium brings the salient features of a particular situation into play with his or her standing commitments and conception of the general principles of practice. While the general principles and standing commitments may guide this teacher's response to a particular set of circumstances, they do not dictate it. Although he or she comes to lessons well-prepared, much of this teacher's practice has the character of improvisation, responding to current conditions and possibilities. There are, of course, constraints on the nature and manner of improvisation. For a teacher's improvisations to count as teaching (and not, for example, as free-floating creativity, self-indulgence, or mere entertainment), they must remain responsible both to standing commitments and to the principles and structures that constitute the practice of teaching. Perhaps there will be times when a new situation prompts a teacher to revise his or her conception of one or more of these principles and he or she may decide that certain prima facie obligations are not really binding. But, to echo Martha Nussbaum, "this never takes the form of leaping above or simply sailing around the standing commitments" (Nussbaum, 1990b, p. 156).

How should a teacher judge the soundness of his or her practical reasoning? In Fenstermacher and Richardson's view, the teacher should judge the soundness of his or her reasoning by assessing the cogency of the underlying arguments. In a strictly instrumentalist view, the teacher should judge the soundness of his or her reasoning by assessing the outcome of his or her actions: if these have resulted in the desired effect—for example, if they have maximized learning of the desired kind in the desired area—the teacher's reasoning was sound and the teacher's practice was competent.

But there is another way, a way in which it is possible to incorporate and nurture a rich understanding of the goods and ends of teaching and to attend to the salient particulars of the circumstances of action. This is the way of narrative redescription. In reflecting critically on his or her practice, the perceptive teacher has a story to tell—a story which relates obstacles overcome or still looming large; conflicts resolved, displaced, or deepened; turning points for better or worse; climaxes and culminations. Neither argument analysis nor retrospective simple weighing is amenable to these ways of speaking.

ACKNOWLEDGMENT

I am deeply indebted to Barbara Morgan-Flemming whose rich and sensitive account of her work as a teacher-researcher has inspired, and challenged, my thinking about practical reasoning in teaching.

REFERENCES

Confrey, J. (1987). Bridging research and practice. *Educational Theory, 37*, 383–394.

Fenstermacher, G. (1987a). Prologue to my critics. *Educational Theory, 37*, 357–360.

Fenstermacher, G. (1987b). Reply to my critics. *Educational Theory, 37,* 413–421.

Fenstermacher, G., & Richardson, V. (1993). The elicitation and reconstruction of practical arguments in teaching. *Journal of Curriculum Studies, 25*(2), 100–115.

Gardner, J. (1985). *The art of fiction.* New York: Vintage.

Morgan, B. (1991, April). *Practical rationality: A self-investigation.* Paper presented at the annual meeting of the American Educational Research Association, Chicago.

Morgan, B. (1993). Practical rationality: A self-investigation. *Journal of Curriculum Studies, 25*(2), 115–124.

Nussbaum, M. C. (1986). *The fragility of goodness: Luck and ethics in Greek tragedy and philosophy.* Cambridge, UK: Cambridge University Press.

Nussbaum, M. C. (1990a). Perceptive equilibrium: Literary theory and ethical theory. In *Love's knowledge: Essays on philosophy and literature* (pp. 168–194). Oxford: Oxford University Press.

Nussbaum, M. C. (1990b). Literature and the moral imagination. In *Love's knowledge: Essays on philosophy and literature* (pp. 148–167). Oxford: Oxford University Press.

Nussbaum, M. C. (1990c). The discernment of perception: An Aristotelian conception of private and public rationality. In *Love's knowledge: Essays on philosophy and literature* (pp. 54–105). Oxford: Oxford University Press.

Pendlebury, S. (1990). Practical reasoning and situational appreciation in teaching. *Educational Theory, 40,* 171–179.

Pendlebury, S. (1993). Practical arguments, rationalization and imagination in teachers' practical reasoning. *Journal of Curriculum Studies, 25*(2), 145–151.

Rawls, J. (1971). *A theory of justice.* Cambridge, MA: Belknap Press.

Sherman, N. (1989). *The fabric of character: Aristotle's theory of virtue.* Oxford: Clarendon Press.

Shulman, L. S. (1987). Knowledge and teaching: Foundations of the new reform. *Harvard Educational Review, 57,* 1–22.

Sockett, H. (1987). Has Shulman got the strategy right? *Harvard Educational Review, 57,* 208–219.

Sockett, H. (1989). Research, practice and professional aspirations within teaching. *Journal of Curriculum Studies, 21,* 97–112.

Taylor, C. (1985a). What is human agency? In *Human agency and language: Philosophical papers 1.* Cambridge, UK: Cambridge University Press.

Taylor, C. (1985b). Self-interpreting animals. In *Human agency and language: Philosophical papers 1.* Cambridge, UK: Cambridge University Press.

Wiggins, D. (1980). Deliberation and practical reason. In A. Rorty (Ed.), *Essays on Aristotle's ethics* (pp. 221–240). Berkeley: University of California Press.

PART II

THE ROLES OF NARRATIVE IN LEARNING

CHAPTER 5

Radicalizing Childhood:
The Multivocal Mind

Brian Sutton-Smith

In this chapter, I want to challenge the view of children's minds which has been constructed by traditional psychology based on the predictive science model. Current theories of child development that have resulted from this research emphasize the "primitive" nature of the early childhood mind and a unilineal path of development; these theories privilege the superior accommodations of adulthood. In place of this currently dominant view, I want to propose what I will call the *multivocal* mind of the child, emphasizing a variety of developmental possibilities children can pursue, the complexity of their thinking, and features of their cognition in which they are commonly superior to adults. While we have, since Margaret Mead's work in particular, striven to recognize other diverse human cultures as inherently worthwhile in their own right and not to be evaluated by spurious comparisons with Western adult male norms, we have not as yet applied such insight to our own children.

What I wish to do in this chapter is to revisit some of my own empirical studies in early childhood literacy, narrative, television, toys, and play in order to support the conception of the sophisticated, complex, multidevelopmental, and multivocal mind of the child.

SOME MASTER METAPHORS

By way of illustrating what I have in mind, I am going to review several of my own research studies which have had relevance to some of the master concepts that have contributed powerfully to psychological thought about early childhood in the past several decades. These master concepts include the role of *scaffolding* in the acquisition of literacy and the role of *structuralism* in the development of children's narratives. Let me make it quite clear

69

that this is not meant to be other than a most partial listing of such master concepts. What I am doing is testing out whether the kind of inquiry that I have in mind is worthwhile. For me, this is the pilot review only. It is not the final product.

Scaffolding

The notion of scaffolding first appeared in an article by Ninio and Bruner (1978) entitled, "The Achievement and Antecedents of Labelling." In this article, the authors demonstrated by videotape recordings of a mother and her infant, between the ages of 8 months and 18 months, how the child learned picture book reading through a process of a ritualized picture book dialogue with the mother. Over 90% of the time the mother calls the child's attention to the pictures in the book by saying "Look," by asking, "What's that?" by next labeling the picture, and then by making a positive feedback response to the infant when it pays attention in some way to the picture. Whatever the child's response, a smile or a grunt, a reaching or a babbling, the mother interprets it as an appropriate response and repeats her labeling. As time goes by, the child enters more fully into the dialogue, following the mother in saying "Look," asking "What is it?" or labeling the picture. The process of reading has begun.

It is a potent demonstration of the role of parent tutoring in the development of literacy and of the interactive role of the parent with the child. Furthermore, it is a powerful demonstration of Vygotsky's "zone of proximal development," by which the child with adult help is lifted beyond its own meager level of competence to a higher level. In his later, somewhat autobiographical work, *Actual minds, possible worlds*, Bruner (1986) acknowledges the Vygotskian source of this idea. Vygotsky, for his part, and in his Marxist voice, was attempting to show the social source of word meanings, how the second signal system of language was drenched with cultural meaning.

Although this was just a single case study with a firstborn male child of a somewhat didactic English middle-class mother whose husband was a schoolmaster, it has become something of a metaphor for the development of literacy. This is due in part to the paradox of American society. Although generally we are not under Vygotsky's obligation to give credit to the social source of language, our psychological tradition follows the metaphor of mechanistic physical science. We tend to believe that we have achieved science when we have found causal connections and predicted outcomes. This case study apparently gives us a wonderful example of such determinism in child development and is exemplary, therefore, both as a piece of science and as a model for tutoring children. The implication is that despite our general vaunting of individuality in American life, our parallel respect for positivistic social science encourages us to believe and find credible very deterministic accounts of human behavior. And what this implies is that we find it easy to believe that behind all the confusion and individuality of human development there really is some single set of universal laws which will ultimately explain the variance in the human condition. In education, likewise, we can have faith in our tutoring because in the long run, even if not immediately, it will be based on a science of human development. I believe Ninio and Bruner's scaffolding metaphor helps to encourage such a mechanistic faith.

Several years after the Bruner publication I set about doing a replication of his study with the aid of Mary Ann Magee, who owned and directed several preschools in Swarthmore, Pennsylvania (Magee & Sutton-Smith, 1983). The intent was to find out something about how a child learns to tell a story. The child, a 23-month-old girl, listened to and participated in story-book reading, picture book reading, personal narratives, and made-up story telling over a period of 9 months. Thirty-six sessions were tape-recorded for a total of 5 hours and 20 minutes, with an average length of about 11 minutes.

The important points to be made for my purposes are that although the American mother, father, and teacher, like the English mother, monopolized the exchanges, taking up to 75% of the recorded time, neither adult nor child were as didactically ritualistic as in the Bruner paradigm. In our studies, adults and children fooled around a lot more, particularly the father and child, who were both given to considerable nonsense. The child's responses were much more diverse than those of the parent's. In the bulk of these responses, the child was original in multiple ways as evidenced by laughter, inventions to the text, her own storytelling, or her own play, despite the fact that most of the adult responses were those of conventional storytelling and despite the fact that this child became more orthodox over time (Sutton-Smith, 1984).

From these studies, what became apparent to us for the first time was the multivocal mindedness which is my key to the radicalization of our concept of childhood. This is one kind of evidence that the child's mind is not a tabula rasa passively awaiting adult intent. If we follow the Russian scholar Bakhtin, as in his *Rabelais and his World* (1984), laughter is the most primitive form of parody and satire by which the sanctity of established ways gets impugned. It is life's basic form of unofficial response. But in addition to this mental alternative, this 2-year-old also plays with the material given, transforming the official scaffolding situation into one of pretense and novelty. Or she becomes her own storyteller, supplanting the adults. She takes on the official role. Or she invents a new text where she is serious but innovates. So here we have a 2- to 2½-year-old child in the tolerant and supportive domain of her parents, acting with possible voices, including her response to the text. In fact, the factor analysis we performed suggests that, according to this method of coordinating the variances, she speaks with at least 12 different voices. The factor differences now are more subtle and more specific, but it is quite reasonable to think of each as a specific form of enactment or a specific voice. This factor analysis, with its total of 20 separate factors required to speak to the 50 coded variables (and covering 75% of the variance of these), speaks to the complexity of what is going on here.

So what should we conclude from this? That the American child in this study is different from the English child in literacy, just as we have learned that Athabaskans (Scollon & Scollon, 1981) are not the same as Carolinians (Heath, 1983; Sutton-Smith & Heath, 1981)? Or should we conclude that 1-year-olds have a more didactic relationship to their parents than 2-year-olds, or perhaps that girls are different from boys? Or that Ninio and Bruner were only concerned with the didactic aspect of their scaffolding and ignored all the other non–target responses of their 1-year-old child, which were in any case largely unintelligible? Or should we conclude that Ninio and Bruner chose only the deterministic aspect of Vygotsky's writings and ignored the more voluntaristic parts (Sutton-Smith, 1988)?

Like other notable Russians of the Stalin era, Vygotsky was not exceptional in the uneasy path he trod between his socially deterministic and voluntaristic accounts (Wertsch, 1985). He has, for example, given us a view of children's play which provides it with a more creative role in human cognition than any other serious theory in developmental psychology. A primary illustration of the zone of proximal development in his work, though ignored in most American readings where the focus is on what adults do for children, is the child's play. He says, "The child always behaves beyond his average age, above his daily behavior; in play it is as though he were a head taller than himself" (Vygotsky, 1978, p. 102). And we all remember his statement to the effect that we should imagine two girls who are sisters playing a game called "two girls who are sisters," as an exemplification of the way in which rule structures are first engendered in play, so that meaning arises and abstracts itself from everyday contextualization. He says, "From the point of view of development, creating an imaginary situation can be regarded as a means of developing abstract thought" (p. 103). If this should be true, and it may well be, it means that play has a direct, not an indirect, relationship to cognition.

In sum, whether approaching the concept of scaffolding through my own alternative research analysis of an example of it, through cultural comparisons such as those of Heath (1983) or Scollon and Scollon (1981), or through an analysis of Vygotsky's theoretical statements, one would certainly not arrive at the singular version of it which became so heralded by the study of Ninio and Bruner. It grossly underestimates both the character and the potential of the child's variability. Undoubtedly, parents play an important modeling role through their repeated interactions with children in rewarding reading situations. What is obscured by that apparent tutorial determinism, and scientifically yielded finding, is the fact that the very notion of scaffolding is, in the light of these other findings, little but a metaphor for parental hegemony and parental control.

Here again, we see what we can observe throughout the scientific journals in psychology, namely, the privileging of apparently singular causal or deterministic findings. The effects are seldom sustained when the more ecological complexes of socioeconomic status, race, or ethnicity are parceled out. The metaphor of positivist science hangs over our journals, maintained almost religiously by minimal and seldom replicated variances. It is a metaphor which subtly supports that side of education that assumes the child is dominantly a tabula rasa. Such monistic mindedness in education presupposes the same mindedness in children. We are all perfectly aware of what that means on the political scene, but often seem to have neglected what it means in everyday schooling.

Structuralism

With structural development and its application to children's narratives, we turn to another metaphor which, as used in developmental psychology, also has deterministic overtones. These have to do not with the antecedents of learning, but with the consequents, not so much with causes as with predictions. The concept of development in the twentieth century is very much a conflation of the notions of progress and evolution. It states a sequence of stages through which a child must proceed toward some higher maturity. It is implied that to know these stages and their sequences is to provide a predictive science of human development. Furthermore, the sequence of stages is said to represent a kind of progress because the final stages clearly require more maturity than do the earlier ones. The master pilot for this version of human development has of course been Piaget (1951), though many major figures such as Freud (1955), Erikson (1951), and Werner (1957) have contributed such schemes. As mentioned earlier, these scientific accounts with their general privileging of the civilized outcomes over the primitive beginnings, when added to the various historical factors mentioned earlier, buttress the role children have as the residual legatees of cultural historicism. They are the ones who if properly guided through the series of appropriate stages, ensure our future, if no longer our salvation.

There is, however, a clear lack of subcultural relativity about all of these systems. The danger of their scientific developmental metaphors is the unwarranted confidence they breed in psychologists and educators that they really know the true directions of development, in this case of narrative. Such confidence has a profoundly negative impact on individual differences. Some attempts have been made, for example, to convert these thin structural analyses of development in stories into rules for teaching children how to write stories.

The grammatical structures of narratives, as analyzed in the work of Mandler (1984) and others, are supposed to reflect children's underlying memory. Here the complexity of a child's ability to recall a story is used in order to infer memory capacity for temporal structure. It is shown that with age children master increasingly complex segments of story structure, whether these are scored in terms of plot, syntax, or the child's own evaluations of story meaning (Peterson & McCabe, 1983). In plot terms, for example, a plot can be seen as involving a beginning, a middle, and an ending (BME). These can be broken down further into six constituents: introductions, preparations, complications, development, resolution, and conclusions.

In my own work with Gilbert Botvin (Botvin & Sutton-Smith, 1977), for example, based on the analyses of the Russian, Vladimir Propp, we broke down those categories into 18 further categories, 92 action elements, 5 elaborations, and 7 markers, and reached a variety of conclusions about developmental change in these. For example, the stories of 3-year-olds are mainly beginnings and endings. It is not until about 12 years of age that the middle developmental section gets equal time.

The problem with our work and with that of everyone else in this field is the assumption that narratives described in this way are a sufficient analysis of what occurs. This classical BME form used by us and others is derived from the myth-of-the-hero narrative found in the folk cultures of urban civilizations, but not in all other folk cultures. These stages in the development of the narrative are not necessarily universal in human development. Many cultures tell tales which do not have resolution. They may attempt resolutions that are failures, or talk of nullifications of threats but without real resolution.

Larger mythic notions about fate appear to be implicated in the traditional tales of each group. Even within our own society, the telling of elementary structural forms does not necessarily imply a poorer story, although younger children will do that more than older children. Some novelists use the more conventional hero tale as their plot outline. Many modern novelists, however, use the more primitive structures in an artistic way. According to Peterson and McCabe (1983, p. 208), for example, Faulkner often ignores the temporal sequencing of his plots, and Hemingway writes like a 4-year-old, in a lean episodic manner, whereas Samuel Beckett, in *Waiting for Godot*, gets by with no orientation, no complication, no resolution, and no evaluation.

Thus, most of our current analyses of children's development through narratives are quite ethnocentric in their interpretation, and decidedly unliterary in their being restricted largely to structural elements. Any teaching of literature based on these analyses alone would be doomed to a philistine result. Not only would it miss much of the literary character of stories (such as figurative effects, images, insights, virtuosity, personality, humor, character, and symbolism), and the particular way in which the stories are told or performed, but it would once again sorely ignore the way in which different writers use structural, literary, or performance effects for the purposes of individualized expression. In his book, *Children's Riddling* (1979), John McDowell has a wonderful account of a 6-year-old boy who knew nothing of the lexical subtleties of riddles, and yet had mastered the fact that they are puzzling questions with arbitrary answers (Sutton-Smith, 1976). This child did well enough to hold the floor in a riddling contest by providing puzzling questions with non-sequitorial but obscene answers.

What I wish to do with my narrative data in the present illustration of multivocality is to show all the unusual things that are left out of the way children tell stories by focusing on the bare bones of narrative grammar alone. By implication, I will also indicate the multivocality that is also there but has so far been ignored. My data this time are to be found in my book, *The Folkstories of Children* (Sutton-Smith, 1981), which is a collection from a New York City public school and a nearby preschool, and contains some 500 stories from some 50 children, 10 each from ages 2 years through 10 years. In each case, I will choose from that percentage of children who take the normative structure and vary it in some individual, often egregious, manner. My point is that the usual kinds of analysis and expectations of childhood leave these examples out of education and out of teacher sympathy.

Plot. Let me begin by comparing a brilliant 10-year-old boy with a brilliant 4-year-old boy. The 10-year-old tells a well-plotted story, and then the 4-year-old tells a non-plotted story, though it has some chronicity (see Stories 1 and 2 below). Which of these would make the best movie?

Story 1

Once Harold was sitting in a restaurant at a table all by himself. Then he noticed there was a female owl sitting down by herself. Mischievously he walked over and asked her what her name was. She said, "Mary Gline." Then Harold thought for a moment and said, "Are you the girl that broke her wing when you were 9 years old?" Then she said, "What's your name and how did you know about my wing?" "Well," said Harold, "I knew about your wing because your name sounded very familiar, so I thought back to my childhood and remembered a girl named Mary broke her wing, and my name is Harold Hoot." Then she said, "You were the kid they called Hoot the Toot." "Oh, yeah," Harold replied, "I forgot about that." Then they started to talk about their childhood and ate dinner together.

After that night they went out to dinner, to movies, and did lots of other things like that. After about a year, they told their parents they were going to get married. Their parents agreed and they had a wedding. They had the most beautiful wedding you can imagine. For their honeymoon they went to Niagara Falls. Then after that they settled down in a nice house in Poughkeepsie and had Bobby and Peter. Last and not least, they lived happily ever after. (Boy, age 10)

Story 2

Once upon a time there was a family of tigers, bears, and lions
and they went out for a wild animal picnic
the wild animal picnic was made of baby rabbits
that's what they ate
they took the rabbits alive and they killed the rabbits at the picnic
and when they ate the rabbits the blood washed out all the meat
where they were chewing so they missed all the parts where
they were chewing
when they missed it they only got a tiny bit of their tooth left
they kept chipping their teeth 'cause they forgot to take
      out the bones
they kept chipping their teeth so much they only had one tooth on
the top and one on the bottom
then they swallowed the rabbit
after they had chipped their teeth and had dinner they went
home and had roasted beef rabbit
then after they swallowed the rabbit and after they had dinner they
went to sleep and they all dreamt the same thing
and that's all.

Phonology. Some, but not all, of the very youngest children are likely to be exceptional in their addition of sound effects to their stories. They use largely alliteration, repetition, or rhyme to create special effects. Here are two 2-year-olds from my New York sample.

Story 3

The cookie was in my nose
The cookie went on the fireman's hat
The fireman's hat went on the bucket
The cookie went on the carousel
The cookie went on the puzzle
The cookie went on the doggie.

Story 4

The monkeys
They went up sky
They fall down
Choo choo train in sky
The train fell down in the sky
I fell down in the sky in the water
I got on my boat and my legs hurt
Daddy fall down in sky.

Shirley Heath provided a similar rhyming example from her African-American South Carolinian sample of a 2-year-old boy storyteller (Sutton-Smith & Heath, 1981).

Nonsense. It is a short step from rhyming to nonsense, and a few children use phonology in that way. Here is a 3-year-old girl trying the researcher's patience.

Story 5

Now there was a pa ka
Boon, goo
There was a dog doo doo
And he didn't like dog doo doo
Then there was a man named Snowball
And he didn't like snow
Cha cha
Doo choo
Cha cha
Doo cho
I named dog doo doo
Christopher say
Dog doo doo
Then there were a boy named Taw taw

O Too too
Then there was a Captain Blooper he had a book and he were very
bad and it hurt him
Then there was a blooper pa pa
Pa pa
There was Superman coming and he hurt both of him knees
Then they were flying and they went right in the ocean and he got
bite from a shark
And he didn't like when he got bite from a shark
Then kla kla toe toe
Tee tah
Caw caw caw caw caw caw caw caw caw caw caw caw caw caw caw
caw caw caw caw caw caw caw caw caw
Now say pah pah kla klee
Sa see
Too tee
Tah tah too tee
Chee chaw
Ta klu
Kli klu
Kla kla
Klu fu
Klee kla
Koo koo
Say say
Klee klee
Klip kla
Klee klee
Klip kla
She she
Fik ahh
Tungoo nah
Ka pa

Popeye the sailor man
Bad guy him be very bad to him
And I spit out a words.

In our sample, by school age, the children did not typically use stories
in these figurative manners, though they sometimes demanded the right to
tell us some rhyme as the price of our admission. More often rhyming or
alliterative effects were restricted to naming characters such as Stupid Loo-
pid or Orangatang Sangatang.

Markers, orientations and morals. Those who study stories often make a great deal out of the children's acquisition of initial and terminal markers, such as, "Once upon a time" and "They lived happily ever after." In this sample, markers didn't make an appearance until the fourth year. The tellers tend to be terse and say simply, "The End" or "That's It." Similarly, their occasional orientations or preludes were equally informal such as 3-year-olds saying, "I'll tell you a real story" or "I've got a story for you." By 5 years of age, children's introductions may be somewhat more complex: "This story has a funny ending." "This is the first chapter." "Now no laughing because sometimes it makes me embarrassed." By age 7, children add drama: "Who will be the survivors of this terrifying story?" By age 8, children show some impatience, "Oh let's just get on with it." And by age 10, children are capable of parody, "Each Thursday a man comes in and takes stories from children." Also by the time children are 10, a comedy orientation appears: "Movie of the year. Three people have died while watching it, twelve of them committed suicide because of it. Here it goes."

My student, Ellen Brooks (1981), spent a year coaxing her small group of mentally retarded children (about 4 to 6 years mental age) to listen to stories on video- and audiotape. All day long they listened to stories and some of them ultimately began to be able to tell and write them—and did so with a most atypical emphasis on markers. Their stories were composed almost entirely of initial and terminal markers. But the most singular example was from the 4-year-old whose librarian mother had read him everything with conventional markers. His parody of markers is in story 6.

Story 6

> Once upon a time the once upon a time ate the once upon a time
> which ate the once upon a time
> And then the once upon a time which ate the once upon a time ate
> the princess once upon a time with the king
> And then the once upon a time died
> Then the end ate the end
> The end
> The end
> Then the end died
> Then the end died
> Then the end died
> Then the end died
> And then the end the end the end died
> The end with a the end
> The end
> The end.

Postscripts or evaluations could be brief from a 6-year-old: "That was a short one." "That's the end of a dumb story." "And the boy learned a lesson." "So they never got him again." From a 7-year-old: "That's the longest one I did. That's because I got most of it off 'Lost in Space.'" From an 8-year-old: "That was tough on my nerves and that's about all I've got to say." Real morals at the end were rare.

Titles. Titles which begin to appear at 5 years in this sample of children have a certain individuality, as follows: *The Fat Dinosaur, The Elephant That Ate Too Much, The Halloween Night, Me and My Teddy Bears, The Bean Bag, The Flower,* and so on. One girl's story, about a fart, is not up to the title, but is certainly original. At age 7, the children gave us: *Freaky Goes to the Bathroom, Frogenstein and Dracula,* and *Burping Nixon*—all sturdy stuff. At age 8, the children's titles become chapter headings, and when the children reach age 10, we get such parodic titles as: *The Living Sour Cream Monster.*

Characters. Characters are, in general, from the children's media world. Twenty percent are television or film heroes and monsters, and about 60% are animals. As these worlds provide children with much fertile fantasy through television, magazines, and comics, many of the children's characters take on a similar madness.

Perverse content. About 15% of this total sample of children achieve striking originality through the perversity of their stories, usually of a scatalogical or sexual nature. By 5 and 6 years of age, we already have a handful of peeing, farting, pooing, and fucking stories. In this sample, this genre does not reach a peak until children reach approximately 10 years of age. (For examples, see Abrams & Sutton-Smith, 1977.)

Complications. While some children show striking originality in all the ways that I have mentioned, in general, only a small percentage, 5 to 10%, are usually so expressive. The area where the majority of children seem to show their originality is that aspect of the plot concerned with the instigation of disequilibrium, the area usually known as the *complication*. In their stories, they show a world of great flux, anarchy, and disaster. Even as early as 2 to 3 years of age, key terms used by these young children in this collection (and in other comparable collections from the 1950s, like that of Pitcher and Prelinger, *Children Tell Stories* [1963]), include such actions as being lost, stolen, bitten, dead, stepped on, angry, hurt, afraid, killed, or crying, crashing down, fighting, pushing, calling the police, running away, or falling down. As Peterson and McCabe (1983) say in their recent story collection entitled, *Three Ways of Looking at Children's Narratives*, "In a nutshell, children are interested in pain, gore, and keystone cop style mishaps, as cartoonists and scriptwriters have known for years" (p. 27).

Young children's preference for these tales of relative disaster, often without any resolution, has to be a major reason why their stories are either avoided or strongly modified by most, but not all, school situations. My own sample was drawn, for example, from a school where considerable license was permitted for this kind of free expression. If in addition to their story disasters, you add their repetitive episodic plots; their preferences for rhyme and alliteration; their nonsense; their obscenity; and their crazy titles, morals, and characters; it is not surprising that most adults, even those who believe they favor creative expression, tend to avoid them. This is one of the clearest cases of children's expression being suppressed as too primitive.

Putting that aside, why do they tell such stories? My own theory is that they tell such stories (when allowed) because they are the kind of stories that make for an arresting performance. An alternative theory might be that the children are being primitive in a Freudian sense, simply expressing more basic instincts. The trouble with that explanation is that all the evidence from their audiotaped bedtime pre-sleep monologues, where being alone they can say anything they like, does not show any such self-display (Kuczaj, 1983). On the contrary, when they are talking to themselves in solitary situations, they tend to talk about everyday, commonplace events. It looks very much as if they put these disequilibrating elements into stories told to permissive peers or adults in order to startle, or at least to capture attention. The mundane disasters of these stories are their personal equivalent of what in the adult world would be the 11 p.m. television news, which has developed the art of keeping the soporific adult awake with "alive on the spot" horrors until the next commercial.

When the 2-year-old introduced earlier (Magee & Sutton-Smith, 1983), for example, first told a story at the end of our 9-month investigation, it was about a bird biting a cat. Perhaps her father paid very great attention to this story when it emerged, because his daughter had had an unfortunate reputation as a biter at the local nursery center. She certainly engaged his attention with her translation of her personal malady into oral literature. The importance of this kind of analysis, if true, is that it points to the very considerable competence of these 2-year-old children in using their own experience in dramatic and even parodic terms. They are already, as it were, distancing themselves from their painful everyday experience and using it in a mocking way as a form of social accomplishment. They have turned their experience into another kind of voice, another kind of commentary on their everyday world.

While these complications have a very personal ring through about 4 years of age in this sample, thereafter the children begin to use familiar content drawn from the mass media, including fairy tales. Generally, the boys are more prone to introduce characters and events from the mass media, with the girls significantly more often centering on domestic matters. The boys seem to find more drama inherent in violence and threat involving space and monsters. The girls more often find their drama in lost pets, abandoned children, or wicked mothers. The girls' dramas more often center on deprivation than on violence. Later, by 8 or 9 years, the children's sense of their own immediate story-setting world begins to creep into some of the tales, and the complications begin to figure parodies of classmates or of their own families. By ten years, there are even complications involving sex and genitalia.

Finally, let me emphasize that this sampling across my 50 children is in no way definitive. Nevertheless, these variations in plot, phonology, nonsense, orientations, morals and manners, characters and complications and perversity, all imply a multiple-mindedness hardly even hinted at yet in prior analyses of children as storytellers.

CONCLUSION: THE MULTIVOCAL MIND

Let me now ask skeptically what has been achieved by this minor array of my own personal empirical ventures. It seems there are at least three possibilities:

The first is that this personal tour has just reminded you of how labile, diffuse, irreverent and *polymorphously perverse* the young can be. Their primitive behavior, when seen through lenses of Heinz Werner (1957) or Sigmund Freud (1955), simply serves to highlight the educator's problem in dealing with childish unruliness. Whether or not these novelties appear creative, they are problematic from a schooling point of view.

The second interpretation might be that all we have exhibited here is the well known range of *individual differences* in these areas of concern. It has long been known in developmental psychology that the best individual predictors of behavior from the very earliest years are genetic phenomena such as temperament. For example, the activity levels, impulsivity, and passivity manifested in the first weeks after an individual's birth are the most enduring of characteristics. Education has always paid theoretical obeisance to these individual differences, but largely has had to circumvent them to get on with the everyday business of schooling, which has been conceived as a monolithic task.

Not surprisingly, therefore, even when extensive work is done with individual differences and styles of cognition, as in the famous work of Cronbach (1957), it has had little impact on education. Even his cognitive styles which are most relevant for this presentation, that is, the distinction between convergent and divergent thinking, have had only a trivial influence. The most recent example of this tradition is *Frames of Mind* (1983), in which Gardner uses the history of genius to suggest basic individual differences in styles of competence. These include spatial, logical-numerical, musical, kinesic, verbal, interpersonal, or intrapersonal skills. In psychology in general, the hegemony of the laboratory prevails over such differences, that is, the experimental, quantitative tradition which searches for general laws of development. This tradition has coalesced with the general egalitarian public tradition of giving all children equality of opportunity, which seems to have meant largely treating all children in the same way. It would be nice if what I have said did increase our sensitivity to individual differences, but there is little hope that it will.

The third interpretation, the one I wish to put before you, emphasizes changing our views of intra-individual minds. All of this material, I argue, implies not just that we are different from each other (the prior implication), but that we are different within ourselves, that we are multivocal creatures, that we hear voices, that we consider multiple possibilities. This is not exactly a new view. It has been gathering force these past decades and threatening the other intellectual hegemonies of this century. In 1890, William James wrote: "The mind is at every stage a theatre of simultaneous possibilities" (p. 288). My argument has been that school has not sufficiently seen itself as a marketplace for this activity of possibility.

In the Future: Schools of Multivocal Consciousness

Let me briefly review the kinds of thought that seem to be leading us to the schools of the future, which we might refer to radically as the schools of multivocal consciousness.

Dreams and daydreams. In current as well as traditional evidence on dreams and daydreams, we have come to take for granted that we are all sources of simply incredible creativity. In dreams we may witness cities that were never built, may hear music of great orchestras, and may engage in conversations that we have never had. The youngest children take some time to discover that their dreams, which are so real, are differently real than everyday waking life. In our scientific tradition, we then teach them to put the dreams to one side except for therapeutic purposes.

Recent neurological research shows that from the point of view of the brain, dreams activate the mind in the same way as their content would in everyday life except that another part of the mind also inactivates the body. This capacity is strangely like that of play or television, where we engage ourselves often more energetically and totally than we do in everyday life, but have ever ready that metacommunicative signal button which says to another, "This is only play. It is not everyday life and it can be turned off at any time." Children's very early command of pretense may well be a product of their knowledge of the difference between sleep and wakefulness.

Studies of daydreaming show that all of us are engaged in this off and on throughout the day and that everyone has imaginary conversations with others. For some they are at times so real that they can actually report the feelings that they instigate, feelings such as those of anxiety, heat, coldness, or sexuality. Similarly, recent work on television fantasies shows that many of us carry around in our heads hundreds of TV characters, (as well as relatives and politicians), with whom we are constantly engaged and whom we even discuss in our conversations with others. I know that in my interior life I have been talking polemically to Frank Sinatra for years. All my daughters talk endlessly to and about the characters in "*General Hospital*." John Caughey, in his book *Imaginary Social Worlds*, says,

> Such vivid transporting experiences characterize all forms of media consumption. Every time an American enters a movie theatre, turns on a media machine, or opens a book, newspaper or magazine, he or she slips mentally out of the real social world and enters an artificial world of vicarious social experience . . . the intensity of the absorbed state leads some researchers to compare media consumption to the trance-like altered states of consciousness induced by drug consumption. Manipulated by a steady stream of dramatic dialogue and tense or amusing interaction the individual becomes so absorbed that the proper label for this role is not "observer" but "voyeur" (1984, pp. 34–37).

If this appeal to your own direct multivocal mind experience does not move you, I suggest a reading of two recent books, by two respected psychologists, Leona E. Tyler's *Thinking Creatively* (1983), which is about the mind as a constant crucible of multiple possibilities, and Robert Weisberg's *Creativity: Genius and Other Myths* (1986), which is against various myths about creative talent and on behalf of that imaginative competence in all of us.

Literature. The most telling account of this kind of mindedness, and basically the source of this chapter, is the recently translated, *The Dialogic Imagination* (1981) by the Russian author Mikhail Bakhtin. He formulates an account of the history of the development of modern consciousness. The novel in its various phases of experimentation is seen as a kind of epistemological outlaw, always revealing new insights into the way people think. Whether or not people once heard voices outside themselves, as in Jaynes's account of the breakdown of the bicameral mind (1976), in Bakhtin's view, these voices are now internalized. Furthermore, the novel acts as a critique of the monoglossic folk assumption that there is just one language and, therefore, one way of thinking about reality. Language differences and differences within a language make mockery of such one-world illusions. It is not incidental that Bakhtin spent most of his life hiding from revolutionary Russia's intolerance for such a heteroglossic view of both language and reality.

Language and philosophy. In language and in philosophy, the inheritor of Bakhtin's satire of official language has been Jacques Derrida (1974) whose book, *Of Grammatology*, engages in an attack on philosophy's diverse attempts to privilege certain states of being or experience, whether in the essentialist Platonic tradition or the more recent phenomenological tradition. He argues in the same vein as Wittgenstein that there are no universal eternal signifiers. Words and their meanings are matters of history and practicality and they are always susceptible to change, as any reading of William Safire's *New York Times* Sunday column "On Language" should indicate. There is no eternal correspondence of word and thing. There is only the convenience and pressure of the time. Derrida says that the normal reaction to a word or thing is "a play of signifiers" in the human mind. He doesn't deny that our needs for communication tie down words to a current consensus. He just argues that this cannot comprise the only model of what the mind is like. It is just as basic for the mind to go off in any direction it pleases.

The problem for children is that their bricolage, their nonsense, and their derangement of sense, is not socialized and accepted. It is therefore seen as inferior, whereas the bricolage of a great writer like James Joyce is permissible. Children naively give us their own uncorrected copies when they speak or write freely for us, whereas adults are generally too sophisticated to bare their minds in that way. The children give us an innocent play of becoming. That surplus of signification which inhabits all our minds in their case gets loose. As adults, we often have to put ourselves in drastically altered circumstances, by travel or culture shock, to once again be reminded by that flood of signifiers with which we become consciously possessed at such times, that our mind is still there speaking in many tongues.

The knowledge disciplines. These contemporary assaults on earlier notions of the constancies of mind and language take place against an even grander assault on the supposed constancy of the knowledge disciplines. Kuhn's attack on the constancy and continuity of the physical sciences is well known, but Michel Foucault's more far-reaching attacks on what he calls the "games of truth" may not be (1977). In a variety of ways, he has sought to show the relativity of the knowledge of various disciplines to their existence as social institutions with coercive social practices. In some ways, my own attack in this chapter on the hegemony of child historicism, in both education and developmental psychology, is an illustration of the way a rhetoric of history is not only a system of knowledge but also a kind of coercion.

To my knowledge, American anthropologists are most aware of this current state of the relativity, not only of our own ethnocentric assumptions but also of our own disciplinary assumptions of all kinds. The illusion in psychology has always been that tne human experiment could be representative of everyday life, and its independent-dependent variable outcomes could be taken as statements of some general laws about universal human nature. Anthropologists have always similarly cherished a similar synecdochal illusion that they could arrive at a statement of the cultural whole by an intensive study of a part, such as a ritual, an initiation, a kinship system, or the like. But the inconstancies of the whole culture and the irregularities of human behavior have rendered these assumptions largely void. It is not that we cannot engage our multiplicitous reflective selves with multiplicitous reflective others in some struggle for an immediate intersubjective consensus, but it is clearly no simple business.

CONCLUDING METAPHORS

So by now you should be asking whether you are meant to read the sampled children's stories as an indication of children's multivocal capacities and not simply as nonsense, nuisance, or irrelevant individuality. And if I say yes to that, you might reply, but surely, the very youngest children are not even univocal let alone multivocal. And to that I might respond (and this would also be a part of our radicalization of the concept of childhood) that while that could be true, perhaps the infants are multisensory or multi-imagic, as, for example, we might suppose that they are from their various forms of play and exploration with the Johnson and Johnson Playpath infant toys (see Sutton-Smith, 1986). Perhaps, indeed, we are here using the term multivocal as a metaphor for the pluralistic play of mind, not as an indication of its particular media expression at any age level.

Incidentally, one can't help but comment on the surrealistic character of modern toys for infants. Vygotsky could talk of children's toys as drenched with social meaning, but he was living in the world of socialist realism where toys were tractors, houses, or milk pails. What indeed would he make of the Playpath infant toys, which are drenched with Bauhaus plumbing and Piagetian circular reactions, and where children play with toys, the ideas for which originated in the noble Genevan's head. Their tracking tubes, clear rattles, Picasso-like visual displays, red rings, balls in a bowl, and spin-a-sound toys, are like voices of the theorist. Fortunately, they can retreat to Donald W. Winnicott's (1971) transitional blanket if they wish. In a way, the infant's situation is like ours and like the one I am talking about, a nice metaphor for the excessive relativity of interpretation in the modern world. As in modern art, nothing need be as it seems.

As a final note, and borrowing from Gregory Bateson's classic *Mind and Nature* (1979) and more recent *Angels Fear* (1987) (with his daughter Mary Catherine Bateson), let us suppose that what I am really talking about is the *multi-metaphoric mind*, and that what our problem is going to be with young children is the understanding of their rich control of that medium. According to Bateson, the basic mentality of humans, animals, and evolution is metaphoric, which means that it moves by homologies, by moving from one form to another in terms of the similarity between the two, or by what Bateson calls "abduction," in contrast to induction or deduction. In these terms, the very young are not just labile, as Werner might say, moving possessedly from one attractive stimulus to the next; or circularly repetitive, as Piaget might say, repeating effective responses to prior stimuli; or moved by contiguity, as the learning theorist might say; or repetitively compulsive, as Freud might say, driven to reenact their anxieties.

Including and transcending all of these, humans' exploratory and playful management might be in pursuit of homology of act or of form. It is certainly true that once children can speak, they move endlessly through the vocalized plural play of metaphor. The other day in a sandpit for example, I watched my 2-year-old granddaughter first pouring the sand and calling it coke, and then rounding it and calling it an egg, and then lengthening the shape and calling it a sausage, and then banging and slapping it with a vocalized rhythm which she called a song, and so on. The properties of the material in the child's hands were "poured" through a vocal string of metaphoric signifiers.

Given the increasing consensus in the philosophy of science that every epistemological act is prefaced by basic metaphors; that all search and inquiry proceeds to the unknown through vague resemblances to the known; and that all science, physical or human, ultimately traces back to the continuing presence of such metaphors; one can take hope that there will be some day a continuity of understanding of the role of metaphors in childhood and their role in adulthood. In such case the search for such continuities, upon which all social construction and science ultimately depend, may give our children a greater dignity and our educators a greater sensitivity than our present certitudes about positivist science or the role of children in our own destiny seem to allow us.

REFERENCES

Abrams, D., & Sutton-Smith, B. (1977). The development of the trickster figure in children's fantasy narratives. *Journal of American Folklore, 90*, 29–48.

Bakhtin, M. M. (1981). *The dialogic imagination.* Austin: University of Texas.

Bakhtin, M. M. (1984). *Rabelais and his world.* Bloomington: Indiana University Press.

Bateson, G. (1979). *Mind and nature.* New York: E. P. Dutton.

Bateson, G., & Bateson, M. C. (1987). *Angels fear.* New York: Macmillan.

Bauman, R. (1977). *Verbal art as performance.* Prospect Heights, IL: Waveland Press.

Berlyne, D. E. (1960). *Conflict, arousal and curiosity.* New York: McGraw-Hill.

Botvin, G., & Sutton-Smith, B. (1977). The development of structural complexity in children's fantasy narratives. *Developmental Psychology, 13*, 377–388.

Brooks, E. (1981). *A description of the development of story telling competence in educable mentally retarded children, ages 7–10 years.* Unpublished doctoral dissertation, University of Pennsylvania, Philadelphia.

Bruner, J. (1986). *Actual minds, possible worlds.* Cambridge, MA: Harvard University Press.

Caughey, J. (1984). *Imaginary social worlds.* Lincoln: University of Nebraska Press.

Clifford, J. (1988). *The predicament of culture.* Cambridge, MA: Harvard University Press.

Cronbach, H. J. (1957). The two disciplines of scientific psychology. *American Psychologist, 72*, 377–388.

Derrida, J. (1974). *Of grammatology.* Baltimore, MD: Johns Hopkins Universlty Press.

Elkind, D. (1981). *The hurried child.* New York: Addison-Wesley.

Erikson, E. H. (1951). *Childhood and society.* New York: W. W. Norton.

Fagen, R. (1980). *Animal play behavior.* New York: Oxford University Press.

Fein, G. (1986). The affective psychology of play. In A. W. Gottfried & C. C. Brown (Eds.), *Play interactions* (pp. 31–49). Lexington, MA: Lexington Books.

Foucault, M. (1977). *The order of things.* New York: Vintage.

Freud, S. (1955). *Beyond the pleasure principle.* London: Hogarth Press.

Galda, L., & Pellegrini, A. D. (Eds.). (1985). *Play, language and stories.* Norwood, NJ: Ablex.

Gardner, H. (1983). *Frames of mind.* New York: Basic Books.

Garvey, K. (1977). *Play.* Cambridge, MA: Harvard University Press.

Heath, S. B. (1983). *Ways with words*. Cambridge, MA: Harvard University Press.

James, W. (1890). *The principles of psychology* (Vol. 1). New York: Henry Holt.

Jaynes, J. (1976). *The origins of consciousness in the breakdown of the bicameral mind*. Boston: Houghton Mifflin.

Kelly-Byrne, D. (1989). *A child's play life: An ethnographic study*. New York: Teachers College Press.

Kuczaj, S. A. (1983). *Crib speech and language play*. New York: Springer-Verlag.

Kuhn, T. (1963). *The structure of scientific revolutions*. Chicago: Chicago University Press.

Magee, M. A., & Sutton-Smith, B. (1983). The art of storytelling: How do children learn it? *Young Children, 38*, 4–12.

Mandler, J. (1984). *Stories, scripts and scenes: Aspects of schema theory*. Hillsdale, NJ: Lawrence Erlbaum.

McDowell, J. (1979). *Children's riddling*. Bloomington: University of Indiana Press.

Ninio, A., & Bruner, J. (1978). The achievement and antecedents of labelling. *Journal of Child Language, 5*, 1–15.

Peterson, C., & McCabe, A. (1983). *Three ways of looking at children's narratives*. New York: Plenum Press.

Piaget, J. (1951). *Play, dreams and imitation in childhood*. New York: W. W. Norton.

Pitcher, E., & Prelinger, E. (1963). *Children tell stories*. New York: International Universities Press.

Schwartzman, H. (1978). *Transformations: The anthropology of children's play*. New York: Plenum Press.

Scollon, N., & Scollon, L. (1981). *Narrative: Literacy and face in interethnic communication*. Norwood, NJ: Ablex.

Sutton-Smith, B. (1976). A developmental structural account of riddles. In B. Kirschenblatt-Gimblett (Ed.), *Speech play* (pp. 111–119). Philadelphia: University of Pennsylvania Press.

Sutton-Smith, B. (1979). *Play and learning*. New York: Gardner Press.

Sutton-Smith, B. (1981). *The folkstories of children*. Philadelphia: University of Pennsylvania Press.

Sutton-Smith, B. (1983). The origins of fiction and the fictions of origin. In E. Bruner (Ed.), *Text, play, story* (pp. 117–132). Washington, DC: American Ethnological Society.

Sutton-Smith, B. (1986). *Toys as culture*. Gardner Press.

Sutton-Smith, B. (1988). Review of *Actual minds, possible worlds* by Jerome Bruner, 1986. *Language and Society, 17*, 298–304.

Sutton-Smith, B., & Abrams, D. (1978). Psychosexual material in the stories told by children. *Archives of Sexual Behavior, 7*, 521–543.

Sutton-Smith, B., & Heath, S. B. (1981). Paradigms of pretense. *Quarterly Newsletter of Comparative Human Cognition, 3*, 41–45.

Tyler, L. (1983). *Thinking creatively*. San Francisco: Jossey-Bass.

Vygotsky, L. S. (1978). The role of play in development. In M. Cole, V. John-Steiner, S. Scribner, & E. Scuberman (Eds.), *Mind in society*. Cambridge, MA: Harvard University Press.

Weisberg, R. W. (1986). *Creativity, genius and other myths*. New York: W. H. Freeman.

Werner, H. (1957). *The comparative psychology of mental development*. New York: International Universities Press.

Wertsch, J. (Ed.). (1985). *Culture, communication and cognition*. Cambridge, MA: Harvard University Press.

Winnicott, D. W. (1971). *Playing and reality*. New York: Basic Books.

CHAPTER 6

Looking for Magpie

ANOTHER VOICE IN THE CLASSROOM

Vivian Gussin Paley

For many years, I have listened to children's stories and have read them the books of our favorite adult storytellers. But lately, I am curious about my own fictions and fantasies. I seek another voice in the classroom, one that will carry me further into the culture of the group, in roles not available to me in my customary teacher mode. I want to join the community of story-tellers that surrounds me. Can my role as observer, listener, recorder, inter-preter, discourser, and connector be expanded to include myth-maker? Can I learn to use my own plots and characters as context and continuity for the ideas I wish to convey?

The children do it quite naturally; for me, it is hard work. However, I begin as they do, with a central figure who will speak for me. As it happens, I have imagined a bird called Magpie who seems to make a specialty of rescuing lonely folks and telling them stories to lift their spirits. That some of these stories touch upon issues and events in the classroom is no coinci-dence.

Certainly no one would deny me this idiosyncratic goal, one that is in the best tradition of Sylvia Ashton Warner, who infused her teaching with Maori myth and symbol. Yet, the image of the storyteller usually meets with resistance when proposed as a general approach to teaching. Stories are pleasant, it is felt, but teaching pertains to what is real and knowable.

Princess Annabella sat on her father's lap and smiled up at him. "But father writes of true things, Magpie, and your stories are only pretend," she said.

"Dear Annabella," Magpie replied modestly. "My stories are no less true than those contained in these piles of books. The story I just told you of the lonely princess who wished to be a bird is as real in your mind as all your other thoughts."

91

"Quite right, Magpie," the prince agreed. "We each tell our stories in different ways. Perhaps the reason I write about birds and draw their pictures is that I too would like to be a bird and fly away." (Paley, 1992, p. 17).

The notion that storytelling is the natural method of teaching in the same way that fantasy is the natural and intuitive medium of play is agreeable to think about but not easy to accept as serious business. Even demonstrating that children's play invariably emerges with character and plot in progress and using this commonly observable phenomenon as evidence that it is the way children think does little to alter a firmly entrenched premise: The primary goals of teaching are "cognitive" and therefore antithetical to play. Storytelling, hard work that it may be, seems too much like play.

Those who tell us that play is the work of children or that the child is the father of the man seldom assimilate these metaphors into a theory of teaching. Play seems as random and sporadic to the teacher as the school curriculum must appear to the child. Neither teacher nor child senses the continuity in each other's reality, though the tracks upon which dramatic play runs present by far the more transparent landscape.

"Pretend we live in a castle," says Lisa to Hiroko, both kindergartners in my class. They have just begun an episode that will continue in various forms throughout this day and spill over to the next.

"Then we hear a noise and it's the wicked monster. And pretend it's a castle with no doors so the monster can't get in but we can get out because we're magic."

"Are we the only magic ones?" Hiroko asks.

"Just us. No one else is alive yet. Only us are born. Pretend that."

The stage is set and Act I has begun. During the remainder of the morning free play another princess is added to the cast, a haunted house is built next door by Dracula and several bats, and a family of mice organize a cheese factory.

"Do bats eat cheese?" a mouse calls in the direction of the haunted house. "We're selling cheese."

"They suck blood," replies Dracula, "but we need cheese for traps."

Meanwhile, Hiroko, in the guise of an invisible butterfly, has flown to the story table. "Once there was three princesses," she dictates, "that lived in a castle that didn't have any doors and they were magic. Then they turned into a invisible butterfly and they never died."

Throughout this day, the castle, haunted house, and cheese factory bind us together in a flow of costumes and furnishings, signs and money, arguments and compromises, plus the inevitable tales of bats, monsters, princesses, and mice. Any reference made to these general topics gains immediate attention. Angelo is sent to the library to bring back the "Antoine" books because the cheese factory idea comes from the numerous adventures of this clever mouse who works as a cheese taster in a Paris cheese factory. We decide to read "Antoine and the Thirty Thieves."

As I connect my curriculum to the children's we meet at a number of intersections: "How much does the cheese cost? There are big chunks and little ones." "What if this whole room had no doors and no one could enter? What would we have to do for ourselves?" "Is it fair to tell Clara she can't be a princess?" About the last, Magpie has a story, for this problem of Clara's rejection is one I would like to deal with in a new way.

A tiny wisp of something flew past Magpie but he could see nothing. Then he felt the tickle of silky wings on his back. "Who's there?" he asked. "Why can't I see you?"

"Because I'm invisible," a voice answered. "I'm a princess who lives in the castle on the hill. It has no doors and my sisters and I make ourselves into invisible butterflies when we wish to go out."

"But, if your castle has no doors, how can someone come in?" Magpie wondered.

"We don't want anyone to come in," said the princess. "We live alone."

Magpie shook his head. "How unfortunate. Just this morning I saw a little girl lost in the woods surrounding your castle. She must have tried to enter but couldn't find the door."

Magpie sensed the wetness of an invisible tear and then heard a tiny whisper. "That girl must feel sad. What will she do?" Magpie did not know.

The little butterfly said good-bye and flew home, wondering what her sisters would say when she told them about the lost child.

A day in the life of a classroom is a many-textured weaving, a shared literacy, a community of urgent themes. The ancient storyteller seated across the fire under a darkened sky, telling of angry gods and magical omens, creates the same effect, the audience repeating and reinterpreting his stories and adding their own.

Story is the essential culture builder and learning tool of any society or family or classroom. The child within us and the children in our classes yearn for stories. It matters not that we no longer sit around campfires originating mythology—or even spend much time on porches gossiping and spinning tales—every child reenacts this ancient means of expression and depends on its form to explain life's deepest concerns.

Children give dramatic utterance to their thoughts because their thoughts are imagined in dramatic form. Listening to their own inner monologues, they know how they wish to be heard in the crowd. The best way to penetrate the other monologues that orchestrate the classroom is to tell a story.

Listen to 5-year-old Aisha as she begins to reveal herself to us. She appears shy at first and does not speak during group times. But in the doll corner she says, "I'm the mermaid," and when she dictates her first story she reinforces the image. "Little mermaid. I'm little mermaid. She swims with the fish."

Her next story carries her further into friendly territory. "The little mermaid swims with her sisters. And they play on the water slide." There are more mermaid stories to follow, sisterly and safe, but Aisha has been making up other stories in various corners of the classroom and playground. She has listened to fairy tales and has painted rainbows and is ready to expand her narrative. It has not taken long because, after all, she has been telling herself stories even before she began to talk.

Little mermaid went upstairs to her room. Then she came back down. Her father said, "If you don't go upstairs and get into bed I'm going to spank you." Then she said, "Oh, well, I'm going to look at a book." Her father said, "No, no, you go to sleep or I'm calling the wicked witch." The little mermaid said, "I'm not scared of the wicked witch."

No one has taught Aisha this story and no one else could invent it. Her singular voice speaks out to us. She will not be intimidated. Perhaps she borrows a page from her family's story: This is who we are, she has been told, and where we come from; these are the legends we value and those are the stories we reject. Aisha, in the meanwhile, has been creating her own legends: This is who I pretend to be and where I live, this is what I fear and how I protect myself, this is the way I attach myself to others.

Aisha examines every image of good and bad, big and little, strong and weak, searching for clues to support the notion that fears can be conquered and safe havens established. She cannot live through the day without stories, real and pretend.

Nor can we. In the absence of a narrative voice we feel disconnected and lonely; we are unable to convince, amuse, intrigue, explain, impress, rationalize, theorize, sympathize, or create attachments. We are barely able to secure attention or be remembered if we do not present ourselves in a role. The child who crawls on the floor meowing and the teacher who describes and imitates the meowing student in a case study perform in the same mode. Without stories, our lives would seem as impersonal and unhinged as the math and social studies workbooks.

Children enter school accomplished storytellers, veteran fantasy players, only to discover quite abruptly that this great passion of theirs is not part of the curriculum. Their talents for imagery and illusion are sent outdoors to play where no teacher can make use of the stories they tell—or even hear them.

The dramatic images that fill the minds of school children are ready to emerge as the text for play the moment the teacher says, "You've done your work, now you can play." Stacks of folders on the teacher's desk are called "work," and what the children have joyfully and purposefully trained themselves to do is called play and is of lesser value.

Yet there are 5 or 6 years of fantasy-making and family stories that precede first grade, giving children most of the character types, plots, and emotional settings with which to think and write about and act out the great and small issues of life—as well as those in the classroom. It is a common and familiar track; no matter at how many stations it stops along the way, we know where we've been and we can somehow anticipate where we're going.

The natural connection between storytelling and learning is obscured in school mainly because we seldom see the classroom as a real and full life, a continuing drama, a world into itself. The inhabitants of a cultural entity need a common mythology by which to explain themselves to one another if they are to weld their disparate elements and establish continuity and purpose in their lives. In a cohesive society, family, or classroom, each member is storyteller and story listener by turn as the train of events moves along a shared network of daily expectations and surprises, histories and fantasies, laws and customs.

Nowhere is this more important than in a classroom for, each year, most children enter a new class as strangers in an unknown land. If we watch and listen, we will see the natural way strangers quickly become participating members of a society: They begin by telling one another stories, building a culture within which to establish the parallel roles of player and student.

"Pretend we're kitties and we're lost in the woods and we hear a strange noise" places a group of children inside a familiar structure of language, metaphor, and magic with which to examine old and new ideas together. A myth-making curriculum is sensible because the children have been practicing the technique all of their lives.

However, what does it mean to teach in narrative form? If the essence of the narrative is the singular voice within a cultural context, then, as in play, each of us must find our own dramatic ways of connecting the social, emotional, and academic events in our own students' lives as well as in our own. When we share a communal life, every story begins in the middle of another story. It is an open-ended, error-free process and the more people who tell stories the greater will be the number of connections made.

A narrative style of teaching can collect a great diversity of people under a common umbrella of understanding. At any age, we reach out to a storyteller because it may be that our own story is about to be told. Story is our simplest connection; you tell me your story and I'll tell you mine.

> Magpie thought about the sad tale he had just heard. Who can say when tears are too many? "I can't answer that question," he said, "but I can offer my own story in return for yours. Would you like to hear how a witch named Beatrix saved my life?"

"I don't have a magpie on my shoulder," protests a second-grade teacher after I describe my fine-feathered alter ego. "When my own children wanted a story the best I could ever come up with was some simple child-hood incident."

Sheila warms to her subject. "Actually they didn't mind a bit. 'Tell me about digging the hole,' they'd say. Or, 'Tell about the peddler.' This was one of their favorites." Now my colleague's face is glowing. "When I was little, girls didn't deliver newspapers in my town. But I wanted so much to have that job I dressed in my brother's clothes and fooled the man who hired the delivery boys. One day the fruit peddler said to my mom, 'I didn't know you had two boys, ma'am, and both such fine lads.'"

Sheila has come alive for me. I see her in overalls and flannel shirt riding a rickety bicycle, her hair tucked beneath a boy's cap, lowering her voice as she greets the peddler early in the morning. How brave she is, venturing out in disguise, in this old-fashioned world she created each night for her son and daughter. How easy it is for me to fill in the unknown parts in her story.

Indeed, she is a storyteller, and she has made me into a story listener. "When I was little" is as magical a beginning as "Once upon a time" or "Long ago in a far off land," all of which promise to reveal secrets and compel us to listen. The children are eager to hear of events that happened before they were born, to imagine the world as a different place, to fill in the unknown scenes.

Whatever must be imagined enters the realm of magic and invention. "When my father was little," a science teacher tells my class, "his family had no electricity and they used big chunks of ice to cool their food." Instantly I picture the ice man urging on his old horse, shouting, "Ice for sale, fifteen cents a piece!" Where did the ice come from? What happened when it melted? Automatically, a story turns over in my mind.

Once upon a time there was a boy named Jack whose job it was to empty the pans of water beneath the king's ice box. One night he dreamed he was sailing away on a swift stream of icy water and when he awoke . . .

The science teacher's voice brings me back to his lesson. He has brought ice cubes for us to melt and is gathering suggestions from the children. Of course we can and should organize experiments to see how quickly ice melts under a variety of circumstances. But once we accept the idea that learning takes place deeply within the imagination, we sense also that fact and fantasy naturally intertwine in the shape of a story.

"Long ago when the world was much younger . . . " a teacher begins, and every student's story-making apparatus tunes up to the rhythm of her song. It matter not if her narrative is drawn from prehistoric times or last week's newspaper. She may have found the concept in the encyclopedia, a childhood incident, a fairy tale, or her imagination. The children are prepared to enter her story, confront its problems, escape its dangers, and discover the unknown. They are also ready to anticipate what might happen, filling in the pauses and ambiguities with alternate plots and characters of their own.

A fact by itself may open a door to the castle but if we place the fact into a story, unforeseen tunnels are revealed as we crisscross and mingle and expand our horizons. For example, let us consider a well-known fact of great importance in our country's history: George Washington was chosen unanimously as our first president and took office on April 30, 1789, after refusing the people's offer to make him a king.

These are astonishing events to think about. Chosen unanimously? Refused to be a king? What sort of person could be so beloved by his people and why would he set aside a throne in favor of an elected position? The facts alone are exciting but if we imagine them in a story the ideas multiply and grow.

"Tell us a true story, Magpie," demands King Bertram. "I want to know something that is really happening right now somewhere in the world."

Magpie perches on the arm of the throne. "My friend Parrot heard this story from a prisoner on a pirate ship. There is a man in a far away land who has refused to be king even though his people have offered him a throne."

King Bertram is shocked. "Refused a crown? Impossible! Why would he not wish to be king? Who is this foolish man?"

"His name, I believe, is General George Washington. He doesn't think a king can be trusted always to rule wisely."

The king is puzzled and saddened. "Magpie doesn't mean you, father," Princess Alexandra assures him. "We know you are a good king."

"Oh, well, continue your story, Magpie. Tell me how this Washington fellow thinks a country can be ruled if not by a king. And, by the way, why are those people so fond of him if he is not a real king?"

The story within a story fits the pattern of our thinking whether we are young or old, but, for the child, who is already preoccupied with fantasy, it is the necessary approach if we are to lend our important fact the full benefit of the child's attention and imaginative playfulness. Parson Weems demonstrated his understanding of the concept when he fashioned a cherry tree morality tale to help explain what sort of person is urged to be king and says no.

The library is, of course, stocked with books that surround particular historical, scientific, and artistic events with intimate stories of people whose lives are vastly changed in unexpected ways. We may debate the merits and authenticity of these sometimes fanciful narratives but we cannot do without them if we are to connect the unknown to our own time and to ourselves.

Fiction blends with fact, not to deceive us, but, rather, to involve us in the emotional issues that underlie every event. Such is the role of storytelling: It helps us interpret and integrate new ideas into our store of familiar images and feelings by dramatizing their meanings and relationships.

Tell me a story and I'll soon think of my own version according to my need at the time. Then your story becomes my story. With practice we can join the children in their never-ending saga of enticements, explanations, and entreaties, disguised as stories, that attempt to persuade others to listen to one voice above the competing chorus.

"Nix, nix, double-nix!" Beatrix protests when Magpie finishes the George Washington story. "Why do great people have to always tell the truth? I can't stand that!"

"But Beatrix," replied Magpie. "People don't trust a person who lies."

The young witch pouts. "Well, it's too hard for me to keep telling the truth."

Alexandra hugs her friend. "You just did tell us the truth, Beatrix. That sometimes you tell lies."

Beatrix grins and twirls around the throne room. "Then I guess

I'm not so bad after all," she sings out. "May I please have some more cherry pie?"

REFERENCE

Paley, V. G. (1992). *You can't say you can't play.* Cambridge, MA: Harvard University Press.

CHAPTER 7

The Role of Narrative in Interpretive Discussion

Sophie Haroutunian-Gordon

How does conversation about the meaning of texts transform the ideas and attitudes of the participants? The answer to this question is complex. I addressed it to some extent in my book, *Turning the Soul: Teaching through Conversation in the High School* (1991). The task of the present chapter is to explore the role that narrative plays in the transformation. By narrative, I mean the activity of telling stories about oneself or others that one knows or knows of, or of referring to partially articulated stories to make points (see Chapter 3 by Witherell, this volume, for a compatible and more fully elaborated definition). In the conversations that follow, one sees discussants weaving stories, or pieces of them, into their comments about the meaning of the text. Indeed, they appear to learn what Wittgenstein (1958) might call a kind of "language game" that uses stories from personal experience to illuminate the meaning of the literary work and, eventually, vice-versa (i.e., the work illuminates the events and views they relate in their stories). This claim is similar to the one made by Kieran Egan (1986) about the use of abstractions in children's stories. They use abstractions to make sense of new knowledge.

Turning the Soul takes the reader back and forth between two high school classrooms discussing Shakespeare's *Romeo and Juliet*. By "discussing," I mean that the students are talking with one another and a teacher or discussion leader about the meaning of the play. Usually (but not always), the discussants work to resolve a question about meaning which has more than one possible resolution, given the evidence in the text.

In what follows, we focus upon a group that is located in a low-income, inner-city school I call Belden High School. The students, members of a special education class, have had little previous experience with interpretive discussion or Shakespeare. The teacher, Margaret Prince, had invited me to lead discussions of the play with her students.

THE BELDEN CLASSROOM

In an effort to focus the discussants on the issues of revenge with which the *Romeo and Juliet* deals, I asked them to write about a time when they took revenge on someone or thought of so doing. What follows are stories that the students produced in response to my request. The first is Colette's:

> Well, my brother Clark is so bad that in front of my friends he dragged me on the ground and kicked me in my face. I was really hurt and I was embarrassed. I called the police to have him arrested because he . . . because he was drunk. Therefore, I am not his child . . . his sister anymore. (Haroutunian-Gordon, 1991, pp. 31–32)

Here, we have a very dramatic story! Indeed, as I tell the reader of *Turning the Soul,* I was not prepared for the intensity of this revelation. But Colette's was not the only powerful example. Here is Sylvia's:

> I have been hurt in many different ways. One of the ways was my mother. It is the ways she acts towards me and my sister. I don't think she should have her picks and chooses between us. You might think that I am jealous of her, but I am not. But that is one of the ways I have been hurt. Although I did not get revenge, I do think of hurting myself at times. What did I do? I went for a long walk one day and I planned not to come back. Why? So I wouldn't say anything I would regret later. I am glad I took this walk because if I hadn't we would have been fighting. (p. 32)

Once again, the content of the writer's paper is stunning—the fact that her anger and pain have been so great that she has thought of hurting herself at times. And what about the foresight and self-control that the story reveals—her decision to take a walk? It may be that the intensity of her daily personal experience has already opened her eyes to the dangers of retaliation.

To explore the meaning of these stories, Mrs. Prince and I question the students:

> *SHG:* That is a very good paper, Sylvia. Can you tell us why you decided not to have the fight?
> *Sylvia:* Because she was pregnant.
> *SHG:* She was pregnant and you didn't want to hurt her?
> *Sylvia:* Uh-huh.
> *SHG:* Well, that is very interesting. How would some of the rest of you respond to that? Is there anyone who would have done something different in that situation?

Michael: I would have just packed my clothes and left.

MP: Why would you do that?

Michael: If my momma had her picks and chooses, I would just have left.

SHG: So you're saying you would have just left, Michael? Would you have left so as not to hurt your mother, or, [as] Sylvia mentioned in her story, [so as not to] hurt [yourself]? Would you have gone off to hurt [someone else]?

Michael: My mother would probably hurt me before I hurt her.

SHG: So you would go off to protect yourself, because you think that if you fought with her you would have been the loser?

Michael: Yeah.

SHG: Marcy, what would you have done in this situation?

Marcy: I never thought about it.

SHG: You never thought about it? Well, just hearing it this time, do you have any response to it?

Marcy: I would be in my room and I would start crying.

Michael: Yeah! Marcy is a crier!

SHG: Why do you think this situation would have made you cry, Marcy?

Marcy: That my mom treat me like that. When she do something like that, I just go to my room and cry and write in my diary about her.

SHG: You would write in your diary. That is very interesting. (Haroutunian-Gordon, pp. 33–34)

The foregoing suggests that these students may not take the discussion as an opportunity to reflect upon issues to which the answer is unclear. When Marcy responds to the question of what she would do in Sylvia's situation by saying that she "never thought about it," it seems that she may believe that she has nothing to say *because* she never thought about it until that moment. Later in the conversation, students seem to recognize that the discussion provides them the opportunity to reflect, and that they need not have a definitive or "correct" response in mind before they respond to a question. Fortunately, Mrs. Prince, who participated in many of the conversations, seemed to encourage the students to reflect openly. Notice her responses to the following story, written by James:

I have been hurt a hundred times by many people. Sometimes it makes me feel good, but most of the time it hurts and I refuse to stand for someone taking a cheap shot at me. Sometimes I am forced to do what I don't want to do to get revenge. It is hard to keep cool. I try not to let anyone blow my top. They think I won't do anything, but I will get them back. I have decided not to be hurt anymore. For in my lifetime I have been hurt too many times. I am going to try to make it better.

MP: That is a good paper, too. It explains something about James and the
way he treats me. I feel better about that. I am glad I read this.

Sylvia: Well, maybe sometimes you treat him wrong and you wait for a
while. That is maybe why he get mad at you real fast and talks back to you.

MP: And he is really afraid of someone taking a cheap shot at him, right? But
I need to ask a question, James. What is a cheap shot?

James: Something that is not expected. You are probably expecting something from that person but you are not expecting a low blow from them. It
is coming but you don't think it is going to come that way. You sit there
and you be shocked and you be hurt. Then you want to get them. So you
just come back another day, another time, another place.

MP: So I said something bad—you thought I would never say anything like
that to you. But it sounds like when you want to get back at somebody,
James, it is to protect yourself. It is not so much to harm the person but to
prevent this from happening in the future.

James: Right. (pp. 34–35)

Here, we see the teacher using the student's story to make sense out of
their relationship in a way that seems to open up its meaning to her. She is,
as it were, using the text (the student's paper) to illuminate the meaning of
her personal experience with him. In order to benefit from their study of
Romeo and Juliet, students need to move back and forth between the text
and their personal experiences, so that at some times they draw upon the
text to explain events in their lives and at others they relate events in their
lives to illuminate the meaning of the text (Gadamer, 1989). Indeed, Colette shows that she has begun to play the game already:

Colette: Sometimes it is not nice to take revenge.

Sylvia: In my house, you had better!

SHG: What are you saying, Colette? Why is it sometimes not nice?

Colette: It is not smart because if you take revenge you could get hurt if you
go back. Just like in my paper as I read when I called the police on my
brother. And then my father told me and they handcuffed him and all this,
and I was about to cry because they were taking him away. I felt sorry that I
had called the police on him. But again, I look at it that he shouldn't have
jumped on me. He jumped on me—I didn't do something wrong. When I
called the police I was crying. I didn't want him to go to jail. But they took
him anyway. When he got out, I thought he was going to jump on me
again. But instead, he told me I did the right thing to call the police. (Haroutunian-Gordon, pp. 35–36)

Here, Colette appears to come to new insight about the incident with
her brother—that taking revenge in that instance caused her pain. Her
reflection may have been advanced by listening to the stories and observa-

tions of others, rather than merely by speaking herself. Recall that early in the conversation she had agreed with Sylvia's decision not strike her pregnant mother, so that even at that moment, Colette may have begun to think about the negative consequences of taking revenge. The exchange between James and Mrs. Prince, which had reference to a difficult moment in their relationship, may have touched her as well.

The students in the Belden classroom seem to bring extraordinary resources to the discussion situation: they have intense personal relationships to draw upon, their daily experiences are powerful and so potentially instructive, and they are willing to share these experiences. Furthermore, some seem able to use personal experience to illuminate the meaning of a text, as did Michael and Marcy after hearing Sylvia's paper. Some also seem able to use the text to illuminate the meaning of personal experience, as did Ms. Prince and Sylvia, having heard James's paper, and Colette in her final remark about the pitfalls of taking revenge.

Yet, when attention is turned to *Romeo and Juliet*, these same students encounter difficulties drawing upon the resources that they bring to discussion. At first, as shall be seen, they show little interest in the text or the opportunity to converse about it. Over time, and through questioning, they come to draw upon their personal experiences—to tell stories—to illuminate the meaning of Shakespeare's play and the events in their lives as well. The telling of stories appears to play a significant role in the transformation that the students undergo.

MISINTERPRETING THE TEXT

Given the "natural resources" that the Belden students bring to the discussion setting, one might expect that they would respond positively to the opportunity to converse about the meaning of *Romeo and Juliet*. Such, however, was not the case initially. To begin with, there was the great gulf that existed between Shakespearean English and the speech to which they were accustomed (Haroutunian-Gordon, 1991, pp. 39–41). The gulf was broadened by the students' lack of experience in actually using the events in their own lives to provide access to the text. At first, they did not seem to believe that their own stories could give them ideas about Shakespeare's story. Consider the following exchange that occurred about the meaning of the nurse's speech, act 1, scene 3, in which she tells about weaning Juliet:

SHG: What does "weaned" mean? Yes, Colette.
Colette: I don't know. Dead?
MP: No. Think! She "weaned" the baby. Colette, [do] you have an idea now?

Colette: Spanked? Slapped?

MP: No.

Colette: You tell us! You're the teacher!

SHG: Wait! Let's try to figure it out. Have you never heard that before? She weaned the baby?

Sylvia: She had an abortion? A miscarriage?

MP: No.

SHG: Now we know this nurse has these two girls who are about the same age, right? Where are you going, Colette?

Colette: I am going to the dictionary because I don't know.

SHG: Wait a minute. Come back here. Read it one more time.

Colette: "Now eleven years; and she was weaned." It means she was pregnant.

SHG: Now this nurse is taking care of two babies, right? And what would a nurse be likely to do? If the nurse had a child of her own and is also taking care of Juliet, which was one of our ideas, what could she do for Juliet? Yes, Colette?

Colette: Take care of them. Breast-feed them.

SHG: Right, exactly. Breast-feed them. If she had a child of her own, she would have milk and be able to breast-feed them. So the word "weaned" is related to breast-feeding. What happens next?

Sylvia: She weans her daughter.

Marcy: Susan doesn't actually have to be her daughter. The nurse is taking care of Juliet and Juliet is not her daughter.

SHG: Is that what you think, Marcy? Yes, Colette.

Colette: The whole thing wouldn't matter if Juliet was dead instead of Susan.
(p. 44)

In this instance, we see what appears to be random guessing on the part of the students in response to the teacher's questions. In addition, the students turn to both the teacher and the dictionary to determine the definition of "weaned" instead of trying to use the text to help them figure out the meaning. I urge them to try the latter, believing that it can be done, given what the nurse says. But the students are highly resistant. After Colette is asked to "read [the passage] one more time," and avoid the dictionary, she complies but follows the reading with what seems to be more random guessing ("It means she was pregnant"). I try to relate the passage she has just read to an interpretation made previously ("Now this nurse is taking care of two babies, right?") and the definition of "weaning," but the students have difficulty following the procedure so as to glean the definition from the text. It appears that they have had little experience using knowledge drawn from daily living to help them interpret puzzling passages in the way I am suggesting.

In a subsequent conversation, another problem arises. Here, students draw upon their own experience all right, but with the outcome of grossly misinterpreting the text, not simply failing to make an interpretation. The exchange focuses upon a passage from act 1, scene 5. The scene is Lord Capulet's party, and Romeo, overwhelmed with feelings of love at his first sight of Juliet, questions the nurse about the girl's identity:

> Romeo: What is her mother?
> Nurse: Marry, bachelor,
>   Her mother is the lady of the house,
>   And wise and virtuous.
>   I nursed her daughter that you talked withal.
>   I tell you, he that can lay hold of her
>   Shall have the chinks [plenty of money].
> Romeo: Is she a Capulet?
>   O dear account! My life is my foe's debt.

The students had some trouble reading the passage aloud, and again I assisted them. Fearing that they had not grasped the text, I began the discussion trying to find out:

> SHG: So what does Romeo know about Juliet now that he knows [that her] mother is the lady of the house? Myrna.
> Myrna: That she is a Capulet.
> SHG: That she is a Capulet because it is [the] Capulet's party, right?
> Colette: Right.
> MP: Thank you, Colette. And so Juliet is a Capulet, right?
> Michael: We don't know that.
> SHG: We don't know that, Michael?
> Colette: And Romeo is a Montague!
> SHG: Wait a minute! Michael is saying that we don't know that Juliet is a Capulet.
> Mason: Michael is playing the fool!
> Michael: No! Doesn't Romeo say "Is she a Capulet?"
> SHG: Yes, he does, Michael—line 119. Now when he asks this, does this mean he does not know whether she is?
> Marcy: No.
> SHG: Does he know or doesn't he know?
> Sylvia: He don't.
> SHG: He doesn't know?
> Marcy: He doesn't know for sure.
> SHG: Wait a minute!
> Michael: He can't be sure just because the mother is a Capulet.
> MP: Yes, Myrna.
> Myrna: You know her mother is one.

SHG: If the mother is a Capulet, is there any way that Juliet is not a Capulet? Henry?

Henry: When her mother got married she could have kept her maiden name.

Sylvia: Her mother could have just wished to be a Capulet. Then her daughter wouldn't be one.

SHG: James, what do you think about this? Is it possible that Juliet might not be a Capulet?

James: Yeah.

SHG: You think she might not be one?

James: It's possible, but she is one, though.

SHG: Is it possible that Juliet could have been a Montague?

[A chorus of "NO!!" fills the air. "That would be crazy!"]

SHG: But could Juliet have been other than a Capulet? Myrna.

Myrna: Yeah. Her mother could have got married and didn't change her name. Then the mother wouldn't be another Capulet.

Sylvia: Yeah! If the mother didn't change her name, then the mother wouldn't be another Capulet.

Richard: But she probably did change it.

SHG: So you think she is a Capulet, Richard? You think there is no question about it? Why would she have to be a Capulet, Richard?

Richard: Because you said so!

SHG: Because I said so? (Haroutunian-Gordon, pp. 74–76)

Here, it appears that the students are using personal experience—the stories of their own lives—to gain access into the meaning of the text. In their experience, women can keep their maiden names when they marry, in which case the child might not take the father's name, so that Juliet might not be a Capulet. Here, the understanding gleaned from personal experience seems to prevent them from attending to relevant textual evidence. Apparently, they have forgotten that prior to Romeo's conversation with the nurse in act 1, scene 5, Juliet's mother has been designated "Lady Capulet" twelve times in the text. This fact alone would indicate that Shakespeare intends us to believe that the woman is married to Lord Capulet, that she has taken his name, and that their child, Juliet, is therefore a Capulet. The students also seem to have forgotten scene 4 in which the young man, Paris, asks Lord Capulet for his daughter's hand in marriage. Indeed, the discussants' personal experience of women marrying and having children but failing to change their names (Henry, Myrna, Sylvia), or wishing to marry or take another's name but not actually doing so, seems to press them with the possibility that Juliet might not have had the name "Capulet," and so, "might not have been a Capulet" (See Haroutunian-Gordon, 1991, pp. 77–84).

Now, when teachers consider using interpretive discussion in schools like Belden, they are often discouraged from doing so before they begin.

Why? For the two reasons suggested here: (1) the students lack previous experience with the approach and so, lack knowledge of the patterns that one needs to follow in order to be successful (e.g., using one's experience to help decipher textual meaning) and (2) the students' personal experience is of such a nature that it will be irrelevant to or interfere with an accurate, appropriate interpretation. While it is true that the Belden students struggled with both difficulties at first, they did move on to more successful conversations, as the exchanges in the next section demonstrate.

INTO THE TEXT

In the following conversation, the students are focused upon act 2, scene 2, of *Romeo and Juliet*. This is the famous "balcony scene" in which Romeo, hiding in the garden beneath Juliet's window, converses with his beloved, despite the fact that he puts himself in mortal danger by so doing. Mrs. Prince raises a question:

MP: Well, one thing I noticed about Juliet is that she never says, "Go home." Why doesn't she tell Romeo to go away?

Colette: Because she is in love with him.

SHG: So she is in love, Colette, but she knows he is in danger. Still, she doesn't tell him to leave.

Colette: Right.

MP: She wants him to be there?

Colette: Right.

Marcy: They love each other.

MP: They love each other but she never tells him to go. Don't you think that is interesting? If you love somebody, and they come to your house, and they are in danger if they stick around—[they] may get hurt—but you never tell the person to go, isn't that interesting? Colette.

Colette: If she don't tell him to go, she is trying to get him hurt.

SHG: Do you think she is trying to get him hurt? Sylvia.

Sylvia: No, she is in love and she wants to see her man. If he leaves and gets hurt, she might never see him again.

Marcy: I think she is trying to tell him to come over to her house.

SHG: So she wants him to come in, Marcy?

Marcy: Yeah.

SHG: But doesn't she worry about it?

Marcy: She said, if they see him outside they are going to get him. She is trying to give him the idea to come into her bedroom.

James: She wants to hide him?

Marcy: No, she doesn't. She wants to get married. (pp. 91–92)

Here, the students create stories about Juliet's motivations that appear to be based upon their personal experiences of young love. As they do so, their views of the text take shape and issues about its meaning begin to emerge. (See Chapter 10 by H. McEwan, this volume, for comments about the educational effects of telling such stories.) For example, Colette begins by saying that Juliet does not tell Romeo to leave the garden because she loves him. Upon further reflection, Colette reasons that Juliet is trying to harm Romeo, since if she were not, she would tell him to leave. The idea that Juliet wishes Romeo harm certainly contradicts the earlier claim that Juliet loves the young man. To Colette's suggestion that Juliet wants Romeo to be hurt, I respond by asking Sylvia what she thinks of that possibility. Sylvia rejects the idea, arguing that Juliet loves Romeo, wants to see him, and fears that she will not see him again if he does leave. This account of Juliet's motivations seems more reasonable to Sylvia, given her experience of love. Perhaps Sylvia's comment raises a new suggestion, voiced by Marcy, that Juliet does not tell Romeo to leave because she wants him in her bedroom. When James asks whether the aim is to hide Romeo, Marcy says no: Juliet wants Romeo in her bedroom not to hide him but because she loves him and "wants to marry him."

So, we have on the floor two opposing views about why Juliet does not tell Romeo to leave the garden. Colette says that the young girl wants Romeo harmed; Sylvia says Juliet wants to see Romeo and fears his being harmed. In addition, Marcy and James contribute two ideas about why Juliet wants Romeo in her bedroom: James wonders whether Juliet wants to hide Romeo, while Marcy believes that "marriage" (lovemaking?) is Juliet's objective. These issues seem to have formed as the students drew upon their personal experiences, speculated about Juliet's motivations, and listened to each other's speculations.

As the conversation continues, Mrs. Prince presses the students to keep thinking about what they would do in Juliet's situation:

MP: It is still interesting to me that Juliet didn't say, "Go away" [to Romeo]. If you really loved somebody, [under such circumstances] wouldn't you tell your loved one [to go]?

James: Juliet is fourteen years old!

MP: But wouldn't you say to your lover, "Please run away. I will talk to you tomorrow"?

Colette: Uh-huh.

Sylvia: Uh-hum.

Richard: I wouldn't.

Colette: Better than for him to be dead!

Marcy: I would rather see him safe.

SHG: So would you send him, Marcy?

Marcy: I would send him so fast.

MP: Now James is suggesting something interesting when he says that Juliet is only 14 years old. Do you think Juliet doesn't tell Romeo to go because she is so young?

Colette: Yeah.

MP: Let's take this a little further. Is it possible that young love can be a little selfish? What do we mean by "selfish," Henry?

Henry: Keeping things to yourself.

Colette: Concerned only with oneself.

SHG: So, Colette, is she thinking about him or herself?

Colette: I think she is thinking about him.

Myrna: Both.

Marcy: Yes, both. She wants him now because her love might get killed.

SHG: So what you are suggesting, Marcy, is that Juliet wants the pleasure of the moment while she can get it. Is that what she is doing?

Colette: No, it's just like you said. She is trying to tell him to wait until they get older.

MP: Is she?

Colette: Yeah.

Marcy: No, they are so in love that they—if they are that in love, they couldn't wait. (p. 93)

Although Marcy says that if her lover were in danger she would "send him so fast," she emphatically denies that Juliet is doing this: "They are so in love that they—if they are that in love they can't wait." This interpretation of Juliet's motives seems to be based upon her experience of what two young lovers would feel and do. Furthermore, James' comment that Juliet is 14 years old suggests that from his experience, people of that age would have difficulty postponing the anticipated pleasure of meeting their lovers.

Here, we begin to see a transformation taking place in the discussants. While at first they had difficulty drawing upon the experiences in their own lives to develop interpretations of the text, they now do so more easily. In telling stories that grow out of personal experience, their ideas about the text, as well as their interest in it, begin to spring from an affective rather than a purely intellectual source. Their personal experiences give rise to different ideas about the text, and issues about its meaning begin to emerge. Colette and Marcy seem to be in genuine disagreement: Colette avers that Juliet does not want the pleasure of the moment—"she is trying to tell him to wait until they are older"—and Marcy insists that they are too much in love to wait.

When issues spring from an affective source, students may sustain discussion for long periods and may open up both the text and personal experience in powerful ways. Such was the case in the class held subsequent to the one above, when Colette opened the conversation with a question before anything else was said. The students were still focused upon the balcony scene, act 2, scene 2, where Romeo and Juliet, having declared their love for one another, make plans to unite in matrimony.

> *Colette*: Why was Juliet so eager to get married?

The fact that this question came from a discussant rather than the leader, together with its power, took me off guard, but I struggled to identify a passage that might be used to explore it:

> *SHG*: Look at the top of page 79. Would you read those two lines again, Sylvia, to see if it helps us?
> *Sylvia*: Juliet. "And all my fortunes at thy foot I'll lay, and follow thee my lord throughout the world."
> *SHG*: What is she saying she is going to do?
> *Sylvia*: Follow him.
> *Marcy*: She wants to be with him.
> *James*: Do whatever he says.
> *SHG*: Why is she so eager to be with him, to follow him throughout the world, do whatever he says?
> *Colette*: She loves him.
> *SHG*: She loves him, Colette? But this has been pretty fast, right? Yes, James.
> *James*: They will run away so nobody will be hurt.
> *SHG*: Are you saying they are going to sneak off?
> *James*: Yes.
> *SHG*: This is a sort of secret thing, then.
> *Colette*: I hope not because they are really going to kill him if he sneaks off and marries her. (pp. 101–103)

Notice how quickly the issues are beginning to evolve here. James has responded to Colette's question of why Juliet was so eager to get married: "They will run away so nobody will be hurt." But Colette's reaction to the plan of "sneaking off" contradicts James's idea. On the contrary, Colette says, "they" will kill Romeo if he sneaks off with Juliet. Colette's comment thereby shifts the issue before the group. Now the question is, What will happen to the couple if they sneak off? rather than, Why is Juliet in such a rush to marry Romeo?

> *SHG*: So you are saying, Colette, that if he sneaked off and married her they would really come after him, right? So instead of being safe and being able to get away, they would be in more trouble?
> *Colette*: I don't know.
> *SHG*: Is this a good idea that Romeo and Juliet have here?

Sylvia: Yes.

James: Maybe to them, but not to others.

SHG: Why is it a good idea to them, James?

James: Because they are in love.

SHG: But is it dangerous?

James: Not to them.

SHG: If they are in love and trying to get away, is this a smart thing to do? You are saying that for them it is [smart] because they will be free, right James? Even with everybody chasing them and everything?

James: They won't have to answer to anybody.

SHG: I see, so they can do what they want. They will be free. But what are you saying, Colette?

Colette: If somebody took my daughter and ran off and got married, I would kill him! (pp. 104–105)

The new issue — what will happen to the couple if they sneak off and get married — acquires intensity when Colette, projecting herself into the role of a father whose daughter elopes with a man, declares: "I would kill him!" In drawing upon her beliefs about a father's reaction to the situation, which she presents to the group as a story, Colette polarizes the issue in a very dramatic way. For while James argues that the lovers will be safe if they run off, Colette, given her sense of a father's response, declares they will be in mortal danger. She asserts that the father in such a situation would pursue the couple, not just leave them to enjoy each other.

Here is an example of how beliefs that arise through one's personal experience, when transformed into stories and used to interpret a text, can focus and intensify the discussion of its meaning. The conversation continues:

SHG: You would kill him, Colette? So you don't think that this plan of sneaking off to get married is a good idea? You think they are going to be in more trouble doing it this way? What would you suggest that they do in this situation?

Colette: I think they should tell someone.

SHG: Should Juliet go to her father and say: Hey, I'm not interested in Paris, but there is someone else I am interested in?

Colette: Yeah! He can't do nothing!

SHG: So you think she would be better off if she went and told her father about it instead of trying to sneak off?

Colette: Right.

Marcy: Just because he couldn't stop them anyway.

James: He could stop them, but he probably has someone else to stop them. But, I think he will be very upset with her if she tells him.

SHG: So would he be even more upset if she came back and said she was married?

Sylvia: [Yes, married] to [Romeo], because he is a Montague and she is a Capulet and Montagues and Capulets don't get along.

SHG: [Anyone else?] Would the father be more upset to know before or after
the marriage?

James: After.

SHG: You say "after," James, why?

James: They were talking to her before. Plus, eating, he would spit out his
food at her.

SHG: So that is what happens if she tells him before, right? What about if she
tells him afterward? What would he do, James?

James: He would be bent out of shape!

Colette: Uh-uh, he would kill Romeo for marrying his daughter.

SHG: James, I am still not sure what you are saying. Would it be worse if she
told her father before or after the marriage?

James: Anyway it goes is bad.

SHG: So it wouldn't make any difference. Colette says it might be worse after-
wards because Capulet might want to kill Romeo. Do you think that is
right, Sylvia?

Sylvia: If she tells him she is going to get married, he will be hurt. He will say,
"Why didn't you tell me before?" She would get a lecture.

Marcy: So that is why she wouldn't tell him?

Sylvia: Yeah. He would probably talk her to death so she would miss her wedding!

SHG: Aha! So Capulet would really try to keep her away from Romeo, right?

Colette: I think if they married, and then she told her father, he would try to
keep her away from Romeo. (pp. 105–106)

Once again the issue has shifted somewhat: Should Juliet tell her father
about the marriage before or after it occurs? This is a shared issue, one to
which several members of the group have contributed. It grew out of questions posed earlier—Why was Juliet in such a rush to get married? What
will happen if the couple sneaks off?—and is the outgrowth of several
persons' attempts to answer these questions. As we have seen, the "answers"
came in the form of stories about human motivation that seem to be based
upon the discussants' personal experience. Marcy and Colette maintain that
the father should be told before the marriage because "he couldn't stop
them anyway," and, worse yet, he would "kill Romeo" for marrying his
daughter. James and Sylvia, on the other hand, argue that the father would
be "very upset" to hear of the wedding plans—that he would "spit out his
food" and "talk her to death so she would miss her wedding."

It seems, then, that these discussants care about identifying Juliet's best
course of action. They seem to appreciate her dilemma, and, indeed, have
worked hard to figure out why she faces it, why she is so eager to get
married. They appear to listen to each other's ideas and draw upon their

own experiences to develop positions. In short, a transformation has occurred: The students care about interpreting the text and use the discussion
opportunity to meet the objective.

EXAMINING THE ROLE OF NARRATIVE

What, then, is the role of narrative in the transformation that appears
before us? On the one hand, it appears that there can be no one answer to
the question, as we have seen stories enter the conversation in many different ways and with varying effects. When Marcy says that she would send
her endangered lover away "so fast," yet insists that Juliet was trying to
do otherwise, her story about herself seems to have little bearing on the
interpretation of the text. When Colette insists that were she a father, she
would "kill Romeo" if he eloped with his daughter, the story profoundly
deepens the understanding of Juliet's dilemma: If a father would be moved
to murder a man who eloped with his daughter, then the course of action
open to the couple is severely limited, as Capulet would never approve of
the marriage were it proposed to him. Then again, when Michael maintains
that Juliet might not be a Capulet because her mother might have retained
her maiden name and given that to her child, the story seems to interfere
with text interpretation. In short, it appears that using stories based upon
personal experience to interpret texts need not bring about a transformation
of one's understanding.

However, when the telling of stories does seem to have a profound
impact — as happens occasionally — the experience appears to connect the
reader affectively with the situation presented by the text. At this level, the
reader feels the joys, pains, and dilemmas of the characters. In such a
situation, the story seems to open up the text, to uncover what lies hidden,
as Gadamer (1989) might say. It makes available to readers ideas about the
characters' motivations which are otherwise unavailable and which link the
reader to the character in a compelling way. If the Belden students have
come to feel that Juliet is "in such a rush to get married" not because she is
young and impetuous but because she has no hope of happiness if she
proceeds rationally and asks her father's permission, then their connection
to Juliet may indeed be lasting. For Juliet faces a dilemma which they see
will not pass with age and which poses profound problems: How is one to
live if one is to give up one's source of happiness? Once the students have
entered the text deeply enough to feel the dilemmas it seems to pose, they
are in a position to experience the great rewards of interpretive discussion.
And once they have tasted its pleasures, the apathetic, nay disbelieving,
attitude toward discussion cannot remain what once it was.

REFERENCES

Egan, K. (1986). *Teaching as storytelling: An alternative approach to teaching and curriculum in the elementary school.* London, Ontario: Althouse Press.

Gadamer, H-G. (1989). *Truth and method* (2nd ed.) (J. Weinsheimer & D. G. Marshall, Trans.). New York: Crossroad. (Original work published 1960)

Haroutunian-Gordon, S. (1991). *Turning the soul: Teaching through conversation in the high school.* Chicago: University of Chicago Press.

Wittgenstein, L. (1958). *Philosophical investigations* (G.E.M. Anscombe, Trans.). Cambridge, UK: Basil Blackwell & Mott.

CHAPTER 8

Narrative and Learning

A VOYAGE OF IMPLICATIONS

Kieran Egan

Jerome Bruner's *Actual Minds, Possible Worlds* (1986) has helped popularize within educational research a conception of the mind that gives renewed prominence to the role of narrative in our ways of making sense of the world and of experience. The conception of the mind as, in whatever degree, a narrative concern (Sutton-Smith, 1988) is supported by a wealth of modern research, from Bartlett's celebrated studies on memory (1932), to Bransford and associates' (1972, 1975) and Rumelhart's (1975) work, to the recent large-scale focus on scripts, schemata, and stories. This research has established, to use Gardner's summing up, "that human subjects do not come to tasks as empty slates: they have expectations and well-structured schemata within which they approach diverse material" (Gardner, 1985, p. 126). While this may seem only to echo a point that Gestalt psychologists earlier in the century took for granted, the additional result of this research has been to give us a more elaborate and detailed understanding of how such scripts, schemata, and stories are deployed in our sense-making.

My aim here is not to explore this research, nor to assess the security of its findings, but rather to assume the validity of its most general conclusion and explore some of its implications for our concepts, theories, and principles of learning. That is, I will consider how focusing on the mind as a narrative concern might affect our ideas about learning in general and also about some of the learning principles we use to guide teaching practice and even curriculum structure. (This is not, of course, to presume that the mind is *only* a narrative concern.)

The general conceptions we may hold about the mind obviously influence in profound ways our ideas about learning. Often it seems that significant changes in general conceptions of mind take some time to percolate through to research programs. This seems currently the case with learning.

Or, at least, there seems some lag between acceptance of a significant narrative component in our mental lives, and elaboration of ideas about learning which clearly reflect that narrative component.

What I want to do here, then, is to briefly examine just one kind of narrative that seems universally engaging to young children—the classic fairy tale. (For another perspective on children's use of fantasy, see Paley's essay in this volume.) I will try to show that an analysis of a few of the most uncontentious observations we can make about these narratives raises quite dramatic challenges to the concepts of learning derived from traditional kinds of research based on nonnarrative tasks. Straightforward inferences from these uncontentious observations also challenge some of the more prominent learning principles that one finds underlying teaching practices and curriculum structuring. This is intended as a very general exploration of how wide and deep through education might run the implications of taking the narrative mind to heart. (Also, see especially Jackson's, Paley's, and McEwan's chapters in this book.)

OBSERVATION 1: THE STRUCTURE OF FAIRY TALES

The classic fairy tales, such as "Jack and the Beanstalk," "Hansel and Gretel," "Cinderella," "Little Red Riding Hood," and so on, have a considerable power to engage young children in Western cultural settings, and children learn and remember their contents quite readily. One of the most obvious structural features of these stories is that they are based on powerful conflicts between security and danger, courage and cowardice, cleverness and stupidity, hope and despair, and good and evil. This feature of these stories has been observed often, and is commonly taken as a reflection of the "manner in which the child can bring order into [his or her] world . . . by dividing everything into opposites" (Bettelheim, 1976, p. 74).

The stories are made up of characters and events that give a concrete form to the underlying abstract binary concepts. The narrative brings such underlying concepts as security/danger, courage/cowardice, cleverness/ stupidity, and so on, into conflict, then elaborates the conflict and finally brings it to some resolution. Two features of these concepts are noteworthy. First, they are abstract, and, second, they are affective.

For the classic fairy stories to make sense, children must in some sense be familiar with security/danger, courage/cowardice, hope/despair, and so on. Children need not, of course, be able to articulate or define such terms to be able to deploy them. It seems that these abstract, binary concepts are constantly deployed by children in making sense of the world and their experience. We can see such concepts structuring children's own invented narratives constantly (Paley, 1981, 1984, 1990). The ubiquity of abstract binary concepts undergirding classic fairy stories and children's invented narratives suggests that their presence is hardly an incidental or casual matter. Also, Lévi-Strauss' observation of their vital role in structuring myths (Lévi-Strauss, 1970) suggests that we might sensibly give them more attention.

Implication 1: Abstractions in Young Children's Thinking

We are familiar with claims that young children's thinking is in some sense concrete, and that if we want to make material accessible to them we need to present it in concrete terms. Such a view has been supported by Piaget's research, of course. But the implication of the above observation is that young children's thinking is also abstract, or at least that abstractions are clearly important and necessary ingredients in children's ability to make sense of the kinds of stories they find readily engaging. And it seems to be the abstractions, especially when organized in terms of binary opposites, that provide access to and engagement with the concrete content. The wanderings of Hansel and Gretel through a medieval forest would not engage interest without the underlying conflict between anxiety and security. So, far from young children being unable to deal with abstractions, in such narratives they deploy easily and readily the most abstract ideas we ever learn. What seems abstract to adults is the *concept* of anxiety, the verbal mark of an experience that we all as children have felt vividly.

This implication yields the hypothesis that to make content most accessible and engaging to young children, it should be organized in terms of abstract binary concepts. That is, it is the combination of concrete content with powerful abstractions that enables young children to understand material most readily. (And we can organize mathematics and science content on such concepts as easily as we can construct fictional fairy stories on them. For examples, see Egan, 1988, 1989, 1990, 1992.)

Implication 2: Relevance to Abstract Concepts

It is commonly claimed—indeed, it seems to be generally accepted as a truism—that children will learn more effectively if what is taught is made relevant to their experience. This has most commonly been interpreted as the learning principle that new knowledge can be made *relevant* by connecting it with what Dewey called the "material of ordinary acquaintance" (Dewey, 1916/1966, p. 258). This, in turn, is most commonly interpreted as requiring some association between what is to be taught and students' everyday experience, environment, or interests. The earlier observation implies that any content can be made relevant to children's experience if we can identify within that content, or can organize it in terms of, the abstract binary concepts children deploy so readily. That is, relevance moves from a principle of content associations to one of finding the appropriate binary abstractions to embody the content.

This implication also challenges a prominent principle used in curriculum design. It is a principle that finds expression in "expanding horizons" curricula. The elementary social studies curriculum has for generations been structured on the assumption that what is most relevant, and thus meaningful, to young children is content to do with themselves, their homes and families, their neighborhoods, and so on. The curriculum is designed to expand gradually outward from these to other communities, the nation, and other nations, building on the concepts familiar from everyday experience.

It is worth noting how ubiquitous this assumption is. Nearly all social studies textbooks justify the structure of the curriculum by reference to this principle as though it is entirely unproblematic: "Thus, kindergarten and first-grade students spend a lot of social studies time studying self-awareness and families because these two topics have a sense of relevance and immediacy to young children" (Ellis, 1986, p. 9). The set of expanding horizons topics is justified because "The social studies program should be built on what the child already knows," (Jarolimek, 1982, p. 12). But consider also the following use of the principle: "The sort of familiarity which a child demands in a story is often a social one, a doing of things which the child expects to have done. Thus *Peter Rabbit* is a manageable story for Carol at two years eight months because of its familiar family setting" (Applebee, 1978, p. 75). But if it is familiarity with the child's experience that makes the story accessible or manageable, wouldn't it be better if Peter was a child not a rabbit? Also, one might wonder about other components of the story, such as the wild wood, which is safe, and the cultivated garden, which is dangerous, as well as the closeness of death in the story. Clearly something other than familiarity with everyday experience makes narratives and their content engaging to children. The one element observed above implies a principle quite at variance with what shapes the social studies curriculum and claims such as Applebee's. Similarly, Jarolimek's claim that the curriculum should be built on what the child knows fails to notice that children also "know" binary concepts such as love/hate, anxiety/security, courage/cowardice, and that through these profound, affective concepts any content can be made accessible and relevant. The key to what children can learn is not simply content associations with what they already know. We can observe medieval forests, galaxies long ago and far away, witches, giants, and space warriors all becoming immediately and vividly relevant to children's interests by embodying abstract affective concepts.

OBSERVATION 2: MEDIATION OF BINARY CONCEPTS

How can we account for the fact that young children are so commonly engaged by a story about a rabbit who wears a nice blue coat and is given cups of camomile tea by his mother? The idea that children's grasp of the world proceeds from the familiar gradually outwards cannot account for one of the most obvious features we may observe in children's narrative intellectual lives—the engagement by the fantastic, by talking middle-class rabbits and endless things outside of their or anyone's experience.

It is difficult to gain evidence of some features of children's conceptual development, because some developments can only be reliably traced by longitudinal studies requiring constant monitoring. For example, it is not clear how children master sets of concepts related to such phenomena as time, space, temperature, and other phenomenal continua (see the discussion in Siegler, 1991). Not only is adequate data hard to come by, but, as Flavell has noted, it is even harder to know how to characterize the mechanisms of development at which the data hint (Flavell, 1984). But we may observe some common procedures, and build simple models that are, while in this case not empirically uncontentious, at least consistent with what data we have. The other support for the model I will describe comes from studies of the thinking of people in oral cultures, and how myths encode information (Lévi-Strauss, 1970). There is also an element of logical necessity in the process. And further, the following observation merits attention because it seems to offer an explanation of what no other theory seems to account for adequately.

If we consider how young children accumulate concepts concerning, say, the temperature continuum, it seems that they first learn the concepts "hot" and "cold." This would seem to verge on logical necessity, given that initial discriminations of temperature would be "hotter than my body temperature" and "colder than my body temperature." Also, any discrimination is built on such binary logic, which most simply distinguishes X from all other things which are not X. Following Lévi-Strauss' observations (1963, 1966a, 1966b), it would seem that it is common then for a mediating concept, such as "warm" to be grasped. Then the child may mediate between "warm" and "cold," inferring the meaning of a concept like "cool," and by a similar process of mediating between binary terms, a set of concepts is discriminated for dealing with the temperature continuum.

Now this might be dismissed as being possibly interesting but no more than an unsupported speculation. It is an awkward speculation, because on the one hand it would be very hard to design experiments to either support or falsify it, and on the other hand it has a nagging plausibility for anyone who has spent much time observing young children's narratives—in which this binary opposition and mediation process appears irritatingly widespread once one has the model suggested.

Another reason for not casually dismissing this model of conceptual development is its potential for explaining the appeal of Peter Rabbit. If this binary discrimination and mediation process is common in children's conceptual development, helping them to gain an efficient and effective conceptual grasp of a whole range of phenomenal continua in the world, what happens when it is applied to phenomena that are made up of discrete opposites? Any continuum allows one to form binary oppositions, set at each end of the continuum, and then to form a concept that mediates between the two extremes. The new concept, such as "cool" between "hot" and "cold," might be seen as a coalescence of the two extremes. But what if the binary terms are "life" and "death," or "human" and "animal," or "nature" and "culture"? How does one mediate between these?

Indeed, discrimination between things that are alive and things that are dead is typically learned very early in our experience, and is certainly presupposed in the most basic stories. It is precisely the fear of death that makes Peter Rabbit's exertions in Mr. McGregor's garden meaningful, and that gives tension to Hansel's and Gretel's adventures. What happens when we mediate between life and death, or when we coalesce these concepts? Well, we get things like ghosts. A ghost is both alive and dead, as cool is both hot and cold. And when we mediate between human and animal? We get things like yetis and sasquatches—creatures that are both human and animal, as ghosts are alive and dead and cool is both hot and cold. And what do we generate when we mediate between things that are natural and things that are cultural? We get creatures like Peter Rabbit. Peter is a rabbit—a natural creature—but he is also human in his use of language, his clothes, and his emotions. That is, the fantasy stories of children are in significant degree made up of mediational categories between the most basic discriminations we make among empirically discrete categories. (This would seem to be a much more economical explanation of the fantasy worlds of young children than those offered in various psychoanalytic theories.)

Implication 3: Learning and Curriculum

From reflecting on the curious content of children's fantasy narratives—and we find similar characteristics in both the classic fairy tales and children's own narratives (Paley, 1981, 1984, 1990)—we are inclined in the direction of a hypothesis about children's learning that is powerful, plausible, and merits research attention. Whatever the conclusion of research about the prevalence of the binary discrimination and mediation procedure in children's learning, the observation about the exotic content raises a further challenge to the expanding horizons model of curriculum organization. It may be that the hypothesized explanation of the mediational categories that fill children's fantasy is the wrong explanation, but the fact of the peculiar categories—such as talking middle-class rabbits, fairy godmothers, hobbits, and so on—carries its own implications.

The expanding horizons model assumes that children's understanding moves most effectively from local and familiar content and experience gradually outward, by means of threads of content association. It is a linear model (even if the line is supposed to "spiral" outwards). An interesting feature of the binary discrimination/mediation model is its ability to account easily for children's engagement with both fantasy and exotic real-life content. Such content forms a prominent part of children's thinking. It is odd that the linear learning principle embedded in the expanding horizons model would seem to be quite incapable of accounting for this feature of children's thinking. Indeed, children's own narratives (see Paley's essay in this volume) jump around to fantasy and the exotic very readily. Any attempt to trace the connections proposed by the expanding horizons model would seem entirely futile. What is also evident in the binary opposites/ mediation model is that the generation of the mediating category is commonly made by a metaphorical leap rather than by a content association. Given the abstraction of the most powerful binary opposites, this is hardly surprising, of course.

The degree to which we impose an expanding-horizons style of curriculum on children, and the degree to which we incorporate its associationist learning principle in teaching, reflects the degree to which we contravene or ignore something important in children's learning. Obviously, children can learn content organized in this fashion, but accepting it as a general truth about children's learning is to adopt an unnecessarily restrictive principle for both the curriculum and for teaching. Jackson's discussion in this volume of the transformative role of certain narratives enlarges on the sterility resulting from the restrictive pseudologic and pseudoscientific principles so commonly used in designing curricula.

CONCLUSION

The simple observation that young children have no difficulty being engaged by the weirdest creatures in the most exotic locales plainly denies the general validity of expanding horizons principles, and those taken for granted even by so sensitive an interpreter of children's stories as Applebee. It might be objected that what is true of being engaged by fantasy worlds does not translate to learning about the real world, that fantasy concepts are not equivalent to realistic concepts. This is a reasonable defensive position for those who wish to defend learning theories derived from non-narrative tasks, but the onus is on them to explain why that should be the case. If our concern is some mechanisms of children's thinking that are brought into focus by reflecting on children's narratives, it seems that we can see at work some forms of thinking that challenge current learning theories. Such theories and principles may prove flexible enough to be able to account for the phenomena observed, and to be able to undercut or deflect some of the implications derived from them, as discussed above. But it is not obvious how they might do that.

A few qualifiers before closing: calling the mind a "narrative concern" does not imply that it is not also a logicomathematical, aesthetic, moral, and so on, concern; focusing on the few characteristics of learning that are addressed above does not imply that these are all there are; suggesting that children use binary opposites and mediation does not imply that children *only* use binary opposites and mediation in learning; suggesting the value of the story in shaping curriculum content does not imply that *all* curriculum content must be shaped by story, all of the time; and focusing on the discourse form of the fairy tale does not imply that children do not grasp and use in learning a wide variety of discourse forms. The few characteristics looked at here might be usefully elaborated and extended by some of the multivocal capacities explored by Sutton-Smith in this volume.

REFERENCES

Applebee, A. N. (1978). *The child's concept of story*. Chicago: University of Chicago Press.

Bartlett, F. C. (1932). *Remembering*. Cambridge, UK: Cambridge University Press.

Bettelheim, B. (1976). *The uses of enchantment*. New York: Alfred A. Knopf.

Bransford, J. D., & Johnson, M. V. (1972). Contextual prerequisites for understanding: Some investigations of comprehension and recall. *Journal of Verbal Learning and Verbal Behavior, 11*, 717–726.

Bransford, J. D., & McCarrell, N. S. (1975). A sketch of a cognitive approach to comprehension: Some thoughts about understanding what it means to comprehend. In P. N. Johnson-Laird & P. C. Watson (Eds.), *Thinking: Readings in cognitive science*. Cambridge, UK: Cambridge University Press.

Bruner, J. (1986). *Actual minds, possible worlds*. Cambridge, MA: Harvard University Press.

Dewey, J. (1966). *Democracy and education*. New York: Free Press. (Original work published 1916)

Donaldson, M. (1978). *Children's minds*. London: Croom Helm.

Egan, K. (1988). *Primary understanding: Education in early childhood*. New York: Routledge.

Egan, K. (1989). *Teaching as story telling: An alternative approach to teaching and curriculum in the elementary school*. Chicago: University of Chicago Press.

Egan, K. (1990). *Romantic understanding: The development of rationality and imagination, ages 8–15*. New York: Routledge.

Egan, K. (1992). *Imagination in teaching and learning*. Chicago: University of Chicago Press.

Ellis, A. K. (1986). *Teaching and learning elementary social studies*. Boston: Allyn & Bacon.

Flavell, J. H. (1984). Discussion. In R. J. Sternberg (Ed.), *Mechanisms of cognitive development* (pp. 187–209). New York: W. H. Freeman.

Gardner, H. (1985). *The mind's new science*. New York: Basic Books.

Jarolimek, J. (1982). *Social studies in elementary education* (6th ed.). New York: Macmillan.

Lévi-Strauss, C. (1963). The structural study of myth. In *Structural anthropology* (pp. 206–231). New York: Anchor Books.

Lévi-Strauss, C. (1966a). *The savage mind*. Chicago: University of Chicago Press.

Lévi-Strauss, C. (1966b, Dec. 22). The culinary triangle. *New Society*, pp. 937–940.

Lévi-Strauss, C. (1970). *The raw and the cooked*. New York: Harper & Row.

Paley, V. G. (1981). *Wally's stories*. Cambridge, MA: Harvard University Press.

Paley, V. G. (1984). *Boys and girls: Superheroes in the doll corner*. Chicago: University of Chicago Press.

Paley, V. G. (1990). *The boy who would be a helicopter*. Cambridge, MA: Harvard University Press.

Piaget, J., & Inhelder, B. (1956). *The child's conception of space*. London: Routledge & Kegan Paul.

Rumelhart, D. E. (1975). Notes on a schema for stories. In D. G. Bobrow and A. M. Collins (Eds.), *Representation and understanding* (pp. 211–236). New York: Academic Press.

Siegler, R. S. (1991). *Children's thinking* (2nd ed.). Englewood Cliffs, NJ: Prentice Hall.

Sutton-Smith, B. (1988). In search of the imagination. In K. Egan & D. Nadaner (Eds.), *Imagination and education* (pp. 3–29). New York: Teachers College Press.

PART III

NARRATIVE IN THE STUDY OF TEACHING AND LEARNING

CHAPTER 9

Working with Life-History Narratives

Michael Huberman

[There is a] difference between people who tell stories and people who construct theories about that which lies beyond our imagination.
—R. Rorty, 1991, "Heidegger, Kundera, and Dickens," in *Essays on Heidegger and Others*, Philosophical Papers, Volume 2

Seldom in the shift of social scientific paradigms and methods has a field come on as quickly and expansively as narratology. Where we were used to tectonic changes in the ways social phenomena were represented and accounted for, we suddenly find narratives everywhere, and all along the epistemological spectrum from realism to postmodernism. Everybody wants in.

Some have come to this terrain by oblique routes. This is largely my case. As an educational psychologist with interests in adult cognition and learning, I had been wrestling with the question of how teachers construe and construct their instructional environments at different points in their career, notably at points of transition or change (Huberman & Miles, 1984). This work, in turn, derives from my earlier concern with what has been called *life-span development* (Huberman, 1972, 1974). This is, perhaps surprisingly, less a philosophical or literary field than a fairly rigorous approach to the study of the human life cycle (for a recent example, see Baltes, Featherman, & Lerner, 1990). It has included perspectives ranging from hermeunetics to neuroscience and has harbored an ecumenical stance, epistemologically speaking.

In the work reviewed in this chapter, a large-scale study of teachers' professional life cycles, the life-span development approach is salient. Conceptually, then, the ground initally seemed well prepared. Methologically, I had settled on narratives furnished by our 160 informants, followed by a mix of predesigned instrumentation. It was the collection of those narratives, along with the successive attempts to condense and draw meaning from them within and across our informants, that propelled me into life history interviews. In this chapter, then, I shall be reviewing some of the substance and method of that study. But I will spend more time on the perplexities of capturing the course of teachers' professional lives as rendered by the teachers themselves, and of progressively moving these stories into a more theoretical universe, all in trying to preserve the life blood of the original material.

THE RETURN OF THE INFORMANT

What is it that life-span researchers, among others, overlooked or undervalued in the 1960s and 1970s, before life-history narratives came fully into their own? After all, we, too, were studying the course of human life, often on the basis of oral and written life histories.

Without launching into an elaborate exegesis, one can say that narratology has come to a full boil with the resurgence of a more Hegelian, "idealist" perspective of social research. If, as many phenomenologists and social interactionists have argued, social reality is a series of interactions, a continuously renegotiated process of understanding who we are and how we relate, a number of things are bound to change in the conduct of empirical research. One such thing—by far the most controversial—is the abandonment of the quest for more stable "laws" of personal and social conduct, although, as we shall see, some schools of narrative analysis have not gone along with that premise, and some seminal work in this field (e.g., Dollard, 1935) has defined individual growth in a social milieu and, at the same time, to make theoretical sense of it.

By highlighting the subjective or interpersonal construction of what one thought were social facts, idealists, along with other relativists, have clearly restored the first person singular: those who create the narratives that others were probably too busy interpreting to listen closely. In effect, until recently, oral or written life histories have been largely discounted as second-class forms of representation (Sarbin, 1986b, pp. 3–4)—as raw data, as quasi-literature, as equivocal understandings. As Cochran-Smith and Lytle (1990) put it, somewhat angrily, we have treated as "low-status" information the "voices of the teachers themselves, and the interpretive frames they use to understand their own classroom practices" (p. 5).

When these primary-source data were not simply left out, they were often excluded from the ensuing analysis. At best, informants' stories figured illustratively in publications, as embellishments. As it happens, teacher talk is usually straight talk: jargon-free, experientially dense, expressive, compelling. So it makes for good anecdotal copy and, at the same time, helps ram home an emerging hypothesis or explanation. It was therefore widely used—and abused.

Even if we restore the narrative to the center stage, an important question remains: Is narratology a qualitatively distinctive way of *presenting* personal and social perceptions, or, rather, the study of a qualitatively distinct way of *representing* those perceptions—a different way of knowing? Do we use temporality, generally in the form of event sequences, to represent memories that are then passed on with verbal, visual, gestural, or written media? Or are such memories actually constituted and shaped in serial form?

In a well-known dichotomy, Bruner (1985) has claimed the narrative to be one of two basic modes of representation, the other being the paradigmatic. One is story, the other is argument (Robinson & Hawpe, 1986). By "story," of course, one can mean fable, myth, parable, and so on, in which case we often end up with both modes of representation—a story and a moral. By the same token, there are many genres—the ethnographic research report is one—which shift from one mode to the other, usually from the descriptive to the inferential or explanatory. In fact, in our life-cycle research, informants did this routinely when recounting their past or their present. The interest in telling the tale of one's professional life was no stronger, in effect, than the need to explain it, to carry meaning to a person who has not had the same experience. In that sense, the interviewer is much like a reader, a listener, a scribe, that is, an audience for a performance which may allow the narrator to make new or deeper sense of his or her own trajectory. More on that point shortly.

Finally, we should bear in mind that finer grained research, like the several studies of schematic knowledge, often results in more differentiated categories of representation. In effect, the narrative is only one such category, taking its place aside the taxonomic, the matrix, and the serial.

NARRATIVE KNOWING AND TELLING

Before taking up the teachers' life-cycle study, let me try to situate it in the larger panoply of narrative forms of representation. In effect, the work on teachers' life histories has drawn much of its legitimacy and its technology from forms in which we find a storied mode of presentation or representation.

First, much current developmental and experimental research has been caught up with different forms of *self-narrative*. At the base is the still controversial thesis that symbolic forms of experience are accompanied by, or immediately converted into, sequential chains actually constituting or representing memory. If this is true, we would actually "know" the world through a series of event sequences—primitive scripts or stories—before representing it in other modes. And if this is how we actually assemble raw experience, it would then constitute, at least physiologically, a more "fundamental" or "authentic" vehicle for expressing it to others, and, I might add, for working with it as a researcher.

The premise that the cognitive roots of self-representation are to be found in narration in its simplest form (Fuhrman & Wyer, 1988; Nelson & Gruendel, 1981)—that we know ourselves as an interwoven series of episodes—is a beguiling one. It assumes that temporality or event sequencing is a sort of primary act of mind, a constitutive way of processing information (Hardy, 1977) and of generating self-consciousness. Polkinghorne (1988), for one, takes this stand:

> We achieve our identities and self-concept through the use of the narrative configuration and make our existence into a whole by understanding it as as expression of a simple and unfolding story. (p. 150)

If this is the case, the narrative becomes the vehicle of choice both in capturing the ways that people actually constitute self-knowledge and in soliciting them to convey personal meaning by organizing their experience along a temporal or sequential dimension. We should remember, though, that developmental studies show children's narratives as transformed fragments of their parents' voices, which suggest a more social epigenesis, and that time is not treated in all languages as a series of chronological units (Nelson, 1989). So we may be caught up here in a theory of developmental sequences that is no better than our previous infatuation with developmental stages. Both entail an arbitrary imposition of order on changes over time (McCabe, 1991), and both may be ethnocentric. There is, in any event, as yet no unequivocal support from physiological or neurological research on this score (Dennett, 1991), one way or the other.

On the other hand, the idea that we *retrieve* knowledge and emotions from memory, consciously or preconsciously, in normative form as a primary (but not exclusive) way of organizing our experience and conveying it to others, is more solidly anchored. The oral narrative—as life history, or simply as everyday storytelling about oneself—would then be a more faithful rendering of personal experience than other modes of expression. Remember, however, that the same argument can be made for a non-normative mode of retrieval from memory or of sense-making to oneself or others. This is probably why, empirically, the two are often intertwined.

But we can make a still stronger case for the usefulness of the narrative in research on teaching. As we shall soon see, telling the story of one's life is often a vehicle for taking distance from that experience, and, thereby, of making it an object of *reflection*. Cognitive psychologists call this "decentering," and it allows, say, a teacher, to escape momentarily from the frenzied busyness of classroom life—from its immediacy, simultaneity, and unpredictability—to explore his or her life and possibly to put it in meaningful order.

Finally, we shall see that some researchers working with teachers have pushed the process one step further. When "de-centering" is in play, there emerges the real possibility of unfreezing one's current vision of oneself and moving it to another place, cognitively speaking. For some phenomenologists, and for many critical theorists, interactive interviewing around teachers' autobiographies is a royal road to *attitude change* and, from there, to a sort of *emancipation* from the grooved ways of thinking about one's work. But the term emancipation is not innocent. It means just what it suggests: a far more critical view of one's place in the profession and of the social organization of the profession more generally (Smyth, 1989). Exploring one's life as a teacher can, and often does, open up alternative ways of reconstruing ways of acting and being in the classroom and, from there, of shaping another career path (Jalongo, 1992).

Finally, emancipation is, for some, the prerequisite for social engagement; we go more easily from here to confronting the social or political determinants of teachers' working lives. The invisible strings of power or influence within the system become more visible, and the desire to understand them, then to act on them, begins to gain momentum.

THE PROFESSIONAL LIFE CYCLE OF TEACHERS

Life-cycle research has been around, to be sure, since philosophers and novelists have been studying lives. The more "scientific" treatment of lives, however, has followed disciplinary tracks, each with its marker studies or conceptualizations. For example, there is a psychodynamic track running from Freud through Henry Murray and Gordon Allport and culminating in Erikson's (1950) eight normative "life-crises" and Robert White's *Lives in Progress* (1952). There is another, more sociological, track beginning in recent times with the "Chicago school" and the revival of the oral history tradition, coupled with the development of symbolic interactionism. Along the way, this school has produced some important studies of adult socialization and career patterning. Still another important influence has been the multivolume studies of life-span developmental psychology that were mentioned earlier.

What do we know in particular about the careers of teachers? Until the late 1970s, precious little, aside from Becker's (1970), McPherson's (1972), and especially Lortie's (1975) seminal studies and, even earlier, a perceptive chapter by Peterson (1964) on secondary-school teachers. Since then, the picture has brightened, although, if you look carefully through the most recent *Handbook of Research on Teaching* (Wittrock, 1986), you will find no mention of biographical studies of the profession.

At present, however, both longitudinal and cross-sectional approaches are flourishing, and the semiclinical life history of a small set of teachers has become a staple in the literature (Lightfoot, 1985; Raphael, 1985; Witherell & Noddings, 1991). Also, some of the most promising work has continued to come from England (Ball & Goodson, 1985; Goodson, 1980/ 1981; Nias, 1989; Sikes, Measor, & Woods, 1985). We are beginning to understand how teachers' careers play out and what, from their and others' perspectives, accounts for these trajectories.

Conceptually, there are several ways of analyzing the professional life cycle of teachers. In my recent work, I have opted for a classic perspective, that of the career. Much of the seminal work on career development has sought, in effect, to identify sequences or maxicycles that can describe the career paths not only of individuals within the same profession, but also of individuals across different professions (Super, 1985). Still, given the perils of thinking in terms of phases, there is a need to move gingerly here, applying an heuristic logic rather than pursuing a quest for normative paradigms.

The career perspective has some virtues. First, it allows us to compare people across professions. Next, it is more limited, more focused than the study of individual lives. Also, it combines both a psychological and sociological perspective into its analytic tissue; we can follow the path of an individual within a larger social structure — usually an organization — and understand how the characteristics of individuals affect their surroundings and how they, in turn, are affected by their surroundings.

In the work reported here, I have restricted myself to the teaching profession and, within it, to secondary-school teaching. At the same time, I studied only teachers, that is, people with no, or very little, administrative responsibility during their tenure. Strictly speaking, then, we are talking about the professional lives of people spending 5 to 40 years in the classroom.

THE SWISS STUDY

The Swiss study (Huberman, 1989a, 1989b, 1993) was not primarily a conceptual study; it stemmed rather from curiosity about what seemed to be irresistible research questions. For example, how did teachers construe their careers at different moments? How did they view younger and older peers? Were there "best years" for teaching? Would they choose this career again? Were there moments when many thought seriously of leaving the profession? Did they feel, as Becker's teachers did, that over the years they were coming to resemble the institution in which they worked, much as some people come gradually to resemble their dogs? Was there an evolution toward greater fatalism or conservatism, as the folk and research literature suggest? What was the quality of the initial teaching experience, and how did teachers overcome the uncertainties and inadequacies of the initial year? Which core features of teaching were mastered at which points in the career cycle, and what, if anything, was done about areas of perceived weakness? How extensive was the burnout phenomenon, and how did teachers contend with it? Which, if any, events in their private lives had the greatest impact on their teaching?

The second motive was more mischevious. As much of the literature on "naive" social cognition has illustrated, people work up explanations for social phenomena based on scant, often distorted data. For example, school officials in Geneva pretended to "know" what happened to teachers over time. The evidential base for this knowledge, of course, was flawed, resting on a few lurid instances and on loose talk in the evening over brandy. More important still, these administrators tended to act — to administer their personnel, to make personnel policy — on the basis of what looked like largely unexamined assumptions. Another objective of the study, then, was to weigh the viability of taken-for-granted interpretations within the educational guild.

Sampling and General Methodology

After addressing a few of these questions in an exploratory phase ($n = 30$), I conducted a more ambitious study between 1982 and 1985, with an interview sample of 160 secondary-level teachers in Geneva and Vaud, of whom roughly two-thirds taught at the lower secondary level and the remainder at the upper-secondary level, pre-university division. There were slightly more women than men, in accordance with the referent population. Four "experience groups" were chosen: those with 5 to 10 years of experience, those with 11 to 19 years, 20 to 29 years, and 30 to 39 years of experience. Within this sampling frame (level, sex, years of experience), a random sample was generated. It contained teachers of all subject-matter areas in equivalent proportions to the population of reference.

Each interview lasted approximately 3 to 5 hours, usually spread over two sessions so that both interviewer and interviewee could reflect on the first sitting. The initial questions were open-ended; later ones used flash cards and, in one instance, a checklist. The data were then transcribed and progressively condensed, then underwent both qualitative and statistical analyses. It was a colossal amount of information.

Parenthetically, the sample size and methodology were meant to close a gap. Most life-cycle studies have tended either toward the diminutive (< 30 informants) or the gargantuan (> 1,500 informants). The idea was to benefit from the tools of clinical and semiethnographic interviewing while having the option of making statistical inferences to a larger referent population.

Phases, Stages, and Randomness

The bulk of the information from this study came from the initial question posed to the informants. Its formulation was open-ended, but in the mode of an ethnographic interview (Spradley, 1979). Put succinctly, informants were asked to review their career trajectory and to see whether they could carve it up into phases or periods. For each phase, they were to provide an overarching name or theme and to note the features constituting that theme. Informants were then taken back in memory to the first year of classroom responsibility when asked to ask themselves some questions, such as "Where was it? What had I done the prior year? What were the pupils like? The building and classroom? What was going on in my life outside teaching?" The interviewer suggested they do the same for successive periods, take notes, review carefully any emerging sequence, and not resume the discussion until they were happy with it. Informants were allowed to reflect on their own for a good half hour.

Clearly, narratives of this kind are not straightforward. They come closest to work in cognitive anthropology when an informant evokes, say, a crucial period in her life, and the interviewer begins to probe for the "names" of other such periods. This study, however, was slightly more intrusive and, possibly, encouraged bias. For example, the archetype of the career as a quest, a pilgrimage which must lead somewhere meaningful, may have been induced. Otherwise, the "pilgrim" may simply have been represented as the plaything of occult forces. By ordering professional life into sequences, a degree of continuity is presupposed from one phase to the next. In the life-cycle literature, however, it is clear that a new phase can never fully be reduced to the components of the preceding one (Huberman, 1993). For a new phase to emerge, there has to be a change not only in the elements but also in the way that these elements are connected or configured. An emergent phase implies new characteristics, ones not previously in the corpus. So each phase constitutes a qualitatively new state, a real *discontinuity*.

Empirically, Elder's (1974) biographical reanalyses of children of the Depression was an elegant demonstration of this thesis (cf. also Gergen & Gergen, 1983). Lives which superficially seemed predictable were not so when examined more closely. The Depression, of course, is a good example of the eruption of the unexpected into the life course. So are wars, sicknesses, sudden changes of circumstances in love and work, accidents, providential encounters, and the like.

Elder's work suggests that whole segments of life events, at least when reconstituted by an outsider, appeared almost accidental. Such a line of inquiry would then imply that only in retrospect does *this* career path, *this* event, *this* choice appear to be logical or inevitable. Paradoxically, even for the person recounting his or her life, the *experience* of that next step will invariably bring on surprises—this supports the discontinuity hypothesis— but seems to be inevitable immediately thereafter.

These remarks pertain, of course, to other types of life history. Virtually all of them are vulnerable to transformations on the part of the informant which are invisible to the researcher and which may be unconsciously derived. In the case of the Swiss study, however, the objective was to provide a temporal "scaffold" for informants to use in reconstructing their professional lives without further constraining the rendering of those experiences.

In effect, aside from the constriction of the data into periods, there were no constraints on the informants. They could create any theme, any sequence, any configuration of features. Also, since this was the opening question, there were no cues inducing a set response. Nor were informants probed for explanations—they were simply asked for a narrative and, once the drawn trajectory was there, were asked only questions of clarification.

Most informants had little trouble drawing the trajectory, identifying distinct phases and affixing thematic titles to each. But they needed time to do it—to retrieve the material, order it, and decide between primary and secondary experiences. Globally, they evoked three kinds of themes: (1) metaphorical themes ("drowning," "settling down," "disenchantment," "getting my second wind"); (2) administrative themes ("during my training," "getting tenure," "moving into the upper secondary"); and (3) historical themes ("the creation of the middle school," "the second big reform," "May 1968"), having to do with structural reforms in the system or with historical events having repercussions on school life.

Varieties of Mindfulness

The length of the resulting narrative, its level of detail and its apparent reflectiveness, as well as individual informants' access to the emotions encountered earlier in their lives, all varied wildly from one informant to another. I had assumed that telling was a stimulant to remembering, that it reinstated temporally meaningful episodes, and thereby provided a frame for talking about the past — for making individual events comprehensible, by having informants become aware of the whole to which they belonged and by identifying the effect that one event in their lives may have had on others (cf. Polkinghorne, 1988, p. 18). Finally, we had given our informants time for reflection — something often underdone in narrative interviewing — while staying with an interactive medium (the interview).

The informants provided all manner of material. Some was so schematic, so undifferentiated that, after several vain attempts to thicken it through questions of clarification, I concluded, probably too hastily, that impoverished minds construe impoverished worlds. Recall that I am talking here about secondary-level teachers, from whom my expectations were high.

One important difference emerged quickly: this same subset of people insisted they had never thought about their careers up to now. They had traversed the seasons of their professional lives, often with satisfactions, but apparently with little mindful monitoring of where they had come from, where they were going, and what the underlying sense of their career had been. Whether this was a problem of retrieval from long-term memory or a simple lack of reflectiveness is a moot question. The informants were carefully questioned for signs of intimidation, suspicion, illness, even organic handicaps. Clearly, there are narratives and narratives, depending on the informant. Care should therefore be taken in making assertions about the connections through narrative back to what Husserl called "pre-predicative experience." Some people have nothing to tell us about their past, in large part, perhaps, because they have told themselves little along the way. This does not mean they couldn't tell us more under different circumstances. As Polanyi's notion of tacit knowledge implies, they probably know far more than they can say. Their energies have gone, instead, to other matters.

Beyond that, another, more generous hypothesis is that these informants may be so enmired in the "natural attitudes" of their work and its circumstances, in its taken-for-grantedness, that there is too little reflective distance to work with. I am reminded here of Malinowski's experience with the Trobianders, who, he claimed, found their beliefs and perceptions so obvious that they remained outside conscious awareness and therefore could not be articulated. It was then Malinowski himself who articulated that worldview in their place — a perilous step to take.

Other teachers in our sample, however, provided precise, richly detailed, spellbinding trajectories that reflected the ambiguities, ambivalences, and contradictions of professional life. They ring true, and this kind of exercise brings that out. Presumably, the teachers came up with these accounts and reflected insightfully on linkages and significances because, as one said, "I think about these things. I've thought about them all my career." Whether we are contending here with differences in individual styles of cognition, in differential access to memory or in more fundamental differences in self-insight is unclear. Experimental evidence suggests, for example, that memories are constituted of events and episodes recalled in broad outlines, with a few specific characteristics for each "chunk" (Loftus, 1979). The rest is filled in. It stands to reason that some have better retrieval capacities than others, or are better fillers-in.

It is worth pausing a moment here to note that these are the kinds of data that drive mainstream social scientists mad. Ambiguity, contradiction, and ambivalence are all bugaboos for measurement, analysis, and interpretation, and rightly so. All reflect inherent complexities of the human condition. And all require expressive forms of representation (such as narratives, real or fictional ones) in order to be captured without gross distortion (cf. Eisner, 1988, 1991). They can mean, literally, many things, to their authors as well as to researchers. In other words, as a set they are not orthogonal and, taken singly, they cannot readily be reduced to alphanumeric codes, be scaled, or be manipulated with probabilistic algorithms. They are best analyzed, as it were, in their own juices, with more phenomenological methods.

Retrospective Coherence

On the other hand, these accounts—much like artistic work—appear to be more coherently organized than is the inherent sloppiness of life over time. Here, we confront one of the classic problems in life histories. Simply put, there is a tendency to reinvent one's past in order to give meaning to one's present. As Ross, McFarland, and Fletcher (1981) put it, people are revisionist historians of their pasts. They selectively recall past behaviors to make them consistent with their current attitudes.

The experimental and clinical evidence is particularly strong on this score. Already in the late 1940s, Hebb (1949) had shown that across adulthood, earlier memories were revised as a function of subsequent experiences. In some cases, however, this was the result of new information and was perceived as a "truer" or "deeper understanding" of one's past. This last point is noteworthy, but does not in itself discount Hebb's thesis.

In the same vein, experimental social psychologists have taken life histories, altered the attitudes of their subjects, then found, as expected, that past events and perceptions were realigned to fit the new set of attitudes (e.g., Ross et al., 1981). In other words, identifiable social influences are at play here. Similarly, more clinical experiments have turned up "mood effects" (Clark & Teasdale, 1982; Cohen, Towbes, & Flocco, 1988). Depressed patients have far better recall of negative life memories than of positive ones: the converse also holds. Others have found an overrepresentation of memories from adolescence and the early adult years (Fitzgerald, 1988), and of memories of highly salient or vivid personal experiences: the so-called "flash-bulb" memories (Brown & Kulik, 1977).

A closer examination of individual lives turns up sequences that are objectively much less ordered and predictable (cf. Cohler, 1982, pp. 206–241). Yet, at any point in the life course, individuals' own accounts are experienced as internally consistent. Why such a concern with coherence?

Clinically, self-consistency helps us to maintain a stable identity, to be the same people to ourselves over time. From that perspective, psychopathology would be a state in which some of our stories have been dislocated, and therapy would be an exercise in story repair (cf. Howard, 1991). Other theorists, such as Paul Ricoeur (1984), posit that we strive, in the narrative of our lives, to recreate the same characteristics as stories or epics: a beginning, a middle, and an end, woven together in a coherent manner.

Presentation of the Autobiographical Self

As astute as the clinical interviewers in the Swiss study may have been, there was no avoiding the ambiguities of interview sessions in which one stranger recounts his or her professional life to another. Even under the best conditions—5 hours of interview time, two sittings allowing for both sides to digest the material and, if needed, to review apparent discrepancies—I was aware of three pitfalls. The first was inherently Goffmanesque: the sense that some people have different stories of their past for different listeners, stories which often mask more unsavory, "backstage" episodes, or which simply create a persona whom the informant feels will satisfy the interviewer without doing too much violence to his own code of ethics or his core ideology.

To be sure, some of this can be attributed to self-delusion rather than to ingenuity, which, once again, raises the issue of access to one's own cognitions and memories. It is true enough, for example, that in the cases in which informants' accounts were matched against those of their peers or students, the different versions did not always coincide, often strikingly so. But do peers or pupils have necessarily more insight than our informants themselves? Had we gone to close relatives, to spouses, to close friends, such tests of trustworthiness might have been more compelling.

Next comes the inescapable situation whereby an informant negotiates and cocreates the meaning of his or her life with the interviewer. This dilemma—that the interviewer inevitably intrudes, thereby shaping some of the resulting material—has had an enormous boost from Bahktin's "dialogism" and, more empirically, from Mishler's work (1975, 1986). The formulation of questions, the tone of voice, the interruptions and encouragements, the initiation or conclusion of a topic, the nonverbal gestures that accompany both questions and responses, and so on are interpreted in ways that are integral to an informant's account and compromise its genuineness. The story, as Mischler argues convincingly, is in many ways a "joint production," an intricate interpersonal ballet:

> . . . repondents learn from how interviewers respond to their questions—restating or rephrasing the original question, accepting the answer and going on to the next question, probing for further information—what particular meanings are intended by questions and wanted in their answers. . . . (1986, p. 56)

There have been other demonstrations of the cocreation of interview data, both through observations and through the study of transcripts (e.g., Brenner, 1982; Garfinkel, 1967). One hypothesis is that much of this is due to the relative status of interviewer and interviewee. In most cases, narrative interviewing implies status asymmetry; the informant feels, justifiably or not, that he or she is being interrogated, however gently, and that self-disclosure beyond a certain point might be imprudent. In this regard, Connelly and Clandinin (1990) speak of "shared narratives," and insist on "equality and trust" to get an authentic self-narrative. To have such complicity, of course, takes time, almost the time of friendship. It cannot be speeded up at will. Nor can we simply assume a community of meaning between researchers and informants. It is doubtful, in fact, that there are shortcuts that would stand up to strict tests of reactivity or reliability, or would even stand up against an informant's sense of being used in return for the privilege of being listened to attentively by a researcher.

Reflectiveness and Consciousness-Raising

Finally, many of the informants, much as in other life history interviews, found that the exercise of reviewing their lives was reward enough for the time spent. They saw this as both a rare occasion for reflection, for putting their professional lives in perspective, and a moment that was theirs: when they talked and an interviewer listened patiently. Here, the merit of the "put-your-career-into-phases" exercise was that the informant was in control of the process. As a result, the phase sequence was already drawn, and the constituent elements of each phase were already noted before the interviewer actually intervened. One intention here was precisely to attenuate the subtle collusion and renegotiation of meaning decribed by Mishler and others.

It is hard to know, after 5 hours of clinical interviewing, to what degree of self-understanding the teachers acceded. Certainly, many said that they had seldom thought about their career in this way, that it provided a new or different perspective, that the ebb and flow of their teaching life, which had seemed accidental, had stronger threads than they had imagined. Here, there are traces of Polkinghorne's image, noted earlier, of the narrative's making one's existence whole by understanding it as an expression of a simple and unfolding story.

For many others who do life-history interviewing with teachers, there is little doubt about this. For Connelly and Clandinin (1988, 1990), as well as for others working in a similar vein (cf. Butt & Raymond, 1989; Grumet, 1988), narrative interviewing is the key to self-understanding and, from there, to change. Their interviews are typically interactive, or are conducted as part of a group process. Analytically, the researchers try to capture generative themes in the life of the informant—the strands that give meaning to the many shifts that accompany the teaching career. Experientially, the process is more like a mutual support group for enacting change in one's life. Narratives can therefore be vehicles for a kind of personal emancipation. But there does not seem to be much hard data beyond self-reports that the narratives themselves are key to the process, especially since many informants seem to come to these groups at a moment of perceived transition. Also, as a mixture of research and consciousness-raising, this approach poses some gritty issues—issues of validity (e.g., the "collusion" problem) and of ethics (e.g., intrusion).

ANALYZING LIFE-HISTORY INTERVIEWS: SOME ASSUMPTIONS

What is the best vehicle for examining narrative interviews? Is there a middle ground between submitting to our material and enforcing our will upon it? This depends largely, of course, on one's epistemology and one's ethics. Still, even among the more "idealist" researchers there are phenomenologists and symbolic interactionists who condense or transform life-history transcripts, then tie them to more generic meaning systems—to archetypes, to constructs, even to theories. It's worth recalling that Blumer himself, the "father" of symbolic interactionism, was theoretically oriented, as were Merleau-Ponty, Ricoeur, and other seminal phenomenologists.

Polkinghorne (1988), an authoritative figure in the study of narrative, takes a relativist stance on narrative inquiry and argues that life histories can and should be analyzed, not just decribed. A valid narrative research report, he feels, "recreates the history that has led to the story's end and draws from it the significant factors that have 'caused' the final event" (p. 171). Such an ending is thereby made "reasonable and believable," much as in the work of historians and therapists. Without seeking generalizable laws, we can answer the question of why something happened—"why things would have been different if the combination of events had been different" (p. 171). Polkinghorne concludes, drawing on Ricoeur (1984), that researchers can legitimately use knowledge "based on rules that describe how humans are prone to act or react under given situations" (p. 173).

These rules apply, Polkinghorne argues, to both imagined and described situations. They are not, however, formal, scientific physical laws, but rather "dispositions to act in certain ways" (p. 173). This is the same position staked out by cultural anthropologists (cf. Geertz, 1983, on the necessity of combining "experience-near" and "experience-remote" knowledge), and one with decent epistemological support (Bhaskar, 1982; Harré and Secord, 1972; cf. Huberman & Miles, 1985).

My own analysis took the form of a series of compressions of the data, inspired in large part by the work of Amadeo Giorgi in psychological phenomenology (1975), itself derived from Merleau-Ponty. Giorgi advances progressively from original transcripts of narratives to summaries that translate the material into a more everyday vernacular. He then condenses the material into what he calls "discriminated meaning units," which are low-inference snippets of the summaries. For example, 10 lines of narrative becomes a meaning unit: "S searches for possible error: distinguishes between 5 hours in oven and 5 hours heating at 90 to 110 degrees" (p. 55). From here, Giorgi moves into more psychological language, in an effort to "respect the phenomenon . . . at hand." So the meaning unit we just saw becomes this: "Reflection on procedures uncovers a 'lived ambiguity'—S now realizes a crucial distinction where previously she assumed an univocal meaning" (p. 55).

The work, as Giorgi himself says, is methodical, systematic, and rigorous. It follows the classic phenomenological paradigm of "returning to the phenomena themselves." They are described, submitted to what is called an "imaginative variation" that gives rise to a comparable, but presumably more profound, or "essential" version of the material. Phenomenologists call this, unfelicitiously, an "eidetic intuition of the structures themselves." In Giorgi's case, there is the further step of venturing, prudently, into a more inferential terrain. This constitutes what Geertz means by an experience-remote corpus, and it is forcibly interpretive, in this instance to be interpreted within a clinical frame.

PROGRESSIVE CONDENSATION IN THE LIFE-CYCLE STUDY

It may be hard to believe that the same procedure was followed for 160 interviews, but this was roughly the case. It took months. There were traps all along the way. As Mishler has shown recently (1991), choices made even in the "cuts" of transcripts—the way they are set up on the page—can lead to different interpretations. Similarly, some version of either discourse analysis or content analysis invariably arises in condensing the data. Both are typically context-stripped. Discourse analysis is fundamentally not about personal meaning, and content-analytic procedures often make the error, pointed out long ago by Jacobson (1960), of sacrificing the sequence of a narrative or a set of narratives (what Jacobson calls the "contiguous" or "syntagmatic") to a thematic focus. In other words, the *succession* of "meaning units" disappears as common themes are teased out across interviews. There is obviously something screwy in a life-history analysis in which the temporal dimension disappears from the narrative.

Having reviewed the earlier part of the process of condensing material, let me illustrate the later phases. Here, the reductive process is far more drastic; it culminates, in fact, in a normative model.

The material, equivalent to Giorgi's "meaning units," was moved to a 25-page protocol with an identical format for the 160 informants. The sequence of themes given by the informant was listed in its sequence, along with its constituent features. This was accompanied by citations which added the context and the particularities. Then began the delicate task of comparing sequences, themes, and features within and across subgroups. This was done with fairly conventional techniques of content analysis, notably those used for sociolinguistic data. The key decision rule was that a common theme had to include either the specific term or a denotative analogue, and that at least two features describing the theme had to be identical. For example, one informant might evoke a "stabilizing" phase (see below) and another a "settling-down" phase, with both using at least two of the same features to describe that period. Protocols were content-analyzed independently, then compared for interrater reliability. Protocols went into the analysis only when these reliabilities passed the threshhold of .80.

This procedure amounts basically to an overlay of individual trajectories. But we should not delude ourselves over the viability of a pooling technique for accounts that, when examined up close, are qualitatively distinct, just as lives are. Even in the best cases, as Wittgenstein (1953) has so convincingly demonstrated, when we analyze meanings, we rarely obtain clearly demarcated boundaries and "essential" defining properties. Wittgenstein's useful alternative explanation is that concepts resemble each other as family members do: they possess certain overlapping features but do not necessarily share one feature in common. If the themes in the study had possessed clearly defined boundaries, then it would have been an indication that the data set had been oversimplified by the analysis.

Obviously, all systems of categorization are arbitrary, including theory-driven ones, which have at least the merit of being coherent and of having a framework for readers to apply the categories to. In effect, too many category systems, or thematic clusters, are sui generis: they simply lie there in the life history, hermetically unconnected to another study with the same focus. Nor is the researcher always aware of how culturally or conceptually provincial he or she may be in trying to tease out themes or generate categorizations for teachers' narratives. Consider Lakoff's (1987) wonderful demonstration of this, in illustrating prototype and folk categorizations, where, for example, "fire, women and dangerous things" constitutes a meaningful, functional category in some African subcultures. It is unlikely that any of us, looking at a teacher's life history in which these three components appeared, would think to put them together as a category—unless the informant did it.

Back to the life-cycle study. The first deliberately analytic product was a chart for each subgroup. Let us look at one that sets out data for women with 5 to 10 years of teaching experience at the lower-secondary level (the "Cycle d'Orientation"). (See Figure 9.1.)

At the far left is the range of years mentioned by these 11 informants for each of the three phases evoked. The themes for the phases (e.g., phase 1: launching a career and initial commitment) are mine, as are the headings in the topmost row: the streams followed by informants prior to teaching. The middle section regroups informants' expressions, with relatively little transformation.

What can we learn here? In this representation, the first phase divides those evoking "easy beginnings" from those with "painful beginnings." "Easy beginnings" involve positive relationships with pupils, "manageable" pupils, the sense of pedagogical mastery, and enthusiasm. Painful beginnings are made up of role overload and anxiety, difficult pupils, heavy time investment, close monitoring by teacher education staff, and isolation inside the school. The numbers next to the themes and over the arrows refer to numbers of informants mentioning the theme (as their "leitmotif") and at least two of its constituent features, as well as to those who followed identical sequences. For the thematic material, at least one-fourth of the sub-group had to share a common theme or sequence for these to be included on the chart. This criterion gets increasingly stringent as sequences are combined and during later phases which some informants do not men-

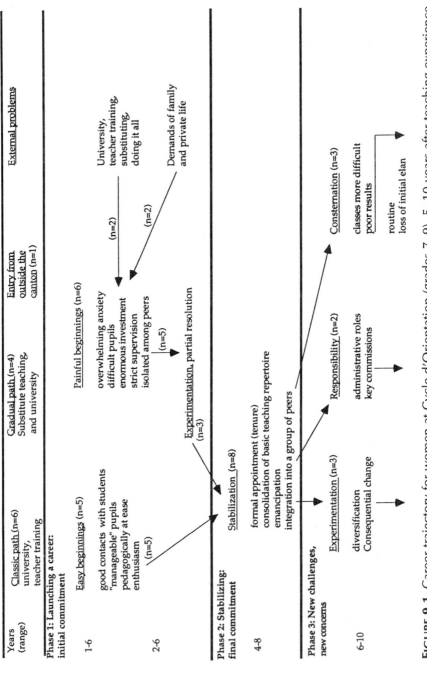

FIGURE 9.1 Career trajectory for women at Cycle d'Orientation (grades 7–9), 5–10 years after teaching experience (n = 11)

tion. But it keeps the process honest, by maintaining simultaneously a temporal and thematic thread in the analysis.

The second phase, "stabilizing," is noteworthy, because it represents a near-archetype for younger teachers. The theme invariably contains two features, and both are present here. The first has to do with pedagogical stabilizing: feeling at ease in the classroom, consolidating a basic repertoire, differentiating materials and lessons in light of pupils' reactions or performances. The second feature has to do with commitment to the profession, which intersects with the moment of tenure. As it happens, each feature here is a staple in the life-cycle literature (e.g., Rosenbaum, 1983), and appears often in empirical work on teachers' careers.

The two remaining features figure in most, but not all, sub-groups. In "affirming oneself," or "emancipation," teachers now feel free to follow their own leads and to confront supervisors more aggressively. In "integrating into a group" of peers means just that, but in many instances it is not achieved at the moment of "stabilization."

The third horizontal block, corresponding to the next period, "new challenges, new concerns," brings us back to another of the modal "phases" reviewed earlier. A subset of informants evokes explicitly a phase of "experimentation" or "diversification" and/or attempts at "consequential change." Once a basic level of classroom mastery is achieved, several informants say, there is a need for refinement and diversity.

On the one hand, they now see that they can get better results and more satisfaction by diversifying their materials and classroom management. On the other hand, they feel, for the first time, the stale breath of "routine." As one put it, "If didn't get some novelty into my teaching, I'd dry up without noticing it." This is reflected in the next period ("consternation").

Also, these experiments typically reach outside the classroom. If not schoolwide, they are at least multiple-classroom, and they typically involve collaborative work. These features are present in virtually all accounts of the "experimentation" phase. When one recalls that there are no stimulus materials here and that informants are not being asked whether they underwent a "stabilizing" or an "experimenting" phase, these data are especially suggestive.

The "experimentation" phase is only one of three possible sequences, and the other modal sequence, "consternation" (see Figure 9.1) is far less upbeat. "More difficult classes," as it happens, tended to characterize teachers evoking "easy beginnings." There is a (sobering) lesson there. Finally, the "responsibility" theme characterizes people whom we will find later in administrative slots; they are clearly on their way up the hierarchical ladder and will soon become, in the eyes of their peers who stay in the classsroom, natives of a different, often suspect, species.

MODAL SEQUENCES

Charts were drawn for each of the 16 subgroups in the study (four "experience groups," both sexes, lower and upper secondary). This took several weeks. Successive analytic overlays were constructed across groups, sexes, and levels, with care being taken to respect the raw data each time that themes, features, or sequences were grouped. We came out of this process with four modal sequences, encompassing 90% of the 133 usable protocols, but representing many fewer sequences than found on any one chart.

Sequence 1. Harmony Recovered

This process is common to the younger groups (5 to 10 and 11 to 19 years of experience), and accounts for 17% of that population.

Painful beginnings ⎯⎯⎯⎯⎯⎯→ Stabilization ⎯⎯⎯⎯⎯⎯→ Experimentation

In virtually all these cases, *the overall theme and the sequence are identical across informants*, and the majority of features for each theme are the same—that is, they mirror those shown on figure 9.1.

Must one begin painfully? Not necessarily, but fully one-third of the sample represented their initial experience that way, defining the first phase exclusively in these terms. Elsewhere in the study our respondents were asked to go over their initial year of teaching in some detail. Close to half recited a familiar litany: a sense of being overwhelmed, continual trial and error, vacillation between excessive strictness and permissiveness, exhaustion, difficulties with pupil discipline, fear of judgments on the part of other teachers and administrators, intimidation by some pupils. Also, these descriptions came *after*, not before, the formal program of teacher preparation—a finding not restricted to Switzerland nor even to European studies. As we know, medical interns talk this way, too, even those well into their internships. So there may well be a (low) threshold to the amount of preparation for actual classroom responsibiity that we can actually *deliver* in preservice programs. It is worth noting that those experiencing the fewest initial difficulties were, predictably enough, teachers who had done a lot of substituting; were from large families; had been scout leaders, camp counselors, or "tourists"—mostly men—who had entered the profession accidentally, just to have a look.

For reasons of limited space, I will outline the remaining sequences and offer a brief explanation of each of them. Interested readers may wish to consult other sources (Huberman, 1989a, 1993) for a fuller description of them.

Sequence 2. Reassessment

Teachers in this group also fall in the range of 5 to 10 and 11 to 19 years of experience.

Let me focus on a "leitmotif" of the reassessment theme: incipient boredom ("Am I going to die with a piece of chalk in my hand?"), leading to doubts about an ultimate career choice ("I made a choice that wasn't really a choice; I backed into teaching. Now it's too late to back out."), after 2 or 3 sour years in succession with difficult pupils, an inconvenient schedule, and nitpicking colleagues or administrators.

What is intriguing about this particular profile is that, superficially at least, it is largely unpredictable from the first phase of one's career. In most respects, these teachers resemble their colleagues, even in the events occurring in their private lives. Nor were we able, in the course of more elaborate statistical analyses of the data set, to pin down the factors that discriminated between these teachers and, say, those moving from a period of "stabilization" to one of "experimentation." Perhaps it is just as well.

Sequence 3. Reassessment: Resolution and Nonresolution

We are now farther along the career cycle and describing teachers with 11 to 19 and 20 to 29 years of experience. Is there life after "reassessment"? Here is the third modal trajectory:

Among teachers describing a phase of "reassessment," the succeeding phase has invariably to do with their success in moving on. One of the more chilling findings of the study came here: among this subset of teachers from 12 to 30 years into the profession, fewer achieved resolution—on their own terms—than did not. Moreoever, their descriptions have the ring of definitiveness; they, at least, see no sign of evolution in succeeding years.

Who are these people? A finer grained analysis of the protocols suggested two groups. One included teachers whose beginnings were so difficult that they had already wondered whether this was their calling. Others skipped through the initial years, then fell upon a tough period that, as the Swiss put it, "broke all their teeth." This shock, together with other ruminations, brought on the first serious "reassessment." Others within this same family felt they had harbored unrealistic expectations toward the profession, toward their colleagues and pupils, and toward themselves. The resulting awareness—"that teaching wears you down, that everyone muddles through . . . that in 20 years I may be like some of the shriveled-up sleepwalkers I see in staff meetings"—seems to come suddenly, one night, like the blow of a hammer.

What characterizes this subset of teachers is the *intensity* of the reassessment phase. What is also distinctive is their impression of reliving that phase at one or several points of their career, of not getting beyond it. This is as true of those who tough it out as of those who take leaves of absence, take courses at the university, throw themselves into new instructional projects, or disinvest massively in school life to follow pursuits elsewhere. These solutions are often tried and seldom work. On the face of it, these data call for a more clinical rereading. They do, however, indicate that, contrary to popular belief within the teaching profession, "reassessment" at midcareer is not necessarily a universal, benign "growth" experience nor necessarily a harbinger of kinder years ahead.

Sequence 4. "Renewal" with a Positive or Negative Outcome

This is the most representative trajectory. Initially, it includes 40% of the teachers in the three experience groups (11 to 19, 20 to 29, 30 to 39 years of experience); though, given the later branching-out of the sequence, this percentage drops off.

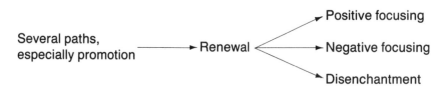

The term "renewal" (other informants speak of "reform" or "major change") here implies structural reform, and is primarily linked to sociohistorical influences: to a series of structural reforms in the Geneva school system between 1962 and 1972, amplified by the so-called "events of May 1968" in Paris (the "students' revolution"). All secondary schools were affected, and many primary-school teachers who taught in the upper grades were assimilated into middle schools. This accounts in large part for the "promotion" theme in the figure.

Now let me explain the ultimate phases. *Positive focusing* is the term I use to describe what respondents spoke of as "cultivating my garden" or "doing my thing" or "specializing," although the term "focusing" was present *explicitly* in 65% of the protocols. The gist was that the "renewal" phase had been expansive and some of the teachers now wanted to concentrate their efforts. This meant focusing on a preferred grade level, subject matter, or type of pupils; disinvesting in school work and increasing outside interests; reducing contacts with peers other than those of one's most convivial group; and avoiding additional administrative tasks or off-hours commitments, not getting involved in schoolwide innovations. The tone was resolutely optimistic, often "self-actualized," but there is a clear sense of pulling back. Something, even, of a narcissist entitlement: "I've done my share; now leave me alone to do what I want with the years left me."

Defensive focusing is also my term. It has many of the same features: specializing, reducing commitments, using seniority to carve out a comfortable schedule, relating only to a small circle of peers. The tone, however, is different. These are essentially people who, like many in the previous sequence, were brought kicking and screaming through the "renewal phase." They are traditionalists who disapproved of the majority of changes enacted and who disapprove of the outcomes. The tone of their remarks is that now, when the dust has settled, they can derive some satisfaction in their remaining years from activities which the system has not yet corrupted.

Disenchantment is a repondent's term, and it carries a sense of bitterness. Most informants approved of the "renewals" and invested heavily in them, but they judged the sequel much like the defensive focusers: amorphous pupils, Babbitt-like administrators, ill-advised policies, mindless paperwork. There are, however, two new chords. First, the themes of "fatigue" and "lassitude" come through clearly. Next, there is bitterness over the failure of the reforms, much of it directed at "turncoat" administrators who caved in when the going got rough. Most of these informants are men—men who stuck around in the classroom after the party, and dealt with the residue. They have not, unlike many of their counterparts, moved on to coordinating or administrative jobs, and they are severe judges of the long-term effects of school improvement projects.

Another reasonable hypothesis is that ambitious, usually externally directed projects may be "out of phase" later in one's career. After the stabilizing comes the experimenting or renewal, and after the renewal comes the limiting and focusing. "Cultivating one's garden," much like Voltaire's Candide after his many, mostly disappointing, adventures, may well be generic to later phases in the teaching career, and elsewhere. It is certainly a leitmotif in the life-cycle literature, with its trend toward greater "interiority," in parallel with gradual physiological shifts. It may, or may not, have to do with the approach of retirement and with intimations of one's mortality, but is consistent with that hypothesis (cf. Jacques, 1965). To the extent, however, that it leads to a disengagement from collective attempts to reshape institutional practices, we have a dilemma that school officials will have to address.

Before ending this section, allow me a final note. If a scenario or modal sequence includes 15 to 20% of a cohort, is that a lot or a little? I have argued that it is a lot, given that our teachers had no "instructions" for generating themes, constitutive features of those themes, or sequences of their trajectories. To be sure, I have grouped some themes or features using the decision rules discussed earlier. Without that there would be 160 unique trajectories which, fundamentally, there are. My claim is that we have captured in each scenario, at a slightly higher level of abstraction, a "cluster," a knot of people undergoing a similar experience as they traverse the teaching career. Each cluster is not large, and cumulatively, looking at the end point of the scenario, they constitute only about 65% of the informants. But they have more in common than any other configuration we can discern. As such, there may well be distinct "families" of career scenarios like the ones we have disclosed. Replications of this study in Zurich and pieces of it elsewhere (Canada, Spain, Belgium) suggest—but do not prove conclusively—that these families are generalizable.

A FINAL CONDENSATION: A MODEL OF TEACHERS' LIFE CYCLE

There simply is not the space here to describe the final, most reductive exercise—that of tying the scenarios to the conceptual and empirical literature on the professional life cycle. I will, however, display the product of that analysis, and comment very briefly on it. Note, however, that I am not positing a term-to-term correspondence between the charts/scenarios and this simplistic depiction of the teaching career (Figure 9.2). Rather, this is meant to be a parsimonious and suggestive ordering of that material into a plausible, perhaps even testable, model.

As the figure shows, there is a single stream at career entry, through the "stabilization" phase. There are then multiple streams at midcareer, converging again into a single path at the end. Depending on the previous

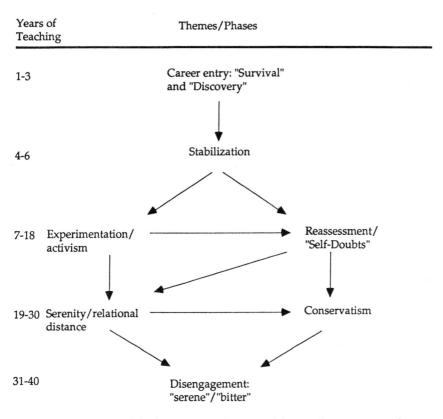

Years of Teaching	Themes/Phases
1-3	Career entry: "Survival" and "Discovery"
4-6	Stabilization
7-18	Experimentation/activism → Reassessment/"Self-Doubts"
19-30	Serenity/relational distance → Conservatism
31-40	Disengagement: "serene"/"bitter"

FIGURE 9.2 Model of successive themes of the teacher career cycle

trajectory, this final phase can be either serene or acrimonious. The most harmonious trajectory would be this one:

Experimentation ⟶ Serenity ⟶ (serene) Disengagement

And the most problematic trajectories would be these two:

Reassessment ⟶ (bitter) Disengagement

Reassessment ⟶ Conservatism ⟶ (bitter) Disengagement

Let me offer a brief explanation of the model: "survival" and "discovery" evokes first, at career entry, the "reality-shock" inherent in taking on the full complexity of the classroom: preoccupation with self ("Am I up to this challenge?"), the gulf between professional ideals and the daily grind of classroom life, the fragmentation of tasks, the oscillation between intimacy with and distance from one's pupils, the apparent inadequacy of instructional materials given the diversity of pupil characteristics (cf. Veenman, 1984). On the other side of the ledger, the "discovery" theme translates the initial enthusiasm of having one's "own" pupils, classroom, materials, and yearly program, as well as feeling oneself a "colleague" among peers. Often the "survival" and "discovery" dimensions co-exist, and the latter allows the novice teacher to tolerate the former. But there are also one-dimensional profiles, and profiles in which these two themes are absent. For example, teachers with little initial commitment to teaching ("I'll just have a look") are not apt to perceive initial difficulties as a matter of "survival" nor to stress the heady aspects of "discovery." They appear to be more detached, even indifferent.

Stabilization. The succeeding phase intersects with the classic life-cycle literature and its treatment of "commitment," "stabilization," and "taking on adult responsibilities" (cf. White, 1952). In teaching, "stabilization" corresponds to a choice (a semi-definitive commitment to *this* profession) and to an administrative act (tenure). That commitment is not a simple affair, for it rules out other possibilities (a career in research or in journalism; an artistic career). This was especially hard for many upper-secondary teachers, who kept other options open for several years. A few even said, after 15 years in the profession, that they essentially hadn't yet decided on what to do with their lives since they had been out of college.

Stabilization also means an affiliation to an occupational community, freedom from direct supervision, and greater instructional mastery and comfort. One has worked up a rudimentary instructional repertoire that fits most situations encountered in the initial 3 to 4 years of teaching, and one is now adding to it, refining it, and molding it to fit one's own, more congenial style of instruction. There is also an attendant sense of relief at having reached this stage, of spontaneity, of pleasure and humor, even a touch of headiness, in the ability to seize the moment, instructionally speaking.

Here, informants stress one or more of the following three aspects: First, as noted earlier, the gradual consolidation of an instructional repertoire leads to attempts to increase one's impact. This brings on a small flurry of "experiments"—with different materials, different pupil groupings, different sequencing. Next, the desire for increased impact in the classroom leads to an awareness of the institutional barriers constraining such an impact and, from there, to attempts to change the more surreal flaws in the school or district. This newfound "activism" can also bring on new responsibilities (as coordinator, as delegate) which in turn open avenues of career "promotion."

Finally, having been a few times around the block, these teachers say they are ready for new challenges. The implicit theme here is an emerging concern with growing stale in the profession, a malady teachers see among older peers.

Taking stock: self-doubts. The symptoms here range from the superficial to the critical—from a desire to reassess one's professional life, to a gnawing sense of routine, to a full-blown existential crisis over staying in or leaving the profession. In all cases, there is a moment of stock-taking, with the realization that other careers will have to be ruled out if one does not act quickly.

Serenity. The gist here is that a gradual loss in energy and enthusiasm can be compensated for by a greater sense of confidence and self-acceptance. To cite an informant:

> I don't worry as much about what can go wrong or what went wrong during the day. I even forget my work when I come home. Mostly, I guess, I don't expect more of myself than I know I can deliver—no more whipping myself for not being perfect. What I have to offer is good enough for me and for the pupils, too.

There is a cognate theme—increased feelings of "serenity" go hand in hand with a sense of greater relational distance vis-à-vis pupils. This has been well-studied: The young teacher moves from the "older sister" role to the maternal role to the grandmotherly role, while her pupils stay relentlessly young, year after year. In part, it is the pupils who age-distance their teachers, not only the teacher who disinvests gradually in relational intimacy. Also, these teachers are now themselves less interested in field trips, in extracurricular activities, and, more generally, in involvements in the personal lives of their pupils.

Conservatism. These are, above all, the "defensive focusers." They complain a lot. They bemoan the new generations of pupils (less disciplined, less motivated, more "decadent"), the more negative public image of educators, the lax or opportunistic nature of school administrators, the lack of commitment to the profession among younger colleagues, and so on. Here, of course, we rejoin the classic life-cycle research that links age and dogmatism, with increasing prudence, resistance to innovations, nostalgia for the past, and more concern with holding onto what one has than with getting what one wants.

Disengagement. In general, the life-cycle literature emphasizes a trend of increasing withdrawal and "internalization" toward the end of the professional career. The tone is mostly positive: a gradual disengaging from investment in one's work to pursue other engagements, and from "instrumental" concerns to more reflective pursuits. We should note, however, that in our sample and in the specific work on teachers' professional life cycle, there are other leads: reactions to frustrated ambitions, distancing from policies and practices of which one disapproves, yearning for calmer years as retirement approaches.

Still, these trends are globally consonant with the literature on professional life cycles. Here, Kuhlen's (1964) thesis is compelling: a sharp curve of expansion, both in activity and career progression, then a gradual, usually fluid, disengagement. But the nature of such a disengagement is controversial. The basic hypothesis is psychological, that of a gradual "internalization" at 40 to 45 years of age, notably among men. This shift, often associated with metabolic changes, corresponds to Jung's concept of "individuation," a shift from instrumental activity to introspective reflectiveness, from the narrow self to the archetypal self.

Others have somewhat similar frames for this gradual shift. For example, Erikson's stages of "generativity" and "ego integrity" are consonant with Jung's, and with Sanford's (1966) ultimate phase of "internalization." On the other hand, sociologists have looked elsewhere for determinisms, and above all to social role pressures (Friedman, 1970; Riley, 1972) to make way for younger blood. Still others have shifted the terms of the debate. For example, Maehr and Kleiber (1981) have argued that professional success means something different to individuals at 55 than it did at 25. At 55, one would have other interests, other investments that might not be associated with professional advancement in a material sense, but that would be equally as active. Reading more, working with 2 to 3 colleagues rather than with 20 to 30, drawing out a modest classroom experiment over several years, even gradually giving more time to private interests, are not necessarily signs of a *lesser* engagement, but simply of *another kind* of engagement.

Finally, like all models, this one has warts, as I noted at the outset. Whatever its conceptual validity, it is admittedly normative, decontextualized, and terribly remote from the original, embodied experiences from which it is derived and which it has lumped together. Even if this clustering has been done with care, and even if the end product squares well with the regnant constructs in the field, the model is probably too reductive of teachers' professional lives. Taken alone, the product is fundamentally too incomplete in comparison with the density, expressiveness, and complexity of the source material. We are simply too far from the particulars. Also, it is likely that, within each phase, there is a recycling through earlier ones. For example, the "experimentation" period probably has moments of "discovery," then of "stabilization." So the appropriate form would be more of a helix than a flow diagram. Doing this, of course, would make such a model all but statistically untestable but would probably enhance its ultimate validity, if only by restoring some of its lifelikeness. Finally, the model underrepresents the more social and economic dimensions that critical theorists have contributed to the conceptual stew (e.g., Clough, 1992).

THE VALIDITIES OF NARRATIVE INQUIRY

When we venture on this terrain, the grounds for the validity or authenticity of life-history interviews, the analytic issues come back to haunt us. Taken at the experiential level, life-history interviewing seems to yield undeniable facts. It could, however, be made of whole cloth, a fable or novella rather than the most faithful and mindful account of a teacher's professional life as that person can or will relate it to a researcher. Not that fables and novellas are to be dismissed so lightly. The naturalist novellas of, say, Fontaine or Balzac or Silone contain an archetypal verisimilitude that keeps us reading them over the generations. They are for good reasons regarded as classics. But the criteria by which we assess their qualities are presumably different from those we would use for objects of nature, of society, or of the mind. Or are they?

Epistemologically, if we choose to remain at the experiential level, the criteria for "validity" have essentially to do with the kinds of things that many phenomenologists insist on: the sense of "intersubjective resonance"— of living the account vicariously, of having it ring true, yet also of reflecting an essential or fundamental truth through and beyond its effect on us. This is essentially Giorgi's position.

The emphasis here is on a sort of "existential investigation." There is first an investigation of an experience (ours or someone else's) as we live it rather than as we conceptualize it. Then there is an attempt to move progressively to what are seen as essential (and therefore transpersonal) themes or what phenomenologists like to call the "structures of the phenomenon." Aside from Giorgi, few have admitted they are making these ontological shifts, much less shown how they have actually gone about doing this transposition from the phenomenological to the genotypal, from what phenomenologists call the "immanent" content to the "eidetic" content.

For example, consider Connelly and Clandinin's (1990) work on teachers' life histories. When it comes to claims of the validity of these accounts, they evoke such qualities as "authenticity," "familiarity," and "economy." The last term, however, also seems to imply pertinence to more than just aspects of a reader's or listener's own experience (cf. Reason & Hawkins, 1988; Robinson & Hawpe, 1986). Connelly and Clandinin, it should be noted, are also interested in "verisimilitude," and in "transferability," and try explicitly to seek out common threads across narratives, be they in the form of teachers' journals, letters, annals, chronicles, or autobiographies.

If we shift paradigms slightly and look at these interviews both as narratives and as requiring some form of corroboration from a third party, the criteria change. Consider Spence (1982), an authoritative source on questions of "narrative truth." Although Spence is more taken up with the narrative than the truth, as it were, his criteria (continuity, closure, the fit of the pieces) apply both to fictional and nonfictional works. He does, however, call for narratives that "carry conviction" (as do the phenomenologists), that "have historical truth" and can be corroborated in some systemic way (pp. 31–34). This puts him in a more "realist" school of thought.

Finally, further along the same continuum we find Polkinghorne (1988). The analysis of narratives has to lead to a "well-grounded and supported" conclusion (p. 175). There must be evidence to buttress the analysis, preferably from other sources, and a "demonstration of why alternative conclusions are not as likely" (p. 176).

But Polkinghorne calls this a test of verisimilitude rather than a test of mathematical or logical validity. He also argues that a "significant" analysis is not statistical but rather "important, meaningful, with consequences." In the same vein, "reliability" is not stability of measurement but rather "trustworthiness" of notes or transcriptions. Polkinghorne claims, too, that these canons are compatible with hermeneutic techniques of textual analysis: the disclosing of "underlying patterns" or of "common plots or themes." He then takes another step on the continuum, by condemning "idiosyncratic results" and calling for other researchers, given the same material, to "agree that the results follow" (p. 176). In the jargon of qualitative analysis, this is known as "auditing" (Guba, 1981). It assumes that more than one account of the narrative will be consistent with the phenomena observed, but that there are agreed-on conventions for determining what a valid analysis of a life history would look like and why some are better than others.

Polkinghorne's stance is close to the "transcendental realist" school (Harris, 1990, Bhaskar, 1982; cf., for an educational researcher's version,

House, 1991), that is, a stance roughly midway between relativism (or idealism) and postpositivism (or realism). And if we line up behind it, as I have done in this chapter and elsewhere (Huberman & Miles, 1985), we are opting for a more classically scientific and more explicit view of how life-history interviews move from the particular to the more abstract. We are, at least indirectly, bent on making theory.

But I have also suggested that once a researcher specifies how exactly he or she makes those same moves when working, say, with narratives, we seem to come out at a very similar place. Thus the example of A. Giorgi, one of the few phenomenologists who exposes in some detail not only his epistemology but also his analytic method, and who, in doing this, seems to shift imperceptibly from phenotypes to genotypes.

Of course, not everyone sees it this way. For example, a deconstructionist or, more generally, a postmodernist would see no differences between my summarizing tables or figures and the kinds of aesthetic devices that a novelist or poet might use (cf. Loriggio, 1990; McLaren, 1992). Both are collections of metaphors and tropes. In this view, data are "managed," variables are "manipulated," and research is "designed" to create the illusion of objective reality (Richardson, 1990, pp. 17–20). From this perspective, even probability tables or theorems are, at the core, rhetorical expressions. To come full circle, this implies in turn that science has to do with the construction of meaning through a particular kind of storytelling (cf. Howard, 1991), and that theories are versions of stories that happen to include episodes or characters that it likes to call "facts." Note that this version of postmodernism has an air of paradox about it. Like the others we have reviewed, it also presents a theory with underlying claims for validity identical to the claims of postpositivists. Indeed, it makes a more extreme rhetorical grab for our attention and consent by having recourse to striking, colorful tropes.

CONCLUSION

Working with life histories brings home sharply, I think, the intrinsic dilemma of doing social science research. The source material, an account of people's lives, is so multifold yet at the same time unique that we seem to be corrupting it from the moment we lay our descriptive or analytic hands on it. Nor do the more indirect or allusive approaches, such as hermeneutics or other forms of psychological and social phenomenology, resolve the problem, as delicate as they try to be. They may even complicate things by assuming that their reexpressions or transpositions leave the source material intact. In fact, they, too, are making these narratives into something qualitatively different, all in using a new semantics. It is no wonder that for some researchers, the closest and possibly the best analogues for these narratives are the "real" ones, the downright literary ones.

Yet it is not quite that simple. In their life histories, some individuals, as I tried to show, present themselves so much like stick figures that their stories make not only for bad literature but also for bad theory; they impoverish their own source material. Others' stories are so delirious that no one else can have genuine access to them — like Faulkner's Benjy (in *The Sound and the Fury*) with the author removed. And still others' stories may be fictions, deliberate and crafted ones, or self-delusive ones, without our being able to determine which. Thus, at least in life-history interviewing, it would seem that we mainly have in mind people who are sufficiently lucid or reflective to recount some of the complexity of their own lives in their stories. This limits our universe of inquiry and, thereby, of generalizability.

On the other hand, it is legitimate to search across teachers' lives for common meanings. For one thing, there are obviously such common expressions and interpretations, especially among teachers of the same generation, of similar backgrounds, and working in similar contexts. Simply spending a few weeks in schools and classrooms makes that clear. It is also legitimate to match those common meanings with ones that try to account for how and why, under these circumstances, people might think or feel or behave as they are telling us they have, either in the past or present. That is presumably what life-cycle research and, more generally, what social science theory try to do.

Just because we researchers have not done that part so systematically up to now does not mean we never will. It does, however, mean that the progressive process we undertake of reexpressing, describing, interpreting, and abstracting, with some of us getting off along the way on epistemological grounds, is not usually adequate to the task. What is?

It would seem we have two options. First, we can contrive methods of description and analysis by which our theories come to correspond more closely to the archetypes or prototypes that lie beneath the richer narratives. These are the elements that constitute great literature, landmark studies in social anthropology, *and* the best social theory we have. In effect, we tend to forget that we also have classic *theories* to call on in moments of analysis and interpretation: the ones that successive generations of educational researchers will invariably turn to when they are stuck, or at some key moment in their careers that indicates they are at the point of undergoing an important conceptual shift.

I would argue that we can sense these archetypes intuitively and can also demonstrate them systematically, even scientifically. Contemporary linguists, for example, have made similar claims (cf. Lakoff, 1987; Roesch,

1975). As it happens, however, intuitive analyses have been unhooked for at least 350 years (using Descartes as a baseline) from rationalist ones, including in educational research. So unhooked, in fact, that we can not even construe them together, and tend to perceive many of those who do as variously opportunist, muddled, or mystical. That perception, I would argue, is a cultural one; other cultures, including many we used to call "primitive," do not seem to have as much of a problem. Although he, too, reflects this dichotomy, Geertz (1980) may have a kindred perspective when he writes that "personal lives do have partly identifiable causes and effects, but the road to discovering them lies less in postulating and measuring them than through examining and inspecting their expressions" (p. 178).

The other solution is to collect the material integrally (not intrude) and leave it intact (not analyze). Heidegger called this "letting things be." This corresponds, in fact, to one of the oldest traditions in qualitative research: the oral history tradition. The interviewer turns on the tape recorder and asks a general, orienting question, usually about the informant's life in relation to a period of social history, then generally gets out of the way. He or she intervenes only when the informant wanders outside the scope of some global questions or when the interviewer cannot make basic sense of the story. As invented and refined by the "Chicago school" of sociology, roughly between 1914 and 1930, the method was used to compile source material for social histories. The interview component was in fact a complement to other data sources, such as family letters, newspaper files, school records, and other archival material. The work of Studs Terkel, for example, is a somewhat journalistic version of this method. In educational research, the methodology has been used the most consistently by social historians (Clifford, 1983; Warren, 1989, 1990).

Researchers in the Chicago-school tradition did not intrude into the oral-history interviewing. They were, however, bent on "triangulating" this material with other data in order to generate and refine social theory. Still, there was no hunting around for archetypes. The social historians, on the other hand, have been more cautious in moving from this kind of source material to explanations, and seem more to want to give the reader a real impact of, say, nineteenth-century teachers' diaries or letters written in frontier towns.

There is, however, at least one contemporary example of a life-history interview in the area of teaching in which the researcher is nearly invisible: Riseborough's (1988) study of a British comprehensive-school teacher who, as I only realized gradually, has in fact broken down emotionally. There has necessarily been some selection within the full transcription; the informant does not begin or end with this account. Despite that, the narrative stands alone, like a novella, but with an undeniable ring of truth.

More important still, Riseborough has no commentary; he simply leaves the reader with the transcribed story. There is only one voice here.

At the same time, the material lends itself readily to a psychological or sociological analysis of the profession, and not only in the specific context from which it originates. The informant fits closely, for example, one of the core scenarios presented earlier. His path can be plotted clearly on the model of the life cycle (Figure 9.2). He is also a textbook case of what can happen to teachers over time when they are worn down by constant stress and boredom (much as in military combat) and buffeted by forces over which they have almost no control. In that regard, he fits like a glove the profile given in dozens of empirical studies, including a subset of Swiss teachers in our sample. This portrait also lends weight to one of the main hypotheses of the Swiss study: *that no matter how private or protected the classroom, the ultimate sources of satisfaction in the teaching career are beyond a teacher's control.* They depend heavily on the assignment of pupils, itself a virtual lottery, and one that is usually played every year. So one year, one class, or one set of classes, can be unforgettable and the next one can be infernal (cf. Huberman, 1993).

Similarly, Riseborough's informant is a textbook case of the more sociopathic aspects of the teaching career: the unmanageable pupils, the deadening curriculum, the indifferent colleagues, the nasty administrators, the shabby material conditions. This is an extreme version of mainstream findings in the literature. At the same time, it is theory-empowering; it depicts the conditions under which teachers of this level, and in these kinds of schools, are likely to thrive or to break down. In doing that, it furnishes some credible leads for redirection in policy and practice.

Finally, I would argue that the account of this informant, together with the people and places he describes, is full of archetypes: the burned-out, middle-aged teacher, the adolescents deadened and made pitiless by a history of school failure and a meaningless curriculum of general culture, the vicious administrator, the cynical colleagues. All could be put in capital letters, as in a modern-day *Pilgrim's Progress.* All seem to come right out of Bunyan or Dickens or Balzac.

Intriguingly, too, one forgets to ask whether this account is true because of its expressive force. But once the question is asked, Riseborough's piece seems both to satisfy the criteria of a good narrative (in its coherence, its plausibility, its pacing, its sense of authenticity, its impact) and of a good piece of oral-history research. In effect, beyond its qualities of internal consistency, we know that it is a good piece of research because we have the empirical studies, the requisite constructs or partly assembled theory, to confirm the substance of the narrative and its several configurations. What is uncertain is whether that knowledge is ultimately a disembodied reflection of what is really driving us, that is, the primacy of the expressive, for which Eisner (1991) has made such a strong case. Or whether, to take another line of inquiry, the encounter of archetypal or prototypical themes in the life history is a meeting ground of our core experiences and the paradigms we generate to account for those experiences — paradigms which, just possibly, can actually transcend them in meaningful, verifiable ways.

ACKNOWLEDGMENT

I am grateful to Margret Buchmann, Judith Warren Little, and John Watkins for their insightful comments. This version is much the better for it.

REFERENCES

Ball, S., & Goodson, I. (1985). *Teachers' lives and careers*. London: Falmer Press.

Baltes, P., Featherman, D., & Lerner, R. (1990). *Life-span development and behavior* (Vol. 10). Hillsdale, NJ: Lawrence Erlbaum.

Bartlett, F. (1932). *Remembering*. Cambridge, UK: Cambridge University Press.

Becker, H. (1970). The career of the Chicago schoolmaster. In H. Becker (Ed.), *Sociological work: Method and substance* (pp. 34–69). Chicago: Aldine.

Bhaskar, R. (1982). Emergence, explanation and emancipation. In P. Secord (Ed.), *Explaining human behavior* (pp. 275–310). Beverly Hills: Sage.

Brenner, M. (1982). Response effects of role-restricted characteristics of the interviewer. In W. Djkstra & J. van der Zouwen (Eds.), *Response behavior in the survey inteview* (pp. 67–84). New York: Academic Press.

Brown, R., & Kulik, J. (1977). Flashbulb memories. *Cognition, 5*(1), 73–99.

Bruner, J. (1985). Narrative and paradigmatic modes of thought. In E. Eisner (Ed.), *Learning and teaching the ways of knowing* (pp. 97–115). Chicago: The National Society for the Study of Education.

Butt, R., & Raymond, D. (1989). Studying the nature and development of teachers' knowledge using collaborative autobiography. *International Journal of Educational Research, 13*(4), 403–420.

Clark, D., & Teasdale, J. (1982). Diurnal variation in clinical depression and accessibility of memories of positive and negative experiences. *Journal of Abnormal Psychology, 91*, 87–95.

Clifford, G. (1983). The life story: Biographic study. In J. Best (Ed.), *Historical inquiry in education* (pp. 56–74). Washington, DC: American Educational Research Association.

Clough, P. (1992). *The ends of ethnography*. Newbury Park, CA: Sage.

Cochran-Smith, M., & Lytle, S. (1990). Research on teaching and teacher research: The issues that divide. *Educational Researcher, 19*(2), 2–11.

Cohen, L., Towbes, L., & Flocco, R. (1988). Effects of induced mood on self-reported life events and perceived and received social support. *Journal of Personality and Social Psychology, 55*(4), 669–674.

Cohen, R. (1991). *A lifetime of teaching.* New York: Teachers College Press.

Cohler, B. (1982). Personal narrative and life course. In P. Baltes & O. Brim (Eds.), *Life-span development and behavior* (Vol. 4, pp. 206–229). New York: Academic Press.

Connelly, F. M., & Clandinin, D. J. (1988). *Teachers as curriculum planners: Narratives of experience.* New York: Teachers College Press.

Connelly, F. M., & Clandinin, D. J. (1990). Stories of experience and narrative inquiry. *Educational Researcher, 20*(4), 2–14.

Dennet, D. (1991). *Consciousness explained.* Boston: Little, Brown.

Dollard, J. (1935). *Criteria for the life history.* New Haven, CT: Yale University Press.

Eisner, E. (1988). The primacy of experience and the politics of method. *Educational Researcher, 20*(4), 15–20.

Eisner, E. (1991). *The enlightened eye: On doing qualitative inquiry.* New York: Macmillan.

Elder, G. (1974). *Children of the Great Depression.* Chicago: University of Chicago Press.

Erikson, E. (1950). *Childhood and society.* New York: W. W. Norton.

Faulkner, W. (1956). *The sound and the fury.* New York: Random House.

Fitzgerald, J. (1988). Vivid memories and the reminiscence phenomenon: The role of self narrative. *Human Development, 31*, 261–273.

Friedman, E. (1970). Changing value orientations in adult life. In H. W. Burns (Ed.), *Sociological backgrounds of adult education* (pp. 39–64). Syracuse, NY: Center for the Study of Liberal Education for Adults.

Fuhrman, R., & Wyer, R. (1988). Event memory. *Journal of Personality and Social Psychology, 54*(3), 365–384.

Garfinkel, H. (1967). *Studies in ethnomethodology.* Englewood Cliffs, NJ: Prentice Hall.

Geertz, C. (1974). From the native's point of view. On the nature of anthropological understanding. *Bulletin of the American Academy of Arts and Sciences, 28*, 1.

Geertz, C. (1980). Blurred genres: The refiguration of social thought. *American Scholar, 49*, 165–179.

Geertz, C. (1983). *Local knowledge: Further essays in interpretive anthropology.* New York: Basic Books.

Gergen, K., & Gergen, M. (1983). Narrative of the self. In T. Sarbin & K. Sherbe (Eds.), *Studies in social identity* (pp. 254–273). New York: Praeger.

Giorgi, A. (1975). Phenomenological method. In A. Giorgi (Ed.), *Phenomenological and psychological research* (pp. 3–17). Pittsburgh, PA: Duquesne University Press.

Goodson, Y. (1980/1981). Life histories and the study of school. *Interchange, 11*(4), 62–76.

Grumet, M. R. (1988). *Bitter milk: Women and teaching.* Amherst, MA: University of Massachusetts Press.

Guba, E. (1981). Criteria for assessing the trustworthiness of naturalistic inquiries. *Educational Communication and Technology Journal, 92,* 75–92.

Hankiss, A. (1981). Ontologies of the self: On the mythological rearranging of one's life history. In D. Bertaux (Ed.), *Biography and society* (pp. 203–209). Beverly Hills: Sage.

Hardy, B. (1977). Towards a poetics of fiction. In M. Meek (Ed.), *The cool web* (pp. 12–23). New York: Atheneum.

Harré, R., & Secord, P. F. (1972). *The explanation of social behavior.* Totowa, NJ: Rowman & Littlefield.

Harris, K. (1990). Empowering teachers: Towards a justification for intervention. *Journal of Philosophy of Education, 24*(2), 171–183.

Hebb, D. (1949). *The organization of behavior.* New York: John Wiley & Sons.

House, E. (1991). Realism in research. *Educational Researcher, 20*(6), 2–9.

Howard, G. (1991). Cultural tales: A narrative approach to thinking, cross-cultural psychology and psychotherapy. *American Psychologist, 46*(3), 187–197.

Huberman, M. (1972). *Adult development and learning from a life-cycle perspective.* Paris: Royaumont.

Huberman, M. (1974). *Cycle de vie et formation.* Vevey, Switzerland: Editions Delta.

Huberman, M. (1989a). *La vie des enseignants.* Lausanne, Switzerland: Delachaux et Neistle.

Huberman, M. (1989b). The professional life cycle of teachers. *Teachers College Record, 91*(1), 31–57.

Huberman, M. (1993). *The lives of teachers.* New York: Teachers College Press.

Huberman, M., & Miles, M. (1984). *Innovation up close.* New York: Plenum Press.

Huberman, M., & Miles, M. (1985). Assessing local causality in qualitative research. In D. Berg & K. Smith (Eds.), *Defining a clinical method for social research* (pp. 351–382). Newbury Park, CA: Sage.

Jacobson, R. (1960). Linguistics and poetics. In T. Sebeok (Ed.), *Style in language* (pp. 350–377). Cambridge, MA: MIT Press.

Jacques, E. (1965). Death and the mid-life crisis. *International Journal of Psychoanalysis, 46,* 502–514.

Jalongo, M. (1992, April). Teachers' stories: Our ways of knowing. *Educational Leadership,* pp. 68–73.

Jung, C. (1930). The stages of life. In *Collected works* (Vol. 8, pp. 749–795). Princeton, NJ: Princeton University Press.

Kuhlen, R. (1964). Developmental changes in motivation during the adult years. In J. Birren (Ed.), *Relationships of development and aging.* Springfield, IL: Thomas.

Lakoff, G. (1987). *Women, fire and dangerous things.* Chicago: University of Chicago Press.

Lightfoot, S. (1985). The lives of teachers. In L. S. Shulman & G. Sykes (Eds.), *Handbook of teaching and policy* (pp. 241–259). New York: Longman.

Loftus, E. (1979). *Eyewitness testimony*. Cambridge, MA: Harvard University Press.

Lorrigio, F. (1990). Anthropology, literary theory and the traditions of modernism. In M. Manpanaro (Ed.), *Modernist anthropology* (pp. 205–242). Princeton, NJ: Princeton University Press.

Lortie, D. (1975). *Schoolteacher*. Chicago: University of Chicago Press.

Maehr, M., & Kleiber, D. (1981). The graying of achievement motivation. *American Psychologist, 37*(7), 787–793.

Mandler, J. (1984). *Stories, scripts and scenes: Aspects of schema theory*. Hillsdale, NJ: Lawrence Erlbaum.

Manicas, P. (1987). *A history and philosophy of the social sciences*. Oxford: Blackwell.

McLaren, O. (1992). Collisions with otherness. *Qualitative Studies in Education, 5*(1), 75–92.

McPherson, G. (1972). *Small town teacher*. Cambridge, MA: Harvard University Press.

Mishler, E. (1975). Studies in dialogue and discourse (Pt. 2). *Journal of Psycholinguistic Research, 4*, 99–121.

Mishler, E. (1986). *Research interviewing*. Cambridge, MA: Harvard University Press.

Mishler, E. (1991). Representing discourse: The rhetoric of transcription. *Journal of Narrative and Life History, 1*(4), 255–280.

Nelson, K. (1989). *Narratives from the crib*. Cambridge, MA: Harvard University Press.

Nelson, K., & Gruendel, J. (1981). Generalized event representations. In M. Lamb & A. Brown (Eds.), *Advances in developmental psychology* (Vol. 1, pp. 131–158). Hillsdale, NJ: Lawrence Erlbaum.

Nias, J. (1989). *Primary teachers talking: A study of teaching as work*. London: Routledge & Kegan Paul.

Peterson, W. (1964). Age, teachers' role and the institutional setting. In D. Biddle and W. Elena (Eds.), *Contemporary research on teacher effectiveness* (pp. 268–315). New York: Holt, Rinehart & Winston.

Polkinghorne, D. (1988). *Narrative knowing and the social sciences*, Albany: State University of New York Press.

Raphael, R. (1985). *The teacher's voice: A sense of who we are*. Portsmouth, NH: Heineman.

Reason, P., & Hawkins, P. (1988). Storytelling as inquiry. In P. Reason (Ed.), *Human inquiry in action* (pp. 79–101). Beverley Hills: Sage.

Richardson, L. (1990). *Writing strategies*. Newbury Park, CA: Sage.

Ricouer, P. (1984). *Time and narrative* (Vol. 1). Chicago: University of Chicago Press.

Riley, M. (1972). *Aging and society* (Vol. 3). New York: Russell Sage.

Riseborough, G. (1988). The great Heddekashun war: A life-historical cenotaph for an unknown teacher. *Qualitative Studies in Education, 1*(3), 197–224.

Robinson, J., & Hawpe, L. (1986). Narrative thinking as a heuristic process. In

T. R. Sarbin (Ed.), *Narrative psychology* (pp. 111–125). New York: Praeger.

Roesch, E. (1975). Cognitive reference points. *Cognitive Psychology, 4*, 328–350.

Rorty, R. (1991). Essays on Heidegger and others. In *Philosophical papers* (Vol. 2). Cambridge, UK: Cambridge University Press.

Rosenbaum, J. (1983). *Careers in a corporate hierarchy.* New York: Academic Press.

Ross, M., McFarland, C., & Fletcher, G. (1981). The effect of attitude on the recall of personal histories. *Journal of Personality and Social Psychology, 40*(4), 627–634.

Sanford, N. (1966). *Self and society.* New York: Atherton.

Sarbin, T. (1986a). *Narrative psychology: The storied nature of human conduct.* New York: Praeger.

Sarbin, T. (1986b). The narrative as a root metaphor of psychology. In T. Sarbin (Ed.), *Narrative psychology: The storied nature of human conduct* (pp. 3–21). New York: Praeger.

Sikes, P., Measor, L., & Woods, P. (1985). *Teacher careers: Crises and continuities.* Lewes, UK: Falmer Press.

Smyth, J. (1989). A critical pedagogy of classroom practice. *Journal of Curriculum Studies, 21*(6), 483–502.

Spence, D. (1982). *Narrative truth and historical method.* New York: W. W. Norton.

Spradley, J. (1979). *The ethnographic interview.* New York: Holt, Rinehart & Winston.

Super, D. (1985). Coming of age in Middletown. *American Psychologist, 40*, 405–414.

Teasdale, J., & Fogarty, S. (1979). Differential effects of induced mood on retrieval of pleasant and unpleasant events from episodic memory. *Journal of Abnormal Psychology, 88*(3), 248–257.

Veenman, S. (1984). Perceived problems of beginning teachers. *Review of Educational Research, 54*(1), 143–178.

Warren, D. (1989). Messages from the inside: Teachers as clues in history. *International Journal of Educational Research, 13*(4), 379–402.

Warren, D. (1990). *American teachers: History of a profession at work.* New York: Macmillan.

White, R. (1952). *Lives in progress.* New York: Dryden.

Witherell, C., & Noddings, N. (Eds.). (1991). *Stories lives tell: Narrative and dialogue in education.* New York: Teachers College Press.

Wittgenstein, L. (1953). *Philosophical investigations.* Oxford, UK: Blackwell.

Wittrock, M. (1986). *Handbook of research on teaching* (3rd ed.). New York: Macmillan.

Yee, S. (1990). *Careers in the classroom.* New York: Teachers College Press.

CHAPTER 10

Narrative Understanding in the Study of Teaching

Hunter McEwan

In this chapter, I aim to tell a story about the philosophy of teaching. It is a story that represents both an attempt to explore the place of narrative in understanding teaching and an effort to bridge the gap that has grown between the practice of teaching and the practice of studying teaching. As Alasdair MacIntyre (1984, p. 208) has argued, human social practices and institutions have histories, and our understanding of these practices is often cast in the shape of a story. This perspective recognizes that practices exist in time and change over time. Their distinctive character is the product of past practice and past efforts to understand them. Stories about practices help us to define our purposes, locate our values, and "fix our affective orientation" to people and things (Egan, 1988, p. 100). And so, even though I wish to argue a point about teaching, it is inevitable that aspects of this argument should take on the characteristics of a story. Indeed, given the historical nature of this project and the importance of setting the discussion within a context that reveals the purposes of philosophers of education, the formal elements of story and argument become difficult to separate. The theme of my narrative is that the philosophy of teaching and the empirical study of teaching have kept themselves at a distance from the practice of teaching and that a narrative approach can provide a step forward in seeking a long-needed reconciliation.

UNDERLYING NARRATIVES IN THE PHILOSOPHY OF TEACHING

Let me start by adding a qualification to my formal claim that I am about to tell a story. The tale I am going to tell seems barely to meet the usual conditions that add up to what we would comfortably refer to as a story. To begin with, the plot is undeveloped—a feature of the subject of my narrative, which is hardly the stuff from which a gripping tale can be spun. But also, I find myself suppressing the "narrative function" (Ricouer, 1981, p. 274)—first, by banishing the major players in my story to the reference section and, second, by dealing with abstract qualities rather than the concrete particulars that are characteristic features of narrative prose. Most academic writing may be viewed as an effort to suppress the impulse to relate a narrative, and, correspondingly, disciplinary standards of composition tend to favor nonnarrative writings over straightforward stories (Marshall & Barritt, 1990; and Zeller, Chapter 13, this volume). On the other hand, there is a respectable philosophical tradition which maintains that argument is to be regarded not simply as a different genre from narrative but as a form that is constructed on narrative foundations, as are all the more developed forms of writing. This tradition stems from the work of Hegel, and as Huberman points out in this volume, Hegelian philosophy is at the root of a flourishing endeavor to apply narrative as a means of understanding social phenomena. The argument of this chapter is informed by this tradition, and my task will be to uncover the implicit narratives that already undergird a good deal of the work of philosophy of teaching as well as some empirical approaches to the study of teaching. I aim to expose what Jonathan Ree (1987) refers to as "integral histories." These stories are not just incidental to the dominant forms, procedures, and aims of a given philosophical tradition but undergird them and offer them legitimacy. By relating these stories, we come to appreciate the power that narratives have over the ways we think about teaching, which is an important step in developing a critical perspective that has a bearing on the ways in which teaching is understood.

Philosophical writings may be usefully viewed as dependent forms that require us to abstract from what comes most naturally—the ability to tell a story. The "disciplined mind" thins out description of intentional states, imagines away time and space, places characters in brackets, and condenses events into generalities. Indeed, the power to form abstractions is considered essential, in varying degrees, to all the sciences. Thus, the suppression of narrative in most scholarly writing is more than just a stylistic preference; it is often regarded as a disciplinary requirement and a demonstration of the scientific ideal that identifies objectivity with the scientist's detachment from the object of study. The vestiges of stories may, nevertheless, be detected in most scholarly writings—the part that has not been dispatched by the requirement to form abstractions and generalizations. Sometimes, however, and especially in periods in which established paradigms are being called into doubt, there is what might be termed a "return to narrative," an effort, that is, to recover and perhaps retell the narratives that form the basis of a particular disciplinary practice.

I wish, then, to place the philosophical discourse about teaching in a more narrative form so that its implicit history is brought out in greater detail. The events that I wish to describe represent an evolving set of practices that extend over some 30 years. They tell about the actions of educational philosophers in relation to their goal of informing us about the nature of teaching.

In pursuing a narrative approach to this topic, I hope to clarify what analytic philosophers have been doing with the concept of teaching and to convey something of the commitment and purpose with which the philosophical conversation about teaching has been sustained. However, my own venture into narrative is not purely an attempt to record past events. I believe that in revealing a number of embedded philosophical assumptions and implications within traditional philosophy of teaching, my narrative will have something useful to say about the empirical study of teaching. I believe also that in pursuing this story I can connect the efforts of analytical philosophers over the past few years to a contemporary conversation that is emerging as a result of a more hermeneutical understanding of teaching. And here I understand hermeneutics as "the study of the operations of understanding in their relation to the interpretation of texts" (Ricouer, 1981, p. 43).

My story, therefore, is one of continuity within a tradition, of following a trail that leads up to the present moment and passes beyond it to open up possibilities for future work. I hope to show, moreover, the important place that analytic philosophy has had in shaping our present understanding of teaching, and how it has contributed to an uninterrupted and evolving conversation undertaken by philosophers and others who study teaching.

One way to understand the practice of philosophizing about teaching is to see it as engaged in a conflict with other disciplines that study teaching. This picture presents a familiar portrait of the philosopher as an interested but disengaged observer—one who stands apart from the study of teaching, but also stands ready to provide either sanction or censure, depending on the theoretical constraints of his or her epistemological beliefs and their entailments. But another theme emerges in the practice of the philosophy of teaching that is linked to the critical function. Here, the role of the philosopher is to reveal the essential nature of teaching. This positive function, as opposed to the negative or critical function, is directed toward a logical analysis or conceptual characterization of the essential formal properties of the concept.

Popular opinion frequently portrays philosophers in their negative role as critics. They are pictured as aloof, removed from the fray, eager to comment on the action and to offer advice (even when it is not asked for), but seldom ready to take up arms and do battle in the trenches. This picture is one for which philosophers mainly have themselves to blame, for it is a consequence of the story that they have spread about philosophy and its mission of discovering unassailable grounds for the knowledge claims of those in other disciplines (Rorty, 1982). Philosophy, so the story goes, is a second-order subject, the queen of the sciences, whose main concern is to license the knowledge claims of those who labor in the first-order disciplines. But does this account of the task of philosophy present a fair picture of what philosophers have been doing over the past few decades in analyzing the concept of teaching? I wish to present the case that it represents only part of the story of the philosophy of teaching and that by reducing this story to a sustained commentary on the knowledge claims of those who do research on teaching is to miss out on something important—the ways in which the philosophy of teaching has itself contributed to our understanding of what teaching is.

Thus, two interconnected themes characterized the conduct of the philosophy of teaching until quite recently: a negative theme, which tells of a conflict between philosophers and those who study teaching, and a positive theme, which describes the quest for a logical description of the essential nature of teachers' thinking—the search, that is, for a logical theory of teaching (Macmillan & Garrison, 1988). These epic themes of conflict and quest may seem a far cry from the prosaic concerns of philosophers of education, particularly those whose interests focus on the nature and study of teaching. But operating, as they do, as implicit narratives, they represent an underlying sense of purpose that informs the task that philosophers have set themselves in the study of teaching. In effect, when we cast ourselves as agents in a struggle and relate our actions to some higher goal, we give meaning to what we do. And this helps to explain why stories are so important and why they play such a vital role in our understanding of the nature of teaching and its study. In the following section, I will provide a more detailed account of these implicit narratives and say something of their consequences and shortcomings.

The Way Things Were: Conflict and Quest in the Study of Teaching

A useful way to make sense of what philosophers of education have been doing with the concept of teaching over the past few decades is to view their actions as part of a prolonged siege of the establishment view of teaching—the one proposed by educational psychologists and particularly by those of a behaviorist cast of mind. C. J. B. Macmillan (1990, p. 199) has described the conflict as an engagement in which philosophers have deployed the critical weaponry of ordinary language philosophy to battle the oversimplifications encouraged by the "behavioral objectives" movement—a ploy that may be compared to firing "smart" weaponry at a large, entrenched, and obsolete enemy force. By participating in this engagement, philosophers of teaching have fulfilled their function as commentators, as representatives of an epistemological task force ready to deny the enemy its territorial gains but professing no territorial ambitions of its own. The principal value of their reflections has been in telling us what teaching is not, rather than what it is. They remind us that teaching cannot be thought of exclusively in behavioral terms, nor by analogy with the functioning of a machine. Teaching is to be understood more correctly as informed action, a rational enterprise of considerable complexity that cannot be reduced to simple stimulus-response mechanisms. Thus, the mechanical metaphors entertained by machine-minded psychologists are, at best, simplifications, and, at worst, distortions or misrepresentations (Taylor, 1985a). Reductive scientific approaches to the study of teaching that aim to describe it in "objective" terms direct attention only to the outward and observable phenomena and take no account of the rich interior lives that teachers lead—their decision making, their plans and deliberations, and their habits of reflection.

This critical or oppositional role has therefore performed an important function, especially in reminding us what teaching definitely is not. However, the critical perspective is not purely negative. In the very act of criticizing conceptions of teaching we improve our awareness of appropriate methods of studying teaching and add to our conceptual knowledge of the subject.

In order to understand how philosophical approaches to the study of teaching have changed, then, it will be useful to trace the positive or constructive work of the philosophy of teaching as it emerges in the often painstaking analysis of the concept of teaching (Kerr, 1974). As a result of this work, a new theme emerges in the story of the philosophy of teaching: the theme of a quest. As Graham shows in his chapter, the quest myth is a potent force that shapes our consciousness about the role of the teacher in Western society. The philosophy of teaching may also be said to possess its own version of the search for the Holy Grail—the educational philosopher in the role of a sort of Sir Galahad engaged in a quest for the essence or true nature of teaching. The goal of this project is to identify teaching in such a way that it can be distinguished from other similar acts—the difference between teaching and explaining, for example.

This essentialist project in the philosophy of teaching, as I shall refer to it, is one that aims to identify those features that distinguish teaching acts from nonteaching acts (McClellan, 1976). Philosophers have aimed to pare away the outer lineaments of teaching to get to the heart of what teaching really is. I have described this project in greater detail elsewhere (McEwan,

1990), but basically it amounts to an effort to set out the necessary and sufficient conditions for an act to be considered an act of teaching. In order to accomplish this task, philosophers have deployed the tools of linguistic analysis to clarify of our understanding of the concept of teaching. Roughly speaking, this means analyzing the linguistic features and relationships that inhabit the uses of the concept, that is, an effort to plot, in Gilbert Ryle's (1945) useful phrase, the "logical geography" of the term.

A more recent development of the essentialist program is to describe what teaching really is in terms of the formal characteristics of teachers' thinking processes. The project has therefore moved away from outlining the different meanings of the verb "to teach" or identifying distinctive intentional states of teaching—such as the intention to produce learning—to portraying the appropriate logical operations implied in the act of teaching (Kerr, 1974, p. 64). Thus, for example, Green (1976) and Fenstermacher (1986) have selected the formal properties of practical reasoning using Aristotle's account of the practical syllogism. Macmillan and Garrison (1988), on the other hand, have explored erotetic logic as a way of locating the logic at the heart of teaching. In another attempt to do roughly the same thing, Shulman (1987) has proposed that the distinctive feature of teachers' understanding arises from a process of "pedagogical reasoning," from which teachers derive a specialized form of knowledge which he calls "pedagogic content knowledge." The result of philosophizing about teaching in this fashion is not merely to criticize certain conceptions of teaching from the outside, but also to set up a philosophical alternative with its own implications and research questions. In short, logical theories of teaching promote the idea of the teacher as a thinker of a certain kind—an advance, perhaps, on behaviorist models which view the teacher more as an automaton.

Nevertheless, in spite of offering a theory of teaching based on richer grounds, the theory is not without its problems. To begin with, it focuses too narrowly on the psychology of the individual and identifies the heart of teaching as a correspondence between teacher thinking and certain specifiable logical forms of thought. Teacher thinking is linked to a limited band of formal operations which, it is alleged, pinpoint the distinctive features of pedagogic reasoning. Unfortunately, this ignores the significance to teaching of a more comprehensive human capacity for thought, the ability to make meaning and interpret meaning for others. The problem with logical theories of teaching, then, is that they take formal argumentation as exemplary, whereas formal thought of this sort presupposes a rich foundation of intersubjective meanings that are already in place in teachers' understanding and integral to their reasoning (Pendlebury, 1988).

A second problem of essentialism in teaching is that in concentrating on what goes on in teachers' heads we lose touch with the rich social contexts in which such reasoning occurs (Sockett, 1987, p. 209). Practical reasoning cannot be given a formal description that is divorced from the practices out of which it arises. And so, any effort to give a description of how teachers think must be rooted in the various practices in which teachers are engaged, rather than in some capacity that transcends teachers' actions and aims to abstract it from them.

Thirdly, there is an implicit prescriptive agenda in this procedure. It suggests that we can improve teaching simply by getting teachers to think in the right way. Such an agenda fails to take account of the rich social context which surrounds teachers' reflective practices and which both inhibits and encourages the ways they think (see Pendlebury, Chapter 4 in this volume).

A major shortcoming, however, of this particular version of the philosophical quest is that it has to a large extent been engaged with describing what teaching is as if it were a slice of life — an act, right now, with a finite set of describable characteristics (McEwan, 1990, p. 194). Priority is given to questions of structure rather than to questions of process, to how things are rather than to how things change. Thus the essentialism of philosophers of teaching may be viewed as an attempt to give a description that divorces teaching from its social history, and this is arguably a limitation in a good deal of empirical research on teaching. We have been busy describing the engagement of teaching as if it occurred in a time capsule, as if the act of teaching were something without a history and without a future. But human practices take place in time and over time. They have histories. And so, if we wish to understand something as an act of teaching, we need to know how it arose and how it has evolved. An example will be useful in clarifying this point. Imagine a classroom in which the teacher has assigned students the task of writing a letter of protest to a political figure. Is this teaching? Possibly. But it is just as likely that it is a self-serving action, an effort to employ the students in achieving the personal or political aims of the teacher. How can we know that the teacher is teaching and not simply being self-serving? The usual philosophical solution to this problem is to appeal to the teacher's intentions and ask if their aim is to bring about learning. But the problem with this move is that it is not sufficient to identify it as a teaching act. After all, he or she could have done it with both aims in mind. We need to know more if we are to settle the issue. In other words, we need to go beyond the individual psychological states of the teacher and ask how these states of mind arose. The obvious way to do this is to tell a story that explores the teacher's motives more deeply, explaining the reasoning that preceded the decision to assign the letter-writing activity, and clarifying the teacher's aims, tying them to the earlier more public standards of professional pedagogic practice. To understand teaching, then, we need to delve into the past, and not just into the past of individual teachers but into the traditions of pedagogic practice within whose orbit teachers think and work. As a result, in order to answer the question of whether someone is teaching or not, researchers need to tell stories about what teachers do. Correspondingly, when teachers reflect upon their actions and endeavor to make them intelligible, to themselves as well as others, they will also tend to cast their accounts in the form of a story.

What does this mean for the philosophy of teaching? It suggests that teaching has a history and that philosophers must give up their essentialist ambitions, their quest for the inner nature and true center of the teaching act. Teaching is not something with a fixed and immutable nature but is subject to change over time. The quest for the Holy Grail of teaching should be abandoned. In response, the philosophy of teaching must also change its methods and aims. Philosophers must find a new language and new reasons to continue their philosophical conversation about teaching. And as they pursue this task, they will also need to redefine their relationship with teachers and other people who make it their business to study teaching.

THINGS TO COME: OTHER VIEWS OF TEACHING

So far, my story may be seen as an effort to give an account of the philosophical engagement with the concept of teaching and the philosophical project of defining the essential nature of teaching. I have placed this discussion within the tradition of ordinary language analysis, a tradition that has been enormously influential in modern educational thought. My story began with the rejection by philosophers of mechanistic reductions of teaching into discrete skills, and their attempt to replace it with an alternative vision of teaching as a distinct form of knowing. This agenda reflects Strawson's account of analytic philosophy as a theory of human action which accepts that there is a "massive core of human thinking that has no history" (Strawson, 1963, p. iv).

I argued, however, that the essentialists are right to begin with a theory of action, but wrong in their efforts to search for the essential nature of teaching. Teaching and teachers' thought processes are not ahistorical. There is no core mental procedure or essential form of thinking that is distinctive to teaching. Many stories could be told that give a different sense to what it is to teach. Teaching, then, is not always and everywhere the same thing.

A similar state of affairs exists, or is emerging, in our understanding of literacy, for it too has its histories (Darnton, 1989). The past efforts of essentialists to define exactly what are the central features of reading and writing processes have recently come under considerable critical fire. Other literacies exist and other traditions have helped to give them shape. Indeed, it has become more accurate to use the plural rather than the singular form and speak of "literacies" instead of "literacy," which conceals the multiform nature of the processes in which readers and writers engage. (Since the plural form, *teachings*, has already been appropriated to refer to the doctrines of some teachers, I suggest that we use the phrase *teaching practices* to reflect our understanding of the various ways that teaching can be practiced.)

Thus, teaching, like literacy, has a history. And, consequently, it might have evolved in ways very different from our own rather restricted and entrenched view of what it is to teach. As is the case with literacy, we may be witnessing new forms of teaching in the process of emerging, new stories and new metaphors that express different purposes and values for the teacher. Feminist writers, for example, have argued that our conception of teaching is too narrowly rational and Socratic. They propose that it must be tied to moral and affective qualities such as caring and concern for others (Noddings, 1984). Their story seeks to connect teaching to its feminine roots in the relationship that exists between mother and child, rather than placing it in cold logical space.

Another story that is current in the literature requires a more critical awareness in the teacher, a capacity not just to think in certain ways but to understand the contingent nature of thought and knowledge. I refer here, following Richard Rorty (1989, p. 74), to the teacher as liberal ironist—a teacher, that is, whose practices reflect his or her awareness of the historical nature of knowledge because he or she thinks "nothing has an intrinsic nature or real essence." This idea is similar to Garth Boomer's (1989) "Epic Teacher," who would seem more at home in the Brechtian theatre than the classroom.

> An Epic Teacher, unlike the naturalistic teacher, would show the students that the curriculum is a construction designed to have certain effects on them. He or she would be continually taking student behind the set of his or her own theatre of performance, to see the scaffolding and the construction technologies. (p. 10)

A more familiar conception of the teacher is implicit in the modern desire to see teaching and teachers as professionals willing to collaborate in the open-ended task of educating students rather than lone operators following a plan laid down according to scientific principles of curriculum design and instructional technique. One way to express this difference is to replace the metaphor of the teacher as an assembly-line supervisor with that of the teacher as a player manager. In yet another approach, conceptions of teaching could be seen as arising from within the subject matter disciplines as part of the stories that they have to tell about what it means to do science or study philosophy or read literature (McEwan & Bull, 1991). Here, the disciplines themselves supply the metaphors for teaching (McEwan, 1992b).

Each of these alternatives is based on what Jonathan Ree (1987, p. 31) calls an "implicit integral history," a narrative that constitutes an argument whose logic ends at the spot where you are now being asked to stand" (p. 32). These histories operate as foundational myths. They give legitimacy to our beliefs and consolation to unreflective habits of mind and practices. In teaching, they present portraits of the teacher as a culminating figure in a particular evolutionary history.

Where, then, does all this leave us with regard to teaching and to our understanding of teaching? In the remainder of this chapter I wish to discuss three related issues that, I believe, are thrown into prominence by the breakdown of essentialism in teaching. The first issue asks the question, How should we theorize about teaching? The second matter deals with the whole notion of what a teaching practice is and the place that narrative has in understanding teaching. The third issue is related to the purpose of theorizing about teaching and raises the question of the future of teaching—the idea that our study of teaching need not limit itself to investigating current practices, but can also begin to explore what teaching might become.

FROM ANALYSIS TO INTERPRETATION

In the previous section of this chapter, I cast uncertainty on the goals of the analytic philosophy of teaching by doubting its capacity to arrive at a true, nonhistorical description of teaching. If there is no core conception of teaching, if the enterprise of identifying a set of intentions, thoughts, and actions that are common only to teaching is an empty quest, then what is the point of theorizing about teaching? The philosophy of teaching, it seems, must take on a new account of itself, or retreat into some obscure corner to play idle word games.

Richard Rorty (1979, p. 315) suggests that when we give up doing epistemology, we find ourselves engaged in an interpretive conversation with ourselves and others. What this means for the study of teaching is that, rather than attempting to anchor our beliefs to unassailable foundations, we must now open our minds to processes of interpersonal understanding. Our search is not to find absolute agreement about what teaching is or is not, but to establish as much agreement as we need to understand it.

Hermeneutics is the discipline in which we aim to make sense of whatever is obscure. As Rorty sees it, hermeneutics is not so much a "successor discipline" to epistemology as an inevitable feature of our understanding when we endeavor to explore meanings and explain how things "hang together" (p. 365). Rorty's claim is, nonetheless, a controversial one. Other thinkers, like Paul Ricouer (1981) and Charles Taylor (1985b), are more inclined to view hermeneutics as possessing methodological procedures and aims, even though they may also agree with Rorty that interpretation is not something that we can entirely suspend and pick up again at will.

The goal of philosophical reflection on teaching changes when the epistemological search for essences is abandoned in favor of a more hermeneutical approach. The point of philosophizing is now to interpret teaching, not to find out what teaching is once and for all, but to find "new, better, more interesting ways of speaking" about teaching (Rorty, 1979, p. 365).

A new aim is to tell stories about teaching in the hope that in saying something new we will learn to do it better. For Rorty (1979, p. 315), and also for Gadamer (1975), hermeneutics is not another method of establishing the truth, it is an expression of hope that we can grow more understanding about the human world. The change that this move inaugurates in the philosophy of teaching replaces the search for essences, and for a logical theory of teaching, with an exploration of the multitude of ways that teaching can be meaningfully understood. This methodological shift is directed away from the atomic division of acts of teaching into constitutive elements, and toward narratives that help to explain how various teaching practices have evolved. The move is from analysis to interpretation, from epistemology to hermeneutics, and from synchronic description and logical argumentation to narrative explanation. We derive an epistemic gain from this move. By abandoning the quest for the essence of teaching, philosophers can view their formal analyses of teaching acts within a more historical context. We can see how the concept of teaching is informed by the various practices in which teachers publicly engage. We can open up our investigations into the nature of teaching practices and note the historical and narrative features of those concepts. The result of this reorientation in the philosophical study of teaching is to close the gap between theorizing about teaching, the empirical study of teaching, and the practices of teachers. We may conclude with Marx that the point of research and theory is not merely to understand teaching but to change it. And change of this kind does not arise as it does through experimentation, observation, and the adoption of an apparently neutral standpoint. Change arises from within by effecting a redescription of the practice in which the inadequacies of prior theoretical and pretheoretical commitments are explained and new, more fruitful avenues of practice mapped out. The reflective engagement with practice is not idle. It serves to express what we do and why we do it. It allows us to adopt a critical stance that may help to bring about a more complete account of our practices. It is fruitful if it enlarges our understanding, explains our previous theories, and leads to improved consequences.

TEACHING, NARRATIVE, AND THE CONCEPT OF PRACTICE

Earlier in this chapter, I linked the idea of narrative with the philosophical discussion about teaching as an act. As a result, the related concept of practice was drawn into the discussion in a new way—not as oppositional to theory, but in a way that demonstrates the interrelatedness of theory with practice.

Past efforts to understand the concept of practice within the field of education have tended to follow the natural sciences model, in which theorizing is regarded as something distinct from the phenomena being studied (Carr, 1987). In this view, a practice is held to be, in itself, an atheoretical object—something theories are about rather than something that is inherently theoretical. The aim of theorizing according to the natural sciences model is to gain greater technical control over the phenomenal world. Thus, the concept of practice has become fixed in our minds as inhabiting the phenomenal world rather than the theoretical world. But to make such a division between theory and practice is to misunderstand the nature of practice. Wilfred Carr (1987) suggests that looking at educational practices through the lens of the natural science model has predisposed us to think that such concepts can be "philosophically analyzed apart from their history" (p. 164). This project, he argues, radically misconceives the nature of action and practice and misplaces the proper task of informing ourselves about educational matters by launching us in a futile search for objectivity:

> By making the twin assumptions that all theory is non-practical and all practice is non-theoretical, this approach always underestimates the extent to which those who engage in educational practices have to reflect upon, and hence theorize about, what, in general, they are trying to do. (p. 164)

By telling a different story about what philosophers have to say about human social practices, Carr provides a set of alternative philosophical questions, which are concerned with describing how theory and practice are interconnected. His solution to the dilemma faced by those who view theory and practice through the fragmenting lens of natural science is to turn back the clock, to retrace the history of the problem of practical reasoning to the starting point and return to the Aristotelian vision of practice as embedded in a theory of rational human agency. Carr points out that Aristotle's concept of *praxis* raises the question of rational human conduct in entirely different ways—ones that avoid technical, rational habits of mind by viewing theory instead as constitutive of practice (p. 168). Aristotle's great insight, here, is to see that human action requires its own terms of explanation and interpretation, and that they are irreducible to those of physical explanation.

By drawing on a more Aristotelian conception of practice, one that has also been developed recently by a number of contemporary philosophers such as Richard Bernstein (1971), Richard Rorty (1979), and Charles Taylor (1985a, 1985b), the philosophy of education has begun to embrace a more hermeneutical approach to theoretical and research questions about teaching. The importance of this move in contemporary philosophy is that it connects the analytical conversation about teaching with a hermeneutic tradition in modern European philosophy and the line of thought that begins with Schleiermacher and progresses through such thinkers as Dilthey, Heidegger, and Gadamer (see Palmer, 1969).

The hermeneutic tradition in modern philosophy is represented by such philosophers as Jurgen Habermas, Hans-Georg Gadamer, Paul Ricouer, and Charles Taylor (see Dallmayr & McCarthy, 1977). This tradition has come to influence Anglo-American thought in recent years, and its impact has spread beyond the narrow circle of specialist philosophers, expanding outwards into the various fields of humanistic inquiry.

What, then, according to hermeneutics, is a practice, and how is narrative thought implicated in our practical reasoning?

In answering this question, I hope to show that it is a mistake for philosophers or empirical researchers to understand or define teaching purely in terms of specific logical operations or by appeal to generalized descriptions of teachers' reasoning processes that abstract these operations from the practices in which they arise. A hermeneutical account of practical reasoning provides a corrective to this way of thinking and proceeding, one that dissolves the dualism between theory and practice (McEwan, 1992a).

Hermeneutics has always pictured knowledge and action as moving in a circular fashion, the so-called "hermeneutic circle." One way to understand this process is to see that practices are never devoid of some level of theoretical or pretheoretical understanding. A certain set of concepts and their relationships, rules, goals, values, distinctions, indeed, the very language in which the practice is made intelligible to ourselves and others, is constitutive of the practice. To engage in a practice, therefore, is to some extent to be able to speak the language of the practice. Changes in the language of a practice are, for that very reason, to be seen as changes in the practice itself. Thus practitioners are people who can give an account of their actions by relating them to some goal and explaining the nature of their behavior. Although this kind of talk may be incomplete or even lacking in coherence, it is always shared, in varying degrees, by the community that engages in the practice. Thus, the meanings implicit in the actions of individuals are part of the common store of meanings of the group. Charles Taylor (1985b, p. 36) makes this point when he tells us that the meanings of practices are intersubjective. Meanings are not imposed from outside but arise within the activity, so there is no sense to the idea of getting outside the practice, no objective standpoint, no neutral language with which to talk about our actions. This does not mean that theorizing is impossible, only the kind of theorizing that tries to engage practices from a neutral and external point of view.

As Taylor (1985b) points out, the aim of theorizing in the human sciences is to give an account of a practice in such a way that goes beyond the self-understandings of its practitioners. "Theories do not just make our constitutive self-understandings explicit, but extend, or criticize, or even challenge them" (p. 94). This goal cannot ignore the present level of theoretical understanding implicit in the practice. Reflection and study set in motion a circular process where old understandings are absorbed in a new synthesis that has the potential to inaugurate a qualitative change in the practice.

A new level of self-understandings and a concomitant change in practice results from the theory. Gadamer refers to this process as one that leads to a "fusion" of old self-understandings with new ideas (1975, p. 30). The process is a cyclical one because it has no beginning and no final end. New understandings impinge on old practices and become, to varying degrees, part of the language that constitutes the new practice. Thus, by changing the language through which we understand practices, we bring about changes in practices and add to their history. This dynamic interchange between theory and practice provides an impetus to any future direction the practice may take by giving utterance to new goals, new procedures, and new concepts, and by establishing new relationships between them.

The point that I wish to extract from this discussion about practices is that the continuity of interactions between acting and thinking is largely a historical process. We encounter practices in the present, at the point of intersection of past and future, but we must understand them as part of a process of change. Our attempts to understand practices are destined to become part of their history as well as to become implicated in the future directions that the practices take. Because practical reasoning is as much about ends as it is about means, the business of understanding practices will require us to tell stories about how they have evolved and with what purpose. Practices require, for their full characterization, descriptions of current actions and language use placed in the context of historical accounts that help to explain how the practices have taken their current shape. A synchronic account is in itself devoid of history, it is a picture of the way things are—a slice of life, like a snapshot. We can only understand the nature of a practice when we set the picture in motion and trace the history of its constitutive elements: the actions, thoughts, language, and intentions that contribute to it and give it character and direction. When we place these descriptions within a historical context and, so to speak, account for the way that the practices have evolved, then we have not merely described them but helped to explain them as well.

But what does "narrative" mean in the sense that it is being used here? Despite the antiquity of the human practice of making and telling stories, the word "narrative" and its cognates, such as "narrativize" and "narrativity," are quite recent terms of art. Their emergence in the reflective language of human action and practice is quite new (Swearingen, 1990). They refer to an open category of discourses that are, in general, involved with the construction and reconstruction of events, including human conscious states, in an order that places them in or configures them in such a way that they imply a certain directedness or orientation to some goal. Informal speech is quite often structured in this way, and so are the products of literary reflection and art. So are our practices, and this is a crucial point, to the degree that the constitutive language of the practice aims to clarify the purposes of the practice. Thus, narrative language is not merely about practice, it is also a part of the practices it constitutes. This conclusion suggests that we should not just become more aware of our practices as partly constituted by narrative, but also, and because of this, begin to see our lives and practices as in some significant way changed by our narrative understanding. Where this makes a difference in teaching is that in addition to coming to understand teaching as a narrative, we must come to practice it as informed by narrative and so come to see our own pedagogic values and purposes as contingent and revisable.

IMAGINING WHAT TEACHING CAN BECOME

The philosophy of teaching, in the analytic tradition, has been engaged in developing one possible narrative among many potential narratives. Part of its influence, perhaps, has been unfortunate because it has excluded the possibility of alternative views of education, but, on the other hand, it has played a vital role in demonstrating the poverty of the behaviorist's mechanical descriptions of teaching.

In accepting a more narrative approach to understanding teaching, however, we are brought to the realization that there may be other, as yet unexplored, ways to make sense of teaching. And if stories include an implicit goal orientation, the philosopher is confronted with an inevitable consequence of theorizing about practice—in relating what teaching is, they are also embroiled in the business of defining what it may become. We must be alert to the fact that in constructing a story we aim to do more than just describe a state of affairs—our descriptions are implicitly prescriptive.

Paul Ricouer (1981) has argued that history and fiction are not hard and fast categories but participate to a certain extent in each other. In telling stories about teaching we are doing more than simply recording how practices arise, we are also potentially altering them. By finding a new language to talk about the practices of teaching—a new language that can, moreover, become a part of the practice itself—we are adding to the history of the practice and participating, for better or worse, in its evolution. Research on teaching, then, in so far as it tells stories about teaching, is inevitably oriented toward changing how teachers think and act because it contributes to changes in the languages that constitute teachers' practices.

One consequence of the power of stories to change the way we do things is that we must recognize the degree to which stories, such as case studies and ethnographies, contribute to educational change. But also, if the point of practical reasoning is not just to gain a better account of our teaching practices but somehow to improve the practices themselves, then it makes sense to use stories that set out to explore the realm of the possible as well as of the real. I refer here to the kind of teaching that Robert Coles describes in his 1989 work, *The Call of Stories*, in which he challenges physicians to explore the moral dimension of their own practices by immersing them in a conversation about the characters and events in imaginative literature. I am arguing for the use of fictional accounts of teaching and the metaphors they employ (for example, D.H. Lawrence's portrait of Ursula Brangwen's first experience of teaching in *The Rainbow* is a powerful expression of the prison metaphor applied to teaching) as a way of opening up other worlds of teaching. The advantage of such a procedure is that it presses us to go beyond the present state of our practices to a consideration of how teaching might be conceived—a consideration, that is, that confronts our own practices and challenges us to reflect more deeply upon them. Imaginative fiction provides an intimate access into teachers' minds and into the practices that they engage in. Jackson's chapter in this volume demonstrates that stories have been employed for millennia as a means of transforming thought and action. Stories have the potential to transform us, through the agency of what Coles (1989) refers to as the "moral imagination," by making the wealth contained in them a part of our own understanding and practice.

In conclusion, the philosophical conversation about teaching has undergone radical change. The story is a complex one, but certain features stand out. First, the role of the philosopher as critic has been dropped in favor of a concept of the philosopher as one whose work is continuous with that of practitioners and those of us who study teaching from other perspectives. Second, the search for the essence of teaching can be called off. A hermeneutics of teaching is more diverse in its interests than its predecessor, which focused on identifying the rational essence of teaching. It represents a sustained effort to find meaning and, in Rorty's (1979, p. 359) words, "to edify" by finding a better language to talk about teaching, and, consequently, by finding better ways to teach.

REFERENCES

Bernstein, R. (1971). *Praxis and action*. Philadelphia: University of Pennsylvania Press.

Boomer, G. (1989, July). *Literacy, the epic challenge: Beyond progressivism*. Paper presented to the Joint Australian Reading Association and Australian Association for the Teaching of English National Conference, Darwin, Australia.

Carr, W. (1987). What is an educational practice? *Journal of the Philosophy of Education, 21*(2), 163–175.

Coles, R. (1989). *The call of stories: Teaching and the moral imagination*. Boston: Houghton Mifflin.

Dallmayr, F. R., & McCarthy, T. A. (1977). (Eds.). *Understanding and social inquiry*. Notre Dame, IN: University of Notre Dame Press.

Darnton, R. (1989). Toward a history of reading. *Writers' Quarterly*, Autumn, 87–102.

Egan, K. (1988). *Primary understanding*. New York: Routledge, Chapman & Hall.

Fenstermacher, G. (1986). Philosophy of research on teaching: Three aspects. In M. Wittrock (Ed.), *Handbook of research on teaching* (3rd ed., pp. 37–49). New York: Macmillan.

Gadamer, H-G. (1975). *Truth and method* (J. Weinsheimer & D. G. Marshall, Trans.). New York: Crossroads.

Green, T. F. (1976). Teacher competence as practical rationality, *Educational Theory, 26*, 249–262.

Kerr, D. H. (1974). Analyses of "teaching." *Educational Philosophy and Theory, 6*, 59–67.

MacIntyre, A. (1984). *After virtue* (2nd ed.). Notre Dame, IN: University of Notre Dame Press.

Macmillan, C. J. B. (1990). Telling stories about teaching. In *Philosophy of Education* (pp. 199–203). Normal, IL: Philosophy of Education Society.

Macmillan, C. J. B., & Garrison, J. W. (1988). *A logical theory of teaching*. The Netherlands: Kluwer.

Marshall, M. J., & Barritt, L. S. (1990). Choices made, worlds created: The rhetoric of AERJ. *American Educational Research Journal, 27*(4), 589–609.

McClellan, J. (1976). *The philosophy of education.* Englewood Cliffs, NJ: Prentice Hall.

McEwan, H. (1989). Teaching and rhetoric. In *Philosophy of Education* (pp. 203–211). Normal, IL: Philosophy of Education Society.

McEwan, H. (1990). Teaching acts: An unfinished story. In *Philosophy of Education* (pp. 190–198). Normal, IL: Philosophy of Education Society.

McEwan, H. (1992a). Teaching and the interpretation of texts. *Educational Theory, 42*(1), 59–68.

McEwan, H. (1992b). Five metaphors for English. *English Education, 24*(2), 101–128.

McEwan, H., & Bull, B. (1991). The pedagogic nature of subject matter knowledge. *American Educational Research Journal, 28*(2), 316–334.

Noddings, N. (1984). *Caring.* Berkeley: University of California Press.

Palmer, R. (1969). *Hermeneutics.* Evanston, IL: Northwestern University Press.

Pendlebury, S. (1988). Teaching: Answering questions or telling stories? In *Philosophy of Education* (pp. 326–337). Normal, IL: Philosophy of Education Society.

Ree, J. (1987). *Philosophical tales: An essay on philosophy and literature.* London: Methuen.

Ricouer, P. (1981). *Hermeneutics and the human sciences* (J. B. Thompson, Trans.). Cambridge, UK: Cambridge University Press.

Rorty, Richard. (1979). *Philosophy and the mirror of nature.* Princeton, NJ: Princeton University Press.

Rorty, R. (1982). Philosophy in America today. In *The Consequences of Pragmatism* (pp. 211–230). Minneapolis: University of Minnesota Press.

Rorty, R. (1989). *Contingency, irony, and solidarity.* Cambridge, UK: Cambridge University Press.

Ryle, G. (1945). *Philosophical arguments.* Oxford: Oxford University Press.

Shulman, L. S. (1987). Knowledge and teaching: Foundations of the new reform. *Harvard Educational Review, 57*(1), 1–22.

Sockett, H. (1987). Has Shulman got the strategy right? *Harvard Educational Review, 57*(2), 213–216.

Strawson, P. F. (1963). *Individuals.* New York: Anchor Books.

Swearingen, C. J. (1990). The narration of dialogue and narration within dialogue. In B. K. Britton and A. D. Pellegrini (Eds.), *Narrative thought and narrative language* (pp. 173–197). Hillsdale, NJ: Lawrence Erlbaum.

Taylor, C. (1985a). *Philosophical papers: Vol. 1. Human agency and language.* Cambridge, UK: Cambridge University Press.

Taylor, C. (1985b). *Philosophical papers: Vol. 2. Philosophy and the human sciences.* Cambridge, UK: Cambridge University Press.

CHAPTER 11

Telling Tales

Ivor Goodson and Rob Walker

This chapter was originally devised as a paper for a conference sponsored by the Social Science Research Council (now the Economic and Social Research Council) at St. Hilda's College, Oxford. In the late 1970s and 1980s, this annual conference became an important forum for sociologists of education in Britain, and a number of the issues and ideas that were discussed at the conference set new directions for research. Later work on narratives has followed along some of the lines anticipated in this essay and the questions raised still have resonance.

The paper reprinted here, with its emphasis on metaresearch concerns, did not fit easily with the broad consensus within the conference on problems of method and purpose. We found ourselves taking issue with other researchers on the following matters:

1. The neglect of the process and force of history, particularly curriculum history, in shaping the strategies available to teachers and students. Our view was that curriculum is not readily subject to rational change but of course constitutes an important element in the culture of schooling. This idea was central to Ivor's Ph.D. thesis (later published as Goodson, 1993) and was to form the basis of the series of studies Ivor published as Falmer Press' Curriculum History series. In the papers given at the original conference, the emphasis was on reporting ethnographic accounts of classroom events, and curriculum issues were given little discussion or significance.

2. The neglect of subjectivity in contemporary sociological thought, both in the sense of a failure to provide an adequate account of the role of the person in sociological analysis, and in the sense that sociological methods gave inadequate consideration to issues deriving from the subjectivity of the researcher in research methods. The very notion of "strategies" as a key concept in analyzing schooling implies a behaviorist and rationalist set of assumptions we wanted to challenge.

3. The assumption that "theory" was solely the product of the work of theorists, not teachers or students, and should be necessarily embedded in a technical language. We were interested in the idea that stories (and narrative enquiry) provided another way of looking at the problem of how to explain classroom and school phenomena.

Of course, it is easier for us to see such concerns in hindsight but, even at the time, we were concerned that the orientation of the conference seemed to be one in which it was assumed that sociological research in education was something done by academics on or to those in schools. Even when notions of "life history" and "story" were raised, it was assumed that the researcher would be the person to capture and analyze someone else's life and someone else's stories; for while we talked a good deal about reflexivity, our concern was with the reflexivity of others, not our own.

While we were dimly aware of these questions, when we tried to act on our assumptions, we found this difficult to do and often fell back on ways of doing research, and a language in which to do research, that were conventional. We have subsequently addressed some of these issues (Goodson & Walker, 1991), but here we focus on the ongoing contest over telling tales about school.

In a note circulated prior to the conference we attempted to summarize our stance. We wrote:

> In essence we express a preference for studies which consider a wide context; record specifics, individualities and idiosyncrasies; and lay out multiple meanings in the documentary style Geertz has labeled "thick description". Some time ago Robert Stake made a similar case for what he called "portrayal" arguing that the evaluator often has to choose, between reporting on "what he can measure most effectively given his modest resources", and "reflecting the nature of the program, with fidelity to the many important perceptions of it". The choice it seems is between focus and fidelity: "what the evaluator has to say cannot be both a sharp analysis of high priority achievement and a broad and accurate reflection of the program's complex transactions. One message crowds out the other". (Stake, 1972)
>
> The decision to adopt analytic *or* descriptive styles (though again perhaps the distinction between them is tenuous and ultimately disappears), is not simply a technical or methodological decision, it is both political and moral. It is a decision that defines the nature of the relationship between the researcher (or evaluator) and those who are the subjects of the research. For the moment we want to note that, where analysis is usually premised upon critique, which then generates problems of legitimation; description tends to accept the status quo, concentrating on actual rather than potential meanings, and so finds itself pressed towards conservatism. We have suggested elsewhere that descriptive

methods are most appropriately used in educational situations that are likely to become dramatically worse. (Walker, 1978)

What follows is a lightly edited version of the original conference paper, in which we extend the implications of this stance. The reader may be frustrated by the lack of current references, but no doubt these will be found elsewhere in this book. Since part of our argument concerns the importance of not neglecting history, we have tried to avoid the temptation to rewrite the original text!

ETHNOGRAPHIES, CASE STUDIES, AND STORIES

One of the implications of our stance is that it draws the researcher away from the established research disciplines, not only from psychology and sociology, but to some extent away too from ethnography, history, and linguistics. And the ties that do remain tend to be technical and methodological rather than theoretical. Rather than pursuing theory, we find ourselves reclaiming some of the linguistic garbage of the social sciences; words like "narrative," "stories," "portrayal," and "pictures" are terms we find attractive.

Terry Denny (1978) has written a paper, "In Defense of Story Telling as a First Step in Educational Research," in which he distinguishes between "ethnography," "case study," and "story telling." For Denny, ethnographies are "complete accounts of some culture-sharing group" and he sets high standards for them. *Ethnographies* "must go beyond depicting what is going on. Excellent descriptive accounts of educational settings may or may not be ethnography . . . ethnography is not a reporting process . . . Ethnographic description is framed by a conceptual system believed by the writer to represent the reasons behind the way things are."

The *case study* has lower, though perhaps no less demanding, aspirations, seeking to describe (or to portray) rather than to analyze and explain but, unlike storytelling, case studies do aspire to completeness, being, in Denny's words, "intensive and complete examinations of a facet, an issue, or perhaps the events, of a geographic setting over time." *Stories*, however, "need not test theory; need not be complete; and need not be robust in either time or depth . . . simply put, if you know what the problem is you don't need a story teller . . . Story telling is unlikely to help in the creation or evaluation of educational remedies, but it can facilitate problem definition."

Despite anxiety about the classical problems raised by storytelling and by case studies (for example, in distinguishing between explanation and description, as well as the technical problems of objectivity, reliability, and validity), we confess that we find Denny's idea an attractive one. Storytelling seems to offer a kind of intermediate technology of research adapted to the study of practical problems in realistic timescales — without the prospect of 10 years' initiation among the dwindling (and probably best left alone) tribes of Primitives.

Public and Personal Meaning

For the applied researcher one of the things that appeals most about the notion of storytelling is that it seems to capture the realm of "personal" meaning, and connects it to "public" meaning. The resolution of what some anthropologists refer to as "emic" and "etic" accounts seems to us to be a theoretical issue with very important consequences for style and presentation. If emic (or insiders' or practitioners') views, realities, or definitions of situations are to be adequately dealt with by research, rather more is required than the insertion in the report of carefully trimmed and framed quotes from the subjects of the research. If the issue is taken seriously, important questions of control are raised. (We have written about these at some length elsewhere, see MacDonald & Walker, 1974; and Norris, 1977.) Unlike orthodox formats for reporting research, storytelling offers the possibility of a form that is authoritative rather than authoritarian in relation to the accounts it gives to its subjects.

For many people, a plea for a return to the journalistic level that storytelling implies will look like a regressive step. It may seem as if we wanted to turn our backs on the accumulated wisdom of the social sciences in the search of a style of description that deals only in superficialities and trivialities. We understand this reaction, but point out that we are not arguing against the social science tradition as such. In our situation, where most of our research is of an applied nature, we feel the need for the emergence of a parallel tradition that does not concern itself solely with scientific study, but attempts to confront educational phenomena more directly; attempting, in Eisner's words " . . . to create, render, portray and disclose in such a way that the reader will be able to empathetically participate in the events described" (Eisner, 1978).

Denny perhaps exacerbates the reaction in calling for stories that are "not . . . robust in time or depth," for this touches on deeply held values in the scientific community. The attraction of stories to us is that they *do* offer some sense of time and depth, but one that seems to emerge from educational events and settings. Think for a moment of the recurring stories that take place in schools, in peer group cultures, in the dynamics of classrooms and staffrooms, and in the principal's office. All these things *can* provide the data for a social science–style analysis, but whether "grounded" or "ungrounded" it seems to us that in the translation they inevitably lose some of their meaning and significance as events. Like the subjects of Paul Willis' *Learning to Labor*, we frequently find ourselves reading the data and skipping the interpretation. For the applied researcher there are always difficult calculations to be made in justifying a necessary degree of abstraction.

To go further at this point and say what we might expect from the pursuit of storytelling in educational research is difficult. To promise too much from storytelling would be a mistake, because first we have to demonstrate what is possible, learn the techniques, and make mistakes. The skills required are in many ways difficult for those of us trained in the social sciences to grasp, for they often run against the grain of all we have learned. The first thing we have to learn is how to record events, instants, interactions, places, and people in ways that make them memorable.

Images and Memories

Addressing the British Sociological Association in 1978, John Berger discussed the relationship between the photograph and the memory. He began by talking about a problem that has arisen in the historical development of photography, suggesting that since photography has created its own uses it cannot really be said to have replaced other processes (like engraving or painting) except possibly human memory. The photograph freezes the instant. But although most early photography was essentially documentary, photographs very quickly became used (in industrial countries at least) for propaganda and for advertising. In discussing this development of the uses of photographs from representation to propaganda, Berger (1978) talked about the connections between a photograph and its meanings:

> Now there are two distinct uses of photography: the private and the public. The private, that is to say, the photographs one has of the people one loves, one's friends, the class one was in at school, etc. In private use a photograph is read in a context which is still continuous with that from which it was taken . . . private photographs are nearly always of something which you have known. . . . The private context creates a continuity which is parallel to the continuity from which the photograph was originally taken. . . . By contrast public photographs are usually images of the unknown, or at best, they are images of things which are known only through other photographs. The public photograph has been severed from life when it was taken, and it remains, as an isolated image, separate from your experience. The public photograph is like the memory of a total stranger, a total stranger who has shouted "Look" at the event recorded.

Berger's distinction between private and public photographs raises the question as to whether it is possible to extend the use of personal meaning into the public domain. Can experience be recorded in ways that make it accessible to others? Is it possible to learn from the recorded experience of others, and if so what can be learned and how?

Even if these things are possible (and the enterprise is surely fraught with difficulties of both moral and technical kinds), the analogy suggests a way forward, for by beginning to make research and evaluation a personal and even a private enterprise, a service to the institution and to the person rather than to the research community, it might be possible to unify the worlds of research and of practice. The essential point concerns, not kinds of information, but the structure of the channels through which information travels. Research creates information, and usually that information is about the relatively powerless, or those with low status in the system, and for the relatively powerful, or high status. When we talk about connecting private and public worlds we mean this in the sense of creating new channels of communication or of revising existing channels.

Quality and the Qualitative

What we have said might be seen simply as a plea for more qualitative or descriptive studies but when we look at the reporting of qualitative data in educational research and evaluation studies, what we often see is usually something equivalent to Berger's notion of the "public" photograph. Utterances are frozen, extracted from their sequence and setting and pinned to the text. They manipulate memory rather than prompting it. The context which gives the quotes meaning comes, not primarily from the data, or even from the researcher's interaction with the setting and the subject, but almost entirely from the culture of the researcher. A context is provided, but it is one that is alienated from the world of the subject. The researcher, like Berger's public photographer, is the stranger who shouts "Look!"

This is not to deny the value of qualitative research; few would doubt that Whyte, Becker, Jackson, Willis, and many others have important things to say. But it is to set extremely high standards for such research in terms of criteria that are elusive and subtle. The essential distinction is that the best of this research enters the world of the subjects and presents it to the outside with understanding and sensitivity, increasing the potential competence of the reader who enters similar situations. Dangers arise when the researcher relies on the extracted and reported speech of commentators who interpret the word of the subjects from an external point of view. When such data are used merely to illustrate points of interpretation they begin to look like the public photograph used for propaganda.

Again we stress that this is not an area of absolutes. We are not making claims for a noninterpretative, empirical science, but merely pointing to an area where difficult judgments are made. And these judgments cannot be entirely prespecified, especially in any form of fieldwork. Inevitably the distinction between "outsider" and "insider" changes as the research progresses. Labov, for instance, suggests that the interviewer is likely to ask different kinds of questions as he or she knows more:

> An initial question, "Do you play the numbers?" would thus give way to "Did you ever hit big?" In talking to deer hunters, an initial question such as "Where do you aim?" would give way to "Is it worth trying a rump shot?" As the outsider gradually becomes an insider, the quality of the speech obtained and the speaker's involvement in it rises steadily. A field worker who stays outside his subject, and deals with it as a mere excuse for eliciting language, will get very little for his pains. Almost any question can be answered with no more information than was contained in it. When the speaker does give more, it is a gift, drawn from some general fund of good will that is held in trust by himself and the field worker. A deep knowledge implies a deep interest, and in payment for that interest the speaker may give more than anyone has a right to expect. (Labov, 1972, pp. 114–115)

We have arrived at an essential dilemma, which is in part social and cultural, for the researcher confuses the accepted grammar of social conduct; but in negotiating the situations that result from such research relationships moral dilemmas are never far from the surface. Acting both as "stranger" and "friend" (in Hortense Powdermaker's [1967] terms) is to exploit gaps in the rules that govern interaction, creating problems for the research ("every nth person cannot be a friend," as Dollard put it), but also raising questions about the research enterprise itself. Like Berger's public photographers, researchers who set out on a qualitative or descriptive study are in a precarious position for they are always in danger of using others to build the world in their own image, and often in a form suited to public consumption.

Returning directly to the analogy with photography it is evident that similar issues of exploitation arise there, especially in social reporting, and that their appearance is no recent phenomenon. Humphrey Spender (1977), for example, seriously pursued the notion of "entry into the world of the subject," and was aware of the insider/outsider dilemma and the ethical questions this raised:

> I think you'll find that Tom [Harrison] has made a revealing comment somewhere about the possibility of getting inside people's homes and of course the main difficulty was always that once you got inside somebody's house then you

were no longer taking an unobserved photograph, so that necessarily the whole process was long-winded and would have taken a long time—one would have to become part of the family . . . also there was a feeling that people who are in impoverished circumstances, people who were out of work, simply did not like their fate exposed, in many ways the photograph would have been an exploitation. This was something I felt very keenly.

Spender's success in gaining access to the moods and moments of his subjects' world is well illustrated in his pictures of Wigan and Bolton in the interwar years. His subjects' reactions is often clear too—as in the picture, taken in a Bolton pub, with the "subject" holding up his hands to try and block the intrusive eye of the camera. Spender's response was often reciprocal, for on a number of occasions he refused to use "scoop" pictures he had taken on newspaper assignments out of a sense of responsibility to his subjects.

On the whole, we tend to feel that photographers, perhaps because of the nature of their medium, are rather sensitive to the subject's view of the photographer and what the process of having the picture taken means in their lives. Researchers, on the other hand, are not very good at documenting this reflexivity. Perhaps, in part, this is because the techniques of research make it easier to hide the moral issue behind the veil of anonymity. Spender's picture is simply one example extracted from a long stylistic tradition in photography, but it is difficult to isolate comparable examples from our traditions of social reportage and analysis. Exceptions include Paul Willis's (1977) Appendix to *Learning to Labor* and Peter Fensham and Lawrence Ingvarson's (1977) study of two contrasting classroom observers. As researchers, we tend to concentrate on describing our own motives and experiences, and seeing other people's actions in terms of generalized problems like "access," "rapport," or "publication." Consult any text on fieldwork methods and terms like this abound, but since Whyte, it is rare to find studies in which the subjects of the research emerge from the reports as people with their own strong and coherent view of the research enterprise. The usual reaction we have to descriptive accounts is that the writer is portrayed as hero. Situations are depicted in ways that present the researcher as the most perceptive and intelligent person there and the only one not vulnerable to false consciousness.

TOWARD AN ETHNOGRAPHY OF ETHNOGRAPHY

We find this significant at a level beyond that of the techniques of fieldwork. In part, it is a question of individual research styles, but more importantly it relates to the culture of research. It may not be simply because of *his* of *her* culture and methods of reportage that the researcher builds the world "in his or her own image"; more likely it is because, like the man's obstructive hands in Spender's photograph, access to the subjects' world has been denied the researcher.

The researcher can only start, and end, at a negotiated stance with his or her own perspective. But such a stance is not only an intellectual position, for it enters the situation under study as perceived authority. The access that *is* granted to the researcher is always to a fragment, and perhaps sometimes to a figment, and often this negotiation between researcher and subject as to what will be revealed amounts to collusion. As a teacher said to one of our research students who was patiently negotiating his way into a school, "Don't worry. Just stay out of my way and I'll make sure you get what you need for your thesis!"

Academic conferences are good places to identify those elements in the style and culture of the researcher that lead him or her in almost all educational settings to the assumption of, or relegation to, the role of "expert" (with all the authoritarian connotations that carries) or to the role of "stranger." Ask yourselves! Are the researchers we are, the people we are? Both the roles of expert and stranger, of course, present severe barriers to anyone aspiring to enter the consciousness of their subjects, and to see the world from their point of view; the fact that we have been pupils and teachers ourselves does not necessarily make things any easier.

We emphasize yet again that we do not see this as simply a technical question or as one with absolute solutions, it is both a moral and political dilemma facing us each time we engage in research. It touches on the rights and duties that the researcher owes to others in exchange for the freedom and license allowed in the role. More widely, it touches on the mainstream of a current critical theme in our societies which concerns how professionals relate simultaneously to their subjects and to other interest groups, including those who employ them.

Closer to home, we note a strong isomorphism between the relationship of researcher to teacher, and that of teacher to pupil. In both cases, there is marked imbalance in the power to control knowledge, especially in the sense of defining realities, as well as a strong resistance in the motivations of the subject. Extending the analogy further we see, for researchers, strong warning signs over attempts to innovate and construct alternatives to the dominant style of the relationship where these touch on questions of power and authority. It is just as naive for researchers to think that they can simply hand over control of research to their subjects as it is for teachers to hand over the curriculum to their pupils. Fraternization in order to gain access to the world of the other easily becomes, not simply a flight from responsibility, but a flight from self-identity. Yet we often find ourselves in situations where, to fully be ourselves would be to sabotage the research enterprise. It is a difficult social and cultural calculus we constantly need to make. Examination of progressive practice in teaching, we believe, reveals several examples of teachers who have attempted to desert their roles in an attempt to enter the culture of their pupils, and who have mostly failed. Examples of "going native" in research are perhaps rarer because innovation and experimentation in research are more unusual than they are in teaching.

The problem for the researcher, as we see it, is to retain a hold on specialized interests and areas of expertise in ways that avoid the temptation, indeed the expectation, that this legitimates control over information and its interpretation. We have to learn to be accountable to those we research at all stages of the enterprise, and to expect our motives to be questioned more openly. It will not be easy for we have a lot to learn, and we need to recognize that it is not only the culture of research that creates inequalities of information control and its interpretation. Patterns of specialization, deference to science, and perceived authority are all ingredients in a situation that precedes us, but which by our actions we often compound.

REFERENCES

Berger, J. (1978). Ways of remembering. *Camerawork, 10.*

Bohm, D. (1974). Science as perception-communication. In F. Suppe (Ed.), *The structure of scientific theories* (pp. 374–391). Urbana: University of Illinois Press.

Denny, T. (1978). *In defense of story telling as a first step in educational research.* Paper presented at the International Reading Association Conference, Houston.

Eisner, E. (1978). Humanistic trends and the curriculum field. *Journal of Curriculum Studies, 10*(3), 197–204.

Fensham, P., & Ingvarson, L. (1977). *Case study research in science classrooms.* Paper presented at the meeting of Australian Association for Research in Education, Canberra, Australia.

Goodson, I. (1993). *School subjects and curriculum change.* London, UK: Falmer Press.

Goodson, I. F., & Walker, R. (1991). *Biography, identity and schooling: Episodes in educational research.* London: Falmer Press.

Labov, W. (1972). Some principles of linguistic methodology. *Language in Society, 1,* 97–120.

MacDonald, B., & Walker, R. (Eds.). (1974). SAFARI 1. *Innovation, evaluation, research and the problem of control* [mimeograph]. CARE.

Norris N. (Ed.). (1977). SAFARI 2. *Theory into practice* [mimeograph]. CARE.

Powdermaker, H. (1967). *Stranger and friend: The way of an anthropologist.* London: Secker & Warburg.

Spender, H. (1977). *Worktown photographs of Bolton and Blackpool taken for mass observation* 1937/8, University of Sussex.

Stake, R. (1972, April). *An approach to the evaluation of instructional programs (program portrayal vs. analysis)*. Paper presented at the annual meeting of the American Educational Research Association, Chicago.

Walker, R. (1978). The conduct of educational case studies: Ethics, procedures, theory. In D. Hamilton & B. Dockerell (Eds.), *Rethinking educational research* (pp. 30–63). Hodder & Stoughton.

Willis, P. E. (1977). *Learning to labour*. Farnborough, UK: Saxon House.

Woods, P. (Ed.). (1980a). *Pupil strategies*. London: Croom Helm.

Woods, P. (Ed.). (1980b). *Teacher strategies*. London: Croom Helm.

CHAPTER 12

Stories of Teaching as Tragedy and Romance

WHEN EXPERIENCE BECOMES TEXT

Robert J. Graham

> Cultures do provide specific types of plots for adoption by its members
> in their configuration of self. Although the content of each life is unique
> to a person, it can share the characteristics of a general plot outline.
> —Donald Polkinghorne, 1988,
> *Narrative Knowing and the Human Sciences*

Anyone who has spent time in a school staffroom or attended a teachers'
conference will need little convincing that teachers are inveterate tellers of
stories. Whether teachers tell stories about themselves and their professional experiences more often than firemen, nurses, lawyers, construction
workers, or computer programmers, I have no way of knowing. But as
Maxine Greene observes, at all levels of education "The sounds of storytelling are everywhere today" (1991, p. ix). Teachers and administrators,
undergraduate and graduate students alike are telling anecdotes and stories
of their experiences of schooling, a collective narrative enterprise for which
there are as many justifications as there are individual lives and stories (Ball
& Goodson, 1985; Witherell & Noddings, 1991). One commonly voiced
justification for this narrative outpouring is that teachers, dealing as they
do with the development and nurturing of young minds, ought at least to
have more than a rudimentary understanding of who they are and how they
have become who they are. These basic ontological concerns with being

and becoming, with growth and change, are inevitably linked to matters of personal and professional identity, and, especially for many women teachers, to the recovery or discovery of their personal and professional voices (Pagano, 1990). Yet as one might suspect, developing self-understanding and an image of oneself as an individual-in-process is neither instantaneous nor without its risks. We all require, as Charles Taylor has put it, "time and many incidents to sort out what is relatively fixed and stable in [our] character, temperament, and desires, from what is variable and changing" (1989, p. 50). And as Taylor goes on to point out, "[Self]-understanding necessarily has temporal depth and incorporates narrative" (p. 50).

However, in spite of the difficulties incurred by biographical and autobiographical approaches to teaching (Graham, 1991) and by narrative inquiry as a research methodology (Connelly & Clandinin, 1991), a link has been clearly established in the minds of teachers and researchers between the telling of stories and the exploration and development of personal and professional voice and identity. And yet what too often gets overlooked in discussions on the place of narrative in education is that the stories and images of teaching that reach public consciousness and that draw the greatest critical attention, are not the fleeting anecdotes or cautionary tales uttered over coffee in the staffroom, but written accounts of teaching, "frozen texts" constructed in particular ways and for specific purposes by human acts of intention. The contours of this public textual territory and the stories and images of teaching it contains have been shaped over time by a variety of forms: novels, films, ethnographies, dissertations, biographies, autobiographies, and the stories of the "new journalism." Whatever the forms are, however, they engage in a process of representing experience in text, a process that calls into play a battery of literary and rhetorical considerations of which most of us are unaware as we sit talking around the table. Consequently, to evince a concern for *how* the multiple images and stories of teaching that circulate in our culture have been constructed by writers both inside and outside the academy, is to show an interest in a rhetoric of inquiry. It is, in Simons' (1990) words, to show "how rhetorical choices function to conceal or reveal, magnify or minimize, simplify or complicate, link or divide, elevate or degrade, sharpen images or blur them" (p. 10).

This concern with a rhetoric of inquiry in education can be linked to a general movement within the social sciences for becoming more self-reflexive over how rhetorical and narrative conventions inform the writing of what White (1978) has called "fictions of factual representation" (p. 121). For if it is true as Nelson, Megill, and McCloskey (1987) believe that "the social sciences float in warm seas of unexamined rhetoric" (p. 16), then greater attention must be paid to the specifically literary, rhetorical, and ideological features of the growing number of published case studies, ethnographies, and narratives by and about teachers that make up the corpus of texts that Schubert and Ayers (1992) have taken to calling "teacher lore."[1] Likewise, if we adopt the constructivist view that language constitutes reality rather than simply reflects it, a rhetorical approach to the stories of teacher lore fulfills two important purposes. First, according to Simons (1990), rhetorical analyses "determine how constructions of 'the real' are made persuasive" (p. 11); and second, rhetorical theory serves as "a storehouse of codified ways of thinking, seeing, and communicating that may be tested for their goodness-of-fit to the matter at hand, and which, once applied to particular cases, provide exemplars for subsequent analyses" (p. 11).

Consequently, this chapter will take as its working examples two stories from the annals of teacher lore, stories written for an audience larger than a dissertation committee, the kind of texts that have "[made] it out of specialized, intellectual bookstores and into regular bookstores" (Schubert, 1992, p. 141). I want to consider separately Jonathan Kozol's autobiographical story of teaching, *Death at an Early Age* (1967) and new journalist Samuel G. Freedman's recent investigative biography *Small Victories* (1990). By uncovering some of the major literary and cultural codes and conventions that these writers have drawn on in order to provide their stories of teaching with much of their persuasive power, I want to demonstrate the extent to which teachers inherit as well as create many of the stories that help us imagine the possibilities and disclose the constraints in the institutional world of teaching. In addition, I want to claim that a rhetorical approach to texts like these from the popular literature of teacher lore will open up fresh sources of dialogue among the growing number of educators interested in the place story and narrative occupies or might be made to occupy, in education. For I am convinced that a concern with how various writers have elected to inscribe in the public consciousness images of teachers, students, and schools, is a political issue of continuing relevance to our profession. If storytelling is as central to the conduct of life as the editors of this volume argue in their introduction, and if story is the medium through which we construct as well as understand our personal and professional lives, then it clearly matters how stories of teaching are told, which stories are told, and who gets to tell them.

TEACHING AND TRAGEDY:
WORKING "BETWEEN GOOD AND EVIL"

In the course of discussing some of the books which appeared in the late 1960s criticizing the state of American public schools, educational historian Diane Ravitch devotes one sentence to summarizing Jonathan Kozol's contribution to that debate, *Death at an Early Age* (1967). She writes, "Kozol, whose book won the National Book Award, recounted a year in a school where the teachers were racist, cruel, and contemptuous of the children" (1983, p. 236). As a verbal brushstroke on the larger canvas of her own historical narrative this is accurate enough, but she declines to elaborate that a major source of the book's success at arousing public indignation and at putting a human face on the inequities of a segregated system of public education can be directly attributed to the book's specifically literary qualities. In particular, Kozol's autobiographical testimony achieves its effectiveness as literature by relying primarily on what White (1973) calls "explanation by emplotment" (p. 7), defining "emplotment" as "the way by which a sequence of events fashioned into a story is gradually revealed to be a story *of a particular kind* [emphasis added]" (p. 7). Therefore, to tell us what "really happened" during the time he taught a racially segregated fourth-grade class in Roxbury, Massachusetts, and to transform the autobiographical facts of his experience into text, Kozol first engages in a "prefigurative" act of imaginative consciousness, an act in which as a writer he "both creates the object of his analysis and predetermines the modality of the conceptual strategies he will use to explain it" (White, 1973, p. 31). Kozol alludes to this process in the foreword to his book. There, he tells us that after he had made an initial attempt at putting his handwritten and random jottings "into some sort of shape and sequence" (p. xi), he "began to see for the first time the overall outline of this book" (p. xi) as subsequent and unexpected events took place at his school. Thus in the process of selecting incidents for their typicality and of transforming chronology into story, Kozol's story moves backwards and forwards in narrative time and by so doing provides a causal and explanatory framework which guides and limits the interpretive range of significance Kozol wishes us to ascribe to these events. As I will show, Kozol's allegory of the besieged liberal conscience constructs an image of the teacher as ethical Manichean, a person continually suspended between good and evil, caught between the guilt of helping to maintain the existing conditions of oppression within the school, and the fear of speaking out against the entrenched racism of a segregated system of public education.

In his prefatory note "To the Reader," Kozol provides a broad hint which invites us to consider his book as a mixture of fact and fiction, part reportage, part literary allegory: "With the exception of certain named public figures, characters in this book do not have counterparts in real life" (p. x). Thus we meet the historically identifiable members of the Boston Education Committee, Mrs. Hicks, Walter Ohrenberger, and Joseph Lee, but we also meet the Art Teacher, the Math Teacher, and the Reading Teacher, emblematic characters in Kozol's local morality play of racism and prejudice, a narrative which only begins to take on an expanded symbolic significance when read against the political background of the civil rights movement, the slaying of the Reverend Reeb in Selma, Alabama, and the visit to Boston by Martin Luther King.

On one level, then, Kozol's autobiographical act of transforming experience into text constitutes what Hart (1970) has termed "a drama of intention" (p. 492), an autobiographical narrative which consists of a "fluctuating mixture of confession, apology, and memoir" (p. 488). In addition, a narrative like Kozol's which explores the dialectical interplay between biography and situation also directs attention to the figurative force of its incidents as synecdoche, a rhetorical strategy in which the characteristics of the whole may be discovered or thrown into relief in the specifics of the part. In other words, by centripetally evoking for a reader the microcosm of his school and by describing how everything from textbooks to systems of punishment help to maintain existing hierarchies of power, Kozol also brings to mind the *other world* of society at large where the differences between *here* and *there* are only differences in degree not in kind.

One immediate implication of Kozol's narrative construction of events is that the scenes that are being enacted daily on the smaller stage of Kozol's segregated elementary classroom are being simultaneously played out with a different cast of characters on the larger stage of the national theater of events. As the drama in his own school and classroom unfolds, Kozol discovers to his chagrin as a liberal, white male, that he not only shoulders personal responsibility for keeping in place an unequal form of education, but that he and his African-American are in fact both prisoners and victims of "the system" itself. Stricken by conscience, he unburdens himself one evening to his friends, shares his hesitation about "braving the certain hostility of other teachers" (p. 124) at his school, about his feelings of having been "appropriated by the Reading Teacher and the Art Teacher," and of being continually "stifled and suppressed" (p. 124). When challenged to take action, Kozol joins a protest rally, only to find himself arrested for civil disobedience and thrown into jail.

If Kozol had been intent on writing a different kind of narrative, this event might have signified that a heightened consciousness (or guilty conscience) is one of the necessary preconditions for taking personal political action, for breaking out of the position of victim and of beginning to take hold of one's destiny. But Kozol's story is not at bottom a story of liberation, of victory and transcendence over the world of experience; this is no *Pilgrim's Progress* or Grail legend with Kozol in the role of Christian or Percival. Kozol's literary antecedents and models are at the same time both Sophoclean and Shakespearean. With appropriate irony, it is not Kozol's gross act of civil disobedience that is responsible for his dismissal from the school, but an act of pedagogical hubris: Kozol challenges the system by teaching African-American poet Langston Hughes' "Ballad of the Landlord" to his class of predominantly African-American children. In the furor that follows Kozol's dismissal for not teaching from the prescribed course of study, for not teaching poetry that "accentuates the positive" (p. 202) and does not dwell with honesty on the suffering of African Americans, Kozol literally becomes the scapegoat, an outcast on whom his fellow teachers and the representatives of the all-white Board of Education heap their collective wrath.

In breaching the accepted conventions of teaching, Kozol not only afforded his students the opportunity to respond to a poem that reflected many of the concerns in their own lives, he also created the conditions for a critical literacy in his students, a verbal outpouring that the Reading Teacher believed could only have been achieved by Kozol's having "induced" or "planted" (p. 164) the word pictures in his students' heads. The crackpot sense of optimism that the Reading Teacher had worked so hard to develop throughout her own career was a cornerstone in a pedagogy of "persuasive enthusiasm" (p. 167), a pedagogy in which she overcame student resistance by the sheer force of her personality. Kozol's actions challenged and exposed this pedagogy as inauthentic, since the responses of Kozol's students to his teaching make it clear that only a pedagogy that demands "[h]onest writing and private feeling" can be the starting point in the teaching of English, as well as "the first place where the world outside and the word within the classroom ought to eloquently coexist" (p. 170).

But Kozol pays a heavy price for letting the world inside the classroom and for getting the word outside into the world. The aim of Kozol's project is not to reconcile inside and outside, to merge and to celebrate the adjustment of the students to their environment through the power of literacy. Kozol's aim, along with the other so-called "Romantic" critics of education at that time (Graubard, 1972), was to transform existing educational arrangements, in particular to dissolve the pernicious untruth promulgated by members of the Boston Education Committee like Joseph Lee that only in a racially segregated public system of elementary education could African-American children enter into secondary education "with every sense of the worth of themselves and confidence in their competence to meet life's problems" (Kozol, 1967, p. 110).

In several key chapters, Kozol's narrative explores the contradictions of trying to teach in an ethically defensible manner when confronted daily by the cynicism and doublespeak of administrators like Joseph Lee and the genteel racism of colleagues like the Reading Teacher. In the circumscribed world of the Boston public school system, Evil is alive and well and thoroughly capable of disguising its true intentions in dissimulative speech and actions. As the ethical Manichean, Kozol is compelled to rationalize a course of action for himself in the space created between acknowledging the pervasiveness of the institutional forces at work in the school and his developing feelings of responsibility for his students. In this situation, the ethical Manichean is compelled to "turn whatever talent he has . . . to the service of the good *as he sees it*" (White, 1973, p. 228). The good as Kozol sees it is to replace the "cheery," "hopeful," and "optimistic" (p. 174) sentiments of the literature his students were required to read and memorize from the course of study with stories and poems which might evoke an "honest reaction" (p. 176) rather than replicate the canned responses from a list of adjectives preselected and approved by the teacher. Consequently, Kozol enters the lists by default as the champion of a pedagogy of personal engagement and voice against the inauthentic pedagogy of feigned enthusiasm with its literature of sentiment and the moral touchstone. But even though his students' writing provides eloquent testimony to the effectiveness of this approach, a sense of doom hangs over the narrative, since Kozol has challenged the system at its most vulnerable point, and like Leviathan, what the system cannot absorb or accommodate, it finds some way to reject.

Throughout this analysis, I have been claiming that in making the transition from experience to text, Kozol prefigured his autobiographical narrative as a story of a particular kind, in this instance as tragedy, an allegory of good and evil in which, as the fools and prisoners of time and circumstance, Kozol and his students share a common identity and fate. And yet, even though Kozol suffers the mental anguish of trying to teach in an authentic manner under nightmarish conditions of chaos and cynical misrule, his articulation of the relationship between the events he narrates does not wholly deny the possibility that there is no way out, that he and his students are mere victims at the mercy of forces over which they have no control. Although the workings of the educational machine keep on inexorably turning, committed only to maintaining the social status quo, Kozol's story proclaims that individual teachers committed to practices that confront rather than gloss over the particularity and situatedness of their students' lives will discover for themselves the existential and essential truth that they can make a difference. And yet, as tragic realist, Kozol also dramatizes the constant state of tension that exists when teachers are compelled to live out their professional lives under the surveillance of a malign and spiteful bureaucracy.

Kozol's story of teaching emplotted as tragedy is a story whose outcome appears to support the conclusion that individual action might seem to count for little in the face of such overwhelming and ineluctable forces and odds. And certainly, Kozol neither minimizes the risks involved nor underestimates the depth and strength of the resistance to individuals who choose to work outside the approved curriculum. But the bureaucratic effort at placing moral blinkers on its teachers ironically becomes a source of insight for a teacher like Kozol. In discovering who he is or might be as a teacher, Kozol risks one publicly approved version of himself and in the process discovers a more authentic source of selfhood. By risking little, both the Reading Teacher and the Art Teacher attempt to construct the plots of their own stories of teaching as comedies, stories which leave unquestioned and undisturbed the workings of power in school and in society. The outcome of Kozol's story fills us with pity and with fear; it interrogates the grounds upon which education as a project of human transformation is built and compels us to justify our attitude towards it and our position in it. For some of us it may feel uncomfortable or even extravagant to begin thinking about teachers and teaching in these dramatic terms. However, as one of the exemplary narratives that we have inherited from the literature of teacher lore, the image of schools, teachers, and teaching dramatized in Kozol's story retains a considerable power to disturb, challenge, and inspire.

TEACHING AS ROMANCE: REWRITING THE QUEST MYTH

In the same way that Kozol constructed out of the facts of his own experience a story of teaching emplotted as tragedy, I believe Samuel Freedman's (1990) contemporary story of teaching deploys the structure of romance to different representational but quite similar ideological effects and ends. My analysis will show how a major source of his story's rhetorical power can be derived from a greater understanding of the structural features of romance as a form of quest myth.[2] Thus, as Kozol appropriated many of the features of tragedy in order to endow his experiences with ideological currency and narrative significance, Freedman has turned to the structure of romance in order to shape his observations of his subject's life inside and outside the classroom into a culturally familiar and equally recognizable story form. The subject of Freedman's story is Jessica Siegal, a high school teacher of English and journalism at Seward High School on the Lower East Side of New York. In his investigation, Freedman clearly did not wish to restrict himself to recording behaviors observed only in the classroom, but includes separate analyses and descriptions of Jessica's family, colleagues, friends, and former teachers, as well as lengthy excursions into the background histories and present circumstances of her favorite and problem students. As Freedman states, "I wanted to explore a community" (1990, p. 6).

When making his case for considering the structure of romance as central to an understanding of literature as a whole, literary theorist Northrop Frye proposed that there were only four narrative movements possible in all of literature.

> First, the descent from a higher world; second, the descent to a lower world; third, the ascent from a lower world; and fourth, the ascent to a higher world. All stories in literature are complications of, or metaphorical derivations from, these four narrative radicals. (Frye, 1976, p. 97)

For romance, in particular, ascent and descent are already foregrounded, since a romance typically begins with a break in consciousness, often signaled by sleeping, dreaming, or forgetting. It is not surprising, then, that Freedman begins his own secular romance of Jessica's journey through the school year with her literally awakening from a bad dream at 4:30 a.m. on the first day of school. Jessica suffers from the kind of free-floating anxiety experienced by many teachers as they mentally rehearse the start of the new school year and as they imagine into being a sequence of different plots and outcomes derived from their interpretation of previous experiences of teaching. As another chapter in her life as a teacher begins while her classroom fills up with a new cast of characters whose individual autobiographies she will come to know (and will help to rewrite), Jessica is portrayed as a woman who has written and revised roles for herself from the raw material of her own autobiography.

For Jessica Siegal, it took "years to develop a classroom presence that felt organic . . . she created from pieces of herself a *persona* that might best be called The Tough Cookie" (Freedman, 1990, p. 29). The classroom persona that she has constructed for herself by drawing on a reservoir of past experience, knowledge, and beliefs, is a response to the realities of surviving as a woman in classroom situations which all too often are uncomfortable and threatening. At 5'3", Jessica is physically small in stature and therefore has learned to develop alternative approaches for maintaining order and for holding her students' attention by becoming a skilled "reader" of her students' moods. And although it is clear that these expressions of personal practical knowledge (Connelly & Clandinin, 1987) can be found in teachers everywhere regardless of gender, their importance here derives from their function in the narrative as reminders that in reading about how this woman has responded bodily and psychologically to her experience, we are also reading a particular kind of story.

Jessica has been compelled to incorporate into her gestural repertoire techniques and ways of behaving that do not come naturally in an effort to compensate for the "natural" authority some men are said to command by virtue of their physical stature. Frye, drawing on the distinction he finds in Dante between force and guile (*forza* and *froda*), argues that women in romances often have to rely heavily on the latter characteristic in order to survive. As Balfour (1988) puts it in discussing Frye's conception of *froda*, "This distinction in genre . . . turns in part on a distinction in gender. Since female characters typically have less force at their disposal . . . they are forced to rely on fraud, guile, craft, and cunning" (p. 58). While none of these characteristics is exclusively female, they are foregrounded in romance, where, unlike the women in tragedies who tend to be victims, in many romances women generally play more forceful roles. And yet, as Balfour rightly goes on to point out, romance itself "is by no means a monument to women's liberation. Romance is . . . very much the product of a 'male-dominated world,' with all its attendant double standards and strategies of oppression" (1988, pp. 58–59).

Nevertheless, what an initial reading of Jessica as the heroine of this secular romance does accomplish is to draw emblematic attention to the well-established fact that the teaching profession by and large is still the particular province of women. This fact is reinforced when Freedman shows us Jessica standing in her bedroom in front of the loom on which she had begun weaving a shawl for her mother. "Now that school has started, she worries that the shawl will lie suspended in the wooden frame for weeks and months, like Penelope's winding sheet, forever unfinished" (Freedman, 1990, p. 43). During the term, Jessica puts her private life virtually "on hold," as grading assignments, preparing lessons, and becoming more deeply involved in her students' lives consumes a disproportionate amount of her time and attention.

In this respect, Freedman creates some of his story's most memorable scenes by showing how Jessica's imaginative descent into the often nightmarish world of her students' life histories, laid out for her in her students' journals and autobiographies, is also the occasion for some serious acts of self-appraisal. These descents into knowledge of her students' fractured lives are mirrored in the narrative by parallel descents into her reflections on the romance of her own biography. As Balfour (1988) puts it, "all romances hold up a broken mirror, a mirror in which a reader glimpses . . . him- or her-self caught in a romantic act" (p. 65). For if, as Jessica reminds her students, "Memory plus distance equals true autobiography" (Freedman, 1990, p. 51), then Jessica herself (and we as readers) takes part in a similar kind of quest as her students in the pursuit of self-knowledge. And yet, at the same time as Jessica remains open to becoming emotionally involved in her students' lives, like Kozol she also comes to realize how deeply ironic the quest for identity truly is in a society still shot through with the contradictions of race, class, and gender. Both Jessica and Kozol provide classroom environments for their students to explore these contradictions, knowing full well the dangers, understanding how difficult the task is of transcending the accidents of birth and social positioning. In this respect, both stories of teaching shift continually "between the two poles of myth and irony, the ideal and the real, always containing both" (Hamilton, 1991, p. 140).

But discovering an appropriate form in which to represent these tensions and contradictions often causes writers to construct stories whose endings involve readers in making some subtle and difficult distinctions. For example, if a story is narratively structured as a romantic comedy it foreshadows a comic resolution, that is, a resolution where an individual's quest results in the recognition of a new identity. Yet, even with this new identity, there is the residual feeling that the individual will remain enclosed within the strictures and constraints of society as it currently exists. If, however, stories are encoded as comic romances, if their protagonists are represented as psychologically empowered through having ascended from the quest for self-knowledge, this narrative movement promotes a concern for the transformation of consciousness as a necessary condition for transcendence. "Comedy remains within the cycle of nature; romance transcends it, for in escaping from ordinary reality, the hero and heroine return to a higher reality" (Hamilton, 1991, p. 142). Nowhere is this tension between accepting reality and longing for transcendence dramatized more clearly as when Jessica Siegel discusses *The Great Gatsby* with her high school seniors.

Jessica begins her yearly exploration of the American Dream always fearful that the message of Fitzgerald's novel might prove altogether too bleak and daunting for most of her students, whose dreams, like those of Kozol's students, are continually deferred. As she surveys her class of "new Americans and native-born outcasts" (Freedman, 1990, p. 244), Jessica knows that "[g]eography and pigmentation may set them apart, but their aspirations are fundamentally Gatsby's, to transcend the bondage of birth and class" (p. 244). Jessica worries that the initial seductiveness of Gatsby's charm will be confounded at the end for her students by his deceit and ethically dubious dealings. From previous experience she knows that in any discussion of the final chapters "the silence can be funereal" (p. 245). Consequently, Jessica approaches the last lesson on *Gatsby* fretting that the ending will stun them into silence. But the voice of reason in Jessica's class is Lun Cheung, a former street-gang member, a peasant boy from China now for a time imaginatively caught up in the fate of Jay Gatsby. Lun Cheung's judgment of Gatsby shows Jessica that her fears for the corruption of her students' basic sensibilities may have been unwarranted. "It doesn't matter if he was a crook . . . he was a genuine person. And genuine is genuine" (p. 257).

But if her students' youthful idealism and belief in the persistence of the

American Dream works to reassure Jessica that the kids are all right and
that some will go on to distinguish themselves, she is not blind to the
obstacles that still must be overcome for even a few to pursue their dreams.
In the face of chronic economic disadvantage, what route to personal fulfillment can Jessica hold out to Lun Cheung and the others? The route that
represents "a kind of Grail" (p. 295) for these youthful questers is to gain a
scholarship and admission to a college or university. Thus Jessica finds
herself thinking as she prepares to accompany four of her students on an
odyssey to upstate New York and a meeting with a university admissions
officer, "*How many . . . [c]an you save?* (p. 335). Jessica perceives her job
as one of "salvage and reclamation" (p. 337); she believes strongly in the
part she must play in this social rescue mission and in the necessity of
making sure her students receive a higher education. Jessica's espousal of
the "solution" of higher education derives less from any abstract philosophical position than from her response to the harsh pragmatics of urban life.
"The only choices that awaited her students, if she could not hurl them
into college, were the menial rungs of the service economy . . . garment
sweatshops, or the lucrative trade of selling drugs" (p. 354). The grail of
higher education may be chimerical and as hard to achieve as ever, but for
Jessica it is still the only goal worth striving for. If she must deal in "selective
truth" (p. 337), or indulge in creative circumlocution when pleading her
students' case with the admissions officer, for her these are simply the
necessary actions in a situational ethic where responsibility to her students
is its first operating principle.

A RHETORIC OF NARRATIVE FORM

In this chapter, I have offered analyses of Kozol's and Freedman's
narratives that take it as axiomatic that as writers, each has derived the
form and shape of their stories of teaching from the displaced structure of
tragedy and romance respectively. As organizing principles around which
the central features of their stories are crystallized, I have shown how both
writers have persuaded us of the plausibility of their portraits of teaching
by evoking images deeply embedded in our psyches as readers, archetypal
images "which may have been developed in the aesthetic realm of literature"
(Harrell & Lingkugel, 1980, p. 411). As part of their rhetoric of reaffirma-
tion, Kozol and Freedman have relied on our awareness of these archetypal
images in order to reinforce the perception that they are also telling particular kinds of stories, stories whose social function is to revitalize neglected
aspects of teachers' work. It would now seem pertinent to inquire into the

extent to which Kozol's and Freedman's aesthetic choices are also the most effective rhetorically for enacting their various ideological commitments and intentions. Fittingly enough, the inquiry into the degree of congruence between rhetoric, genre, and ideology, raises the issue of whether these aesthetic choices imply an identifiable politics. For clearly, any inquiry into the rhetoric and politics of narrative form entails important consequences for all writers and researchers on education who are moving towards narrative modes of inquiry.

In offering a way to begin thinking about the ideological implications of historical texts, White (1973) draws on the distinction he finds in Karl Mannheim's *Ideology and Utopia* between "situationally congruent" and "situationally transcendent" ideologies (p. 68). The former are "generally accepting of the social status quo" (p. 68), while the latter are "critical of the status quo and oriented towards its transformation or dissolution" (p. 68). In this respect, the resolutions of both Kozol's and Freedman's stories are situationally transcendent, although the final mood or tone of each is in keeping with the overall atmosphere developed throughout the course of the narrative. Jessica voluntarily resigns from Seward High as a way of allowing her to concentrate her energy into finding alternative ways to help students succeed. In Freedman's words, "she feels a twinge, but not a big one. She never wanted to be the solitary heroine; she never wanted to be the last of the just. She only wanted to be part of something" (1990, p. 418). Jessica's desire to be part of something, in particular to be part of a larger movement for social justice, has taken Jessica from radical journalist in the 1970s to subversive amanuensis on behalf of her minority students in the late 1980s. The sites of Jessica's activities may have altered but she cannot shake her commitment to getting her students to conceive of their lives as a continuing process of self-renewal, to conceive of themselves as capable of writing themselves into, and hence of rewriting, the social text.

Kozol, however, was denied the freedom of choosing to leave his teaching position and had to endure a public humiliation at the hands of the Boston School Committee. The irony in Kozol's dismissal is compounded for him when he receives an offer to teach at a wealthy suburban school, a school whose students enjoy all of the privileges that were being systematically withheld from his ghetto children. Kozol's story ends with his return to the ghetto, chastened by his experiences but still committed to working to transform existing social relationships. His final words are eerily prophetic in the light of the subsequent racial disturbances of the late 1960s, and more recently, of the riots in Los Angeles in the wake of the Rodney King verdict:

there has been an increasing growth of black nationalism in the Roxbury ghetto. . . . It is not difficult to understand why this would seem desirable, and it is very hard for someone who lives among the Negro people to argue against it, much as he might consider it unwise. (Kozol, 1967, p. 214)

From the foregoing discussions of these stories of teaching, I have shown that an awareness for the structure of romance makes plausible a reader's acceptance of the *pathetic fallacy*, where the cycle of nature is analogous to the movement of descent and ascent, disappointment and recovery, that often makes up a teacher's bodily and psychological experience of the teaching year. Similarly, when a story of teaching is encoded as tragedy it can create an image of the teacher as an ethical Manichean, an individual caught between good and evil, committed to doing the right thing although never entirely certain of its outcome nor fully aware of the forces ranged against its success. In addition, romance allegorizes teaching as a quest; in particular, a romance plot characterizes the drive towards human fulfillment and in this sense is implicated in matters of identity creation. Understood this way, an awareness for teaching as romance places the utopian impulse back at the center of the educational agenda and draws attention to the aesthetic aspects involved in acting upon the idea of teaching as a moral craft. Thus, Kozol's and Freedman's use of tragedy and romance are particularly effective narrative forms for dramatizing issues of moral uncertainty, self-questioning, and social critique.

Finally, I believe that as readers, writers, and researchers on education, a rhetoric of inquiry can put us closer in touch with many of the codified ways our culture has developed for telling stories, the kinds of stories whose function is to persuade readers to accept particular versions or constructions of the social reality of teaching. Through cultivating an understanding for how certain literary forms can be mobilized to privilege and reinforce as well as to challenge and oppose commonly held images of teachers and teaching, we may thereby develop a greater awareness for the way narrative works more generally as a powerful ideological force in society. In this respect, then, the existence of tragedy and romance as major cultural forms of storytelling ought to remind us that education is at once a narrative and political enterprise, and that the more we know about narrative and what it entails, the more we will also come to know about the storied nature of the politics of personal experience.

The author gratefully acknowledges the assistance of Research Grant No. 410–1964–91 from the Social Sciences and Research Council of Canada in the preparation of this chapter. The author also thanks Lori Downey, Kieran Egan, Marlene Milne, Allan Neilsen, and John Willinsky for their comments on earlier versions.

ENDNOTES

1. According to Schubert:

Teacher lore includes stories about and by teachers. It portrays and interprets ways in which teachers deliberate and reflect and it portrays teachers in action. Teacher lore can be presented through teachers' own words, and through the interpretations provided by experienced teacher/researchers who . . . report on and interpret stories of other teachers who have influenced our perspectives on teaching. (1992, p. 9)

2. It was a major part of Northrop Frye's literary theoretical project to show how what he took to be the four pregeneric plot structures or *mythoi* (tragedy, comedy, romance, irony) could be used to justify the claim that they work synchronically to organize all literary works within a literary universe (Frye, 1957). These pregeneric plot structure or *mythoi* operate for Frye as the abstract fictional designs that structure sequences of narrated events in such a way that we can begin to recognize them as stories of a particular kind, stories that express in powerful ways our collective anxieties, fears, hopes, and dreams. As A. C. Hamilton states, Frye's archetypal criticism "turns readers inward to that work's core, [to] the myth that expresses their central concerns" (1991, p. 127). But in order to show how these myths are made plausible for a reader, Frye had constant recourse to the key concept of *displacement*, a term whose general features he borrowed from Freud. For Frye, a writer is never free to tell a purely imaginative story or myth, but is compelled to accommodate the story to a reader's awareness of reality, to things as they are in the physical world. It is therefore through the workings of displacement that readers come to recognize how the original outline of a story which had its beginnings in myth has been preserved as the feature which continues to give its present shape. As the primary mode of displaced myth which structures many of the stories of discovery and heroism our culture privileges as its secular scripture and which we continue to teach in our schools, Frye offers romance as the mode which provides the "structural core . . . [of] man's vision of his life as a quest" (Frye, 1976, p. 15).

REFERENCES

Balfour, I. (1988). *Northrop Frye*. Boston: Twayne.

Ball, S., & Goodson, I. F. (1985). *Teachers' lives and careers*. London: Falmer Press.

Connelly, M. F., & Clandinin, D. J. (1987). On narrative method, biography and narrative unities in the study of teaching. *Journal of Educational Thought, 21*(3), 130–139.

Connelly, M. F., & Clandinin, D. J. (1991). Narrative inquiry: Storied experience. In E. C. Short (Ed.), *Forms of curriculum inquiry* (pp. 121–153). Albany: State University of New York Press.

Freedman, S. G. (1990). *Small victories: The real world of a teacher, her students and their high school*. New York: Harper & Row.

Frye, N. (1957). *Anatomy of criticism.* Princeton, NJ: Princeton University Press.

Frye, N. (1976). *The secular scripture: A study of the structure of romance.* Cambridge, MA: Harvard University Press.

Graham, R. J. (1991). *Reading and writing the self: Autobiography in education and the curriculum.* New York: Teachers College Press.

Graubard, A. (1972). *Free the children: Radical reform and the Free School movement.* New York: Pantheon.

Greene, M. (1991). Foreword. In C. Witherell & N. Noddings (Eds.), *Stories lives tell: Narrative and dialogue in education* (pp. ix–xi). New York: Teachers College Press.

Hamilton, A. C. (1991). *Northrop Frye: An anatomy of his criticism.* Toronto: University of Toronto Press.

Harrell, J., & Lingkugel, W. A. (1980). On rhetorical genre: An organizing perspective. In B. L. Brock & R. L. Scott (Eds.), *Methods of rhetorical criticism: A twentieth-century perspective* (pp. 404–419). Detroit: Wayne State University Press.

Hart, F. R. (1970). Notes for an anatomy of modern autobiography. *New Literary History, 1,* 485–511.

Kozol, J. (1967). *Death at an early age: The destruction of the hearts and minds of Negro children in the Boston public schools.* Boston: Houghton Mifflin.

Nelson, J. S., Megill, A., & McCloskey, D. N. (Eds.). (1987). *The rhetoric of the human sciences: Language and argument in scholarship and public affairs.* Madison: University of Wisconsin Press.

Pagano, J. (1990). *Exiles and communities: Teaching in the patriarchal wilderness.* Albany: State University of New York Press.

Polkinghorne, D. (1988). *Narrative knowing and the human sciences.* Albany: State University of New York Press.

Ravitch, D. (1983). *The troubled crusade: American education 1945–1980.* New York: Basic Books.

Schubert, W. H. (1992). Readings as resources for teacher lore. In W. H. Schubert & W. C. Ayers (Eds.), *Teacher lore: Learning from our experience* (pp. 140–147). New York: Longman.

Schubert, W. H., & Ayers, W. C. (1992). *Teacher lore: Learning from our experience.* New York: Longman.

Simons, H. W. (1990). The rhetoric of inquiry as an intellectual movement. In H. W. Simons (Ed.), *The rhetorical turn: Invention and persuasion in the conduct of inquiry* (pp. 1–31). Chicago: University of Chicago Press.

Taylor, C. (1989). *Sources of the self: The making of the modern identity.* Cambridge, MA: Harvard University Press.

White, H. (1973). *Metahistory: The historical imagination in nineteenth-century Europe.* Baltimore: Johns Hopkins University Press.

White, H. (1978). *Tropics of discourse: Essays in cultural criticism.* Baltimore: Johns Hopkins University Press.

Witherell, C., & Noddings, N. (1991). *Stories lives tell: Narrative and dialogue in education.* New York: Teachers College Press.

CHAPTER 13

Narrative Rationality in Educational Research

Nancy Zeller

Several researchers (Connelly & Clandinin, 1990; Egan, 1989; Gee, 1985, 1989; Wolf, 1985; and the contributors to this volume) have begun pursuing issues related to narrative and research on teaching. McEwan, in his chapter, "Narrative understanding in the study of teaching," considers various reporting forms. He is drawn to the "intimate access" afforded by imaginative fiction and fictive strategies. A useful undertaking, he concludes, would be to find "a better language to talk about teaching" — with the ultimate goal of improving practice.

In this chapter, I would like to explore the possibility of a better language to talk about teaching and about case study research in education. After briefly assessing current rhetorical practices in educational research, I will demonstrate some alternative narrative strategies. These strategies rest on two fundamental assumptions about case reporting. The first assumption is that the primary goal of a case report is to create understanding (versus prediction and control), and, as Gudmundsdottir argues in this volume, to create new meanings. The second assumption is that a case narrative, unlike a technical research report, should be a product rather than a record of research.

THE RHETORIC OF INQUIRY

The codification of traditional or "positivist" research rhetoric, according to Bazerman (1987), is found in the *APA Publication Manual*, which has become the style manual of choice for many of the social sciences and education. APA writing conventions are designed to create the appearance of objectivity (the absence of bias) so that the rhetoric of research reports or articles will be consistent with the objective methodology on which they rest. These conventions, according to Bazerman (1984), include "(1) the use of the objective, third person point of view, (2) emphasis on precision, with mathematics as a model, (3) avoidance of metaphors and other expressive uses of language, and (4) support of claims with experimental, empirical evidence from nature" (pp. 1–2).

A striking difference between nonpositivist and positivist research appears to be in their respective reporting modes, with nonpositivists often choosing the case report in preference to the APA-approved, four-part scientific article. Ironically, while many researchers in the human sciences have rejected a positivist conception of objectivity in research methodology, they have not rejected its influence over their writing style.

Stake suggests that for case studies, a "writing style that is informal, perhaps narrative, possibly with verbatim quotation, illustration, and even allusion and metaphor" is more appropriate than a technical reporting style (pp. 6–7). Many other researchers (for example, Agar, 1990; Anderson, 1987; Atkinson, 1990; Hammersley & Atkinson, 1983; Krieger, 1984; Mulkay, 1985; Van Maanen, 1988; and Zeller, 1987, 1990, 1991, 1993) have suggested that case reporters consider such models as new ethnography, new journalism, creative nonfiction, or even fiction. But, rather than being open to a range of rhetorical possibilities, the social science research writer *qua* writer most often seems constrained.

According to Lincoln and Guba (1985), the case report method has many advantages for the naturalistic inquirer (and, perhaps, for other qualitative inquirers as well). First of all, they argue, case reporters can easily accommodate the multiple realities they encounter in any given study. Naturalistic researchers, who see objectivity as an impossible goal, reap a second advantage in constructing case narratives: they can depict clearly their own interaction with the site and the resulting biases. Another advantage pertains to the issue of causality: since naturalists do not accept the idea of linear causality, they can use the case report to describe or demonstrate the range of mutually-shaping influences present in the case. Finally, according to Lincoln and Guba, case reporters benefit by being able to readily portray in the case narrative "the value positions of investigator, substantive theory, methodological paradigm, and local contextual values" (p. 42).

Narrative Techniques for Case Study Research

Narrative techniques, along with description and summary, have great potential value for the case report writer. Three types of nonfiction writing—the nonfiction novel, ethnography, and especially new journalism—are useful models for case reporters who wish to discover a narrative style more reflective of the underlying assumptions of nonpositivist inquiry. Many people see a strong connection between social science and new journalism. Sommer (1975) observes that both "rely on participant observation as their major research method . . . upon first-person access to the people and places to be written about." Hollowell (1977) points to another connection between qualitative inquiry and new journalism: "By revealing his personal biases, the new journalist strives for a higher kind of 'objectivity.' Much that is characteristic of the new journalism may be found in case study research. The basic reporting unit, for example, is not the datum— the piece of information—but the scene" (Wolfe, 1973, p. 50). Prolonged engagement—a hallmark of qualitative inquiry—is also practiced by new journalists, who stay with respondents long enough for scenes to unfold before their eyes.

Because there appear to be many similarities, in belief and action and in method and purpose, between new journalists and qualitative inquirers, the writing strategies and techniques employed by new journalists would seem to be appropriate models for case researchers to consider. The two passages that follow illustrate how case reporting might be improved by more expressive writing forms than those in current use. The data chosen for treatment relate to a number of issues of varying degrees of importance that emerged during a case study of Landmark College. The major issue overarching the entire study concerned the increasing tendency by many institutions to strengthen admission, performance, and graduation standards while, at the same time, extending college access to such underserved, nontraditional student groups as minorities, reentry women, displaced workers, and learning disabled adults. Several other issues important to Landmark students, faculty, staff, and the community emerged during the study, the most intriguing of which concerned attitudes about and experiences of African-American students. In the field, I found it difficult to make sense of the conflicting stories I heard about the experiences of African-American students at Landmark College. I discovered later that as I began to construct narratives from these conversations and observations, the issue began to take shape—like a blurry Polaroid snapshot gradually coming into focus. This experience, beginning with confusion and ending in narrative, gave me a better understanding of the phrase "narrative ways of knowing."

The following is an example of traditional narration as it could be used within a case report. This segment illustrates a first person–involved observer narrative, which gives the writer a central role in the action; an alternate approach would be a third person–panoramic point of view, which allows the writer to fade into the background.

The Black Flap, or When I Got Called a Racist (Gulp)

When I was a little girl, I used to visit my aunt and uncle in Landmark. My visit usually occurred in July or August; so, what I liked best was going fishing where it was cool—in a little stream lined with river willows about 5 miles out of town. My uncle would rig up an old cane fishing pole and let me thread the worm on the hook. I loved to swing the line out and watch the red and white bobber quiver on the water's surface. For lunch we'd light a small campfire and cook some of the fish right there on a stick. Nothing tastes better than a fish that was swimming around in a cool stream 30 minutes ago cooked over an open fire.

In the evening after the drive back, I'd sit on the porch swing with my aunt and watch the moon and stars come out and smell the sweet phlox and listen to the crickets in the dark.

I don't ever remember seeing a black person in Landmark in those days. But, black people have always lived there, I've since learned, just in a different section—what was called "the Station."

Naturally, as I started my case study, I was curious about how urban black kids felt about coming to Landmark, with its isolated location and slow, southern ways. So, as I began talking to people, I began probing about how life was for black students at Landmark College, little knowing that this line of inquiry would embroil me in turmoil and controversy, and, eventually, a charge of racism.

I later came to understand that basically three things happened to cause the "black flap." First, Gretchan Fisher made the comment that blacks didn't seem to value education as much as whites. Second, I pressed hard to find out if other faculty and students agreed with her. Third, several faculty members in one of the academic divisions overreacted.

But, let me start at the beginning. Gretchan Fisher was one of the first faculty members I interviewed. A trim, well-groomed, somewhat flamboyantly dressed woman in her early 60s, Mrs. Fisher had taught composition for Landmark's English department for many years and thus could provide me with an oral history of both the department and the college. A gregarious individual, she seemed to enjoy telling me about earlier days, when classes were smaller and students seemed smarter.

To help students "hear" their errors, she liked to read their papers out loud—with a dramatic flourish. Even though this technique was "very valuable," now there are too many students in her classes for her to practice it. This increasing number of students at Landmark concerns her, especially the growing proportion needing developmental writing.

"It was a sad, sad day when we had to dispense with personal treatment because of sheer numbers," she lamented.

The number of black students taking developmental writing has also grown, a trend that troubles Mrs. Fisher — perhaps because of her failure to help them learn how to write.

"Black students are more likely to be in developmental writing than Comp 101. Blacks don't seem to value education as much as whites . . . that makes for an intergenerational problem," she commented.

As I met with more faculty members, I found myself disturbed by the way faculty members talked about black students; their comments seemed patronizing in an us-them way. Even though the Landmark faculty and staff seemed to believe that they were not at all prejudiced, I was not so sure they were free from thinking in stereotypes: in a discussion about setting realistic educational and occupational objectives, for example, one faculty member told me, "If a student is in developmental reading and is prelaw or preoptometry, he's black."

A couple of months after my meeting with Gretchan Fisher, I constructed two questionnaires — one for faculty and one for students. In addition to demographics and some other items, I included statements from the faculty and students whom I had interviewed; I asked respondents to indicate their agreement or disagreement with these statements, using a Likert-type scale (5 = Strongly Agree, 4 = Agree, 3 = Undecided or No Opinion, 2 = Disagree, 1 = Strongly Disagree). Naturally, I included Gretchan Fisher's statements: "Black students don't seem to value education as much as White students do," which became item 69, and "Blacks are more likely than Whites to show up in a remedial class," item 63. I was later to discover that "show up" was an unfortunate choice of words, for some faculty pointed out that the problem was that black students too often didn't "show up" when they were supposed to.

A copy of the faculty version of the questionnaire was mailed to each faculty member at the college. Since address labels had been glued to the back sheet of the questionnaire and some respondents neglected to remove the label, I inadvertently discovered the identity of some of the respondents. (This later led to the discovery that Gretchan Fisher "disagreed" with both of her own statements about black students.)

Respondents for the student version of the questionnaire were sought in various developmental classes and writing classes, such as

English Composition 101 and 102, Business Communications, and Technical Reporting. Such a sample seemed likely to provide a rough cross-section of students with regard to major, educational objective, and demographic factors. On both faculty and student versions of the questionnaire, I urged respondents to add written comments on the back . . . which is how and where I got called a "racist" — by both students and faculty!

The commotion all started in the reading department. An instructor thought items 63 and 69 were deliberate racial slurs, even though they were prefaced by the statement, "Please react to the following statements made by L.C. students, faculty, and staff." This instructor went to the department chair, who, upon reading the offending items and noticing some other items that made her uneasy, shared in the concern. And, the department chair, having made up her mind that the questionnaire was objectionable, never once varied from her attitude nor her resolution that her students wouldn't participate.

The mounting alarm among the reading faculty quickly became an almost perceptible stir among the faculty in the English department. The chair, only mildly alarmed by the uproar, but uncertain as to how it would all turn out, protected himself by telling his faculty to do nothing . . . yet.

The speech department, which had been asked to administer the questionnaire in a developmental class with 17 students, was never heard from again.

Math faculty, totally puzzled by the hubbub, were the first to return their questionnaires — tied in neat packets and clearly labeled.

The Humanities dean, exasperated by all this distracting excitement a week before finals (and somewhat embarrassed by the faculty's lack of research sophistication), told the department chairs to have the faculty begin administering the questionnaires immediately.

Most of the faculty complied; their packets arrived sporadically over the next 6 weeks. The only packet of questionnaires I received from the reading department came from an instructor whose good will was so universal and respect for authority so complete that she quite literally couldn't help herself.

Now that I have had time to think about the "black flap," I realize that because of it I have learned more about Landmark College than I could have through any simple questionnaire or series of interviews and observations. While there is very little of the detached, objective, rational world of traditional scholarship at Landmark, there is much of the mystifying, emotionally charged world of human beings.

Narration is the primary technique of the dramatic novelist. It is also an important technique in nonfiction because it provides the excitement of events occurring in a closed-in arena. It invests the subject with interest and meaning and effectively conveys both the tone and sequence. In the preceding narrative, events unfold much as they occurred. By using narrative to focus on an event, the qualitative research writer can connect and explain fairly lifeless research findings in richer ways than can a bare list of facts.

NARRATIVE STRATEGIES FROM THE NEW JOURNALISM

The technical similarities and philosophical resonance between the new journalism and nonpositivist inquiry suggest that case reporters can learn much from new journalists about how to write satisfying case narratives. Four writing devices have been identified by new journalist Tom Wolfe (1973). These help new journalists, when portraying real events and real people, to achieve the immediacy or concrete reality or narrative truth found in fiction, especially in novels of social realism. They are:

- Scene-by-scene construction, the telling of a story in scenic episodes
- Character development through full recording of dialogue
- Use of a third-person subjective point of view, experiencing an event through the perspective of one of its participants
- Full detailing of the "status life"—or rank—of participants in a scene, their "everyday gestures, habits, manners, customs, styles of furniture, clothing, decoration, styles of traveling, eating, keeping house, modes of behaving toward children, servants, superiors, inferiors, peers, plus the various looks, glances, poses, styles of walking and other symbolic details that might exist within a scene" (Wolfe, p. 32).

The following is a revision of "The black flap" using a scene-by-scene strategy (and considerably more data).

The Black Flap, Version 2

Gretchan Fisher graciously welcomed me to her tiny, but neatly arranged office and offered me a seat.

"There's not much space, I'm afraid," she said.

A slender, well-groomed woman in her early 60s, she had taught composition for Landmark's English department for many years and, thus, could provide me with an oral history of both the department and the college. She was quite a talker and seemed to enjoy telling me about earlier days, when classes were smaller and students seemed smarter. She told me she was an artist as well as an English teacher and showed me the visual aids she had created to teach sentence structure.

"I'm a great believer in visuals, especially for developmental students," she said.

To help students "hear" their errors, she liked to read their papers out loud—with a dramatic flourish. Even though this technique "is very valuable," there are too many students in her classes nowadays for her to practice it.

The increasing number of students concerns her, especially the growing number of students needing developmental writing. She commented that "students don't like being sent down to developmental writing," so she likes to meet with them individually to talk with them about it, but with the increase in the number of students, this kind of contact becomes difficult.

"Now it's hard to get to talk to them with so many students. It was a sad, sad day when we had to dispense with personal treatment because of sheer numbers."

Many English department faculty members expressed a dislike of teaching developmental writing, but Gretchan Fisher didn't.

"I love the teaching of it . . . but grading papers is a big bore, especially with developmental students."

The increasing number of black students in her classes troubles Gretchan Fisher, perhaps because of her failure to help them learn how to write.

"Black students are more likely to be in developmental writing than Comp 101. Blacks don't seem to value education as much as whites . . . that makes for an intergenerational problem," she commented.

"Hum," I thought. And I copied it down.

That was my first mistake. My second came months later when I included these statements on the questionnaires I prepared for faculty and students to fill out.

The first hint I had that anything was amiss came in a phone call from Barb Loftus.

"Nancy, we've got a little problem here. The chair of the reading department doesn't want to give the questionnaire to her students because of those two questions about blacks."

"What's wrong with the questions?"

"Well, she thinks black students will be offended and think the questions are racist."

"That's ridiculous! . . . You and the dean read over the questionnaire before I had it copied and sent to faculty members to administer . . . did either of you see anything wrong with those questions?"

"No . . . but we probably should have given it to the reading chair to review . . . that may be why we're having trouble now. She may feel like she's been left out."

"Barb, does she understand that those statements are virtually verbatim quotations from a college faculty member and that I'm merely trying to see if others share this view of blacks?"

"I pointed that out to her. I also said, 'Don't you want to know the answers to some of these questions? Don't you want to know if we've got some problems?' But, it doesn't seem to make any difference. She thinks students will believe that the college is behind the questionnaire and that the faculty and administration are harboring racist attitudes."

"Good grief. I don't know what to do . . . I really would like responses from those students in my sample."

"Let me talk to the dean and see if he can convince the reading chair to participate."

"Okay. I'll be down on Monday to pick up the first batch of questionnaires. Maybe things will have calmed down by then."

This conversation took place on Thursday afternoon. The following Monday morning, I walked into Barb's office a little before noon and discovered that far from having calmed down, faculty members throughout the building were in a low-level uproar over my questionnaire.

"Now the English department is involved," was Barb's greeting. "The chair has decided that none of the students in his classes will take the questionnaire until the controversy is settled."

Stunned, I asked, "What is going on?"

"Most of the developmental instructors grew up in Landmark and have degrees in elementary education. They're very protective of their students and probably do more mothering of them than they should. Also, part of what they're promoting to students is self-esteem, and they think your questionnaire threatens that. The nondevelopmental instructors may be more sophisticated about research, but it's almost like a closing of the ranks."

"I can't believe this is happening . . . !"

"I talked to the dean earlier this morning. He's going to tell the faculty to go ahead with administering the questionnaires, and he's going to talk to the department chairs this afternoon."

Barb gave me the faculty and student questionnaires that had already been completed and mailed back to her office.

The first faculty response I looked at was not designed to put my mind at rest. On the page with the now notorious questions 63 and 69, I found screaming back at me the words:

"Racist! Racist!"

And, on the back, was this accusation:

"This survey is biased and bigoted — an insult to both students and faculty."

I looked at another faculty response. Here, next to item 63, I found this remark:

"Racist statement, I do not like this question."

Speechless, I packed the surveys in a box and trudged back to the motel. After dinner, I started going through the student questionnaires, in the grip of a kind of morose compulsion.

In the first batch, taken from classes in writing and math, I found several students who challenged questions 63 and 69. One young man accused me of being careless: "dumb question, dumb question. . . . As a Black student, I didn't appreciate questions 63 and 69. There could have been a much better way to word those questions. The next time you write a student questionnaire be more careful in what you write." Another young man took action: "I refused to answer questions 63–69 on the bases of the questions did not seem to have been asked in total fairness to Blacks. Furthermore, I feel the questions are totally unrelated in racial ways to this survey." His classmate was even more blunt: "This is a bullshit question."

A male student from the Study Lab also was offended: "I think the question that you asked were all heading toward Blacks and I didn't really like them. I think any Black person is just as smart as the next White guy, if not smarter!! I happen to be Black and live with a White family. They don't think I'm lacking in education, so why should I let you put my race down."

One young black woman stated her simple opposition: "I myself disagree with numbers 63 [and] 69." Another challenged me: "On you[r] next survey, replace the Black students with the White student[s] in their capabilities." Another asked, "Why so many comments or put downs about Black students for [questions] 63 and 69?" Another commented, "To me it seem that they are picking on the Black folks. You making it sound that they are dumb and they don't care about their education. I think nomber[s] 63 [and] 69 are very offensive [to] the Black people."

Another young black woman accused me of racism: "I strongly disapproved of the statments made in questions 63 and 69. If you didn't believe that yourself you would not have included it. What you have implied I don't feel is true because there are many Blacks with a higher education than Whites, now and in the past. Education is a very important thing not only to Whites but to Blacks also. I want you to remember one thing, there are as many White bumbs as there are Black one[s]. As for Landmark College I like the school because I was looking for small school so that I can get myself ready for the real world before going on to a big college, and LC is really what I was looking for. The next time you make out a questionnaire pleas[e] reword your questions when referring to different peoples."

I looked around the motel room and felt the palpable presence of legions of black students — all of them mad as hell at me. They didn't understand the purpose of my questionnaire; how could they? They were being attacked . . . again . . . and, to them at least, the attack was pretty much like it had always been. I began to see their faces — the anger and the hurt — and I discovered a new, personal understanding of the term "multiple realities."

Later in the evening, after going over the questionnaires more carefully, I made the gratifying discovery that several white students objected to the "racist" questions.

One young white man commented, "this is petty," while another wrote "false . . . I feel your [question] is not necessary," and another wrote, "very offensive."

Several young white women were outspoken in their criticism. One wrote, "I think some of your questions were extremely prejudise and un-called for! Just because a person is Black doesn't mean that they are not as intelligent as Whites. And it doesn't mean that they won't show up for class. They have as much right as an White or other to attend college. At least L.C. has a program to help in the areas that you are having problems in." Another commented on item 63, "This is offensive and racist." On item 69 she said, "This is also offensive."

But, to soften my optimism about the goodheartedness of L.C. students, I found that the last student questionnaire contained this bold criticism of the college:

"To [*sic*] many niggers."

After a troubled night, I returned to the college in the morning and sought out Denise O'Quinn, whom I discovered I had met some years ago. I was lucky to find her in a tiny office trying to dig out from under a pile of student papers. I brought up the "black flap."

"Nancy, this is really interesting! Conversation in the faculty lounge hasn't been this lively in months."

"What's going on?" I asked with a sinking feeling. "There seems to be a kind of mass hysteria that is spreading throughout the building."

"Well, the English department chair is just being cautious—he can't make up his mind whether anything is wrong with the questions or not."

"Doesn't anyone around here know the difference between asking for an opinion and revealing a prejudice?" I wailed. Denise ignored me.

"I was in the faculty lounge yesterday and asked a few of the faculty if they had seen national surveys with questions like these. I told them we'd look pretty foolish if these questions were, in fact, taken off a national poll."

"What'd they say?" I asked, hopefully.

"Well, it's even more bizarre than you think. One of the instructors and her husband think you are using this study as a ruse to spy on Landmark."

"WHAT ??!" I giggled. "You're joking, right? . . . You're not joking. . . . Well, what in heaven's name do they think I'm trying to find out?"

"They haven't got that far yet."

"I CAN'T BELIEVE THIS IS HAPPENING!"

Later that day, I arranged to meet with the director of the black Student Center. (I guess I was looking for an "expert" to tell me I wasn't a racist.) I found the center on the outskirts of the campus in a little clapboard house built during a construction boom in the 1920s. Its new director, a woman counselor in her early 30s, is one of only three professional black employees out of over 400 at the college. This woman moved to Landmark a few years ago when her husband was selected to serve as pastor for a small Baptist church in the black community. To supplement their meager income, she began working at L.C. 3 years ago as a part-time counselor, and recently was appointed to her new position at the center.

With a triple layer of concern, that of a professional counselor, a pastor's wife, and a black, the director readily admitted that black students coming to Landmark College were more likely to need remedial instruction than their white counterparts.

"That's true . . . they're much more likely to end up in developmental," she stated emphatically. "Luckily, though, most black students feel pretty comfortable taking developmental classes."

She told me about her ideas to improve the current developmental studies program.

"Peer tutors or student tutors are not appropriate," she argued. "Black students need more mature tutors. They need more than 1 hour sessions . . . more intensive assistance is needed."

She is troubled, however, by the overall lack of African-American student involvement in campus life.

"Black students don't get involved in campus activities as a whole, such as student government or social activities. . . . That is a problem."

Her face clearly communicated, "I've got my work cut out for me!"

Having left the somewhat comforting atmosphere of the black Student Center, I found Barb back in her office. She assured me that the dean had asked all faculty to cooperate and administer the questionnaire.

He must not have much influence, though, for I never heard from the reading department.

Now, after looking over the surveys one last time, I have developed a kind of affection for the student who wrote,

"I personally feel that this survey SUCKS!!"

CONCLUSION

Many are now arguing for compelling, innovative, expressive rhetoric in research in education and the human sciences. Atkinson (1990) notes that the "ethnographic text too often seems to treat its own language as a transparent medium." Such a careless simplification of the communication process presents a clear danger for ethnographers whose texts, in Atkinson's view, ought to be more self-aware (p. 178).

I have attempted in this chapter to demonstrate how narrative strategies, especially those used by the new journalists, may serve as models for case reporting. Narrative holds the appeal of interest and identification and offers perpetual possibilities for enlarging the access to, and possibly the impact of, educational research.

Those who view expressive writing strategies as unseemly should remember that a writer, according to Jacques Barzun (1971), "contrives means and marshals forces that the beholder takes for granted"; when a writer speaks of his craft, he means "quite literally that he is crafty" (p. 65). Social scientists, too, need to be "crafty" in the sense that Barzun implies. Using photography as a metaphor for writing, anthropologist Renato Rosaldo (1987) argues that such scheming is an unavoidable—even natural— part of any creative act:

> It is as if one imagined that photographs told the unadorned real truth without ever noticing how they were constructed. Their images, after all, are framed, taken from particular angles, shot at certain distances, and rendered with different depths of field. (p. 3)

In the same way, it is by *design* that the case narrative becomes not simply a record of experiences, but a product of the case study. And, it is through the process of crafting the case narrative that the social scientist becomes not simply an objective narrator of experience, but a narrative filter through which experience is shaped and given meaning.

REFERENCES

Agar, M. (1990). Test and fieldwork: Exploring the excluded middle. *Journal of Contemporary Ethnography, 19*(1), 73–88.

Anderson, C. (1987). *Style as argument: Contemporary American nonfiction.* Carbondale: Southern Illinois University Press.

Atkinson, P. (1990). *The ethnographic imagination: Textual constructions of reality.* London: Routledge & Kegan Paul.

Barzun, J. (1971). *On writing, editing, and publishing.* Chicago: University of Chicago Press.

Bazerman, C. (1984). Modern evolution of the experimental report in physics: Spectroscopic articles in Physical Review, 1893–1980. *Social Studies of Science, 14.* Beverly Hills: Sage.

Bazerman, C. (1987). Codifying the social scientific style: The APA Publication Manual as a behaviorist rhetoric. In J. Nelson, A. Megill, & D. McCloskey (Eds.), *The rhetoric of the human sciences: Language and argument in scholarship and public affairs* (pp. 125–144). Madison: University of Wisconsin Press.

Connelly, F. M., & Clandinin, D. J. (1990). Stories of experience and narrative inquiry. *Educational Researcher, 19*(5), 2–14.

Egan, K. (1989). *Teaching as story telling: An alternative approach to teaching and curriculum in the elementary school.* Chicago: University of Chicago Press.

Gee, J. P. (1985). The narrativization of experience in the oral style. *Journal of Education, 167*(1), 9–35.

Gee, J. P. (1989). Two styles of narrative construction and their linguistic and educational implications. *Journal of Education, 171*(1), 97–115.

Hammersley, M., & Atkinson, P. (1983). *Ethnography: Principles in practice.* London: Tavistock.

Hollowell, J. (1977). *Fact and fiction: The new journalism and the nonfiction novel.* Chapel Hill: University of North Carolina Press.

Krieger, S. (1984). Fiction and social science. *Studies in Symbolic Interactionism, 5,* 269–287.

Lincoln, Y. S., & Guba, E. G. (1985). *Naturalistic inquiry.* Beverly Hills: Sage.

Mulkay, M. (1985). *The word and the world: Explorations in the form of sociological analysis.* London: George Allen & Unwin.

Rosaldo, R. (1987). Where objectivity lies: The rhetoric of anthropology. In J. Nelson, A. Megill, & D. McCloskey (Eds.), *The rhetoric of the human sciences: Language and argument in scholarship and public affairs* (pp. 87–110). Madison: University of Wisconsin Press.

Sommer, R. (1975). New journalism and new sociology compared. In M. Fishwick (Ed.), *New journalism* (pp. 241–249). Bowling Green, OH: Bowling Green University Popular Press.

Stake, R. E. (1978). The case study method in social inquiry. *Educational Researcher, 7,* 6–8.

Van Maanen, J. (1988). *Tales of the field: On writing ethnography.* Chicago: University of Chicago Press.

Wolf, D. (1985). Ways of telling: Text repertoires in elementary school children. *Journal of Education, 167*(1), 71–88.

Wolfe, T. (1973). *The new journalism.* New York: Harper & Row.

Zeller, N. (1987). *A rhetoric for naturalistic inquiry.* Unpublished doctoral dissertation, Indiana University, Bloomington.

Zeller, N. (1990, June). *A rhetoric for naturalistic inquiry: Writing the case report.* Paper presented at the University of Iowa Project on the Rhetoric of Inquiry (POROI) Conference on Narrative in the Human Sciences, Iowa City.

Zeller, N. (1991, April). *A new use for new journalism: Writing the case report.* Paper presented at the annual meeting of the American Educational Research Association, Chicago. (ERIC Document Reproduction Service No. ED 334 257)

Zeller, N. (1993, January). *The transformational power of narrative.* Paper presented at the Sixth Annual Qualitative Research in Education Conference, Athens, GA.

About the Contributors

Kieran Egan is a professor of Education at Simon Fraser University, British Columbia, Canada. Among his books are *Primary Understanding: Education in Early Childhood; Romantic Understanding: The Development of Rationality and Imagination, Ages 8–15; Teaching as Story Telling*; and *Imagination in Teaching and Learning.*

Ivor Goodson is a professor at the University of Western Ontario and the Frederica Warner Visiting Scholar in the Graduate School of Education and Human Development at the University of Rochester. At Western, he is a member of the Faculties of Graduate Studies, Education, Sociology and The Centre for Theory and Criticism. He is the author of a range of books on curriculum and life history studies. They include *School Subjects and Curriculum Change, The Making of Curriculum, Biography, Identity and Schooling* (with Rob Walker) and *Studying Teachers' Lives*. He is the Founding Editor and North American Editor of *The Journal of Education Policy* and the National Editor of *Qualitative Studies in Education.*

Robert J. Graham is an associate professor in the Department of Curriculum: Humanities and Social Sciences, Faculty of Education, The University of Manitoba, Winnipeg, Canada. He is the author of *Reading and Writing the Self: Autobiography in Education and the Curriculum* published by Teachers College Press. Some of his other publications in the areas of language education and narrative approaches to teaching have appeared in *English Quarterly, Canadian Journal of Education, Journal of Aesthetic Education, Journal of Curriculum Studies, Teaching and Learning*, and the *Journal of Educational Thought*. He is currently conducting a series of case studies into the nature and importance of personal myth in the life histories and careers of several preservice and experienced teachers.

Sigrun Gudmundsdottir is associate professor at the Pedagogical Institute at the University of Trondheim. Her most recent work appears in the 1994 issue of *Zeitschrift fur Padagogic*, a leading German-language education journal.

Sophie Haroutunian-Gordon is associate professor and Director, Master of Science in Education Program, Northwestern University. She is the author of *Turning the Soul: Teaching Through Conversation in the High School*, (University of Chicago Press, 1991), *Equilibrium in the Balance: A Study of Psychological Explanation*, (Springer-Verlag, 1983), and co-editor, with Philip Jackson, of *From Socrates to Software: The Teacher as Text and the Text as Teacher*, (National Society for the Study of Education, eighty-eighth yearbook, 1989). Her current research looks at conversations about the meaning of texts as they apply to the teaching of mathematics and science.

Michael Huberman is a visiting professor at the Harvard Graduate School of Education and Senior Research Associate at the Network, Inc. He has been interested in life cycle research since 1971, when he published *Adult Development and Adult Change*. He is the author of several books, numerous chapters and articles, the most recent of which was *The Lives of Teachers*, the English translation of *La Vie des Enseignants*.

Philip W. Jackson is the David Lee Shillinglaw Distinguished Service Professor in the Department of Education and Psychology at the University of Chicago. He is the author of *Life in Classrooms, The Practice of Teaching*, and *Untaught Lessons* and is co-author (with J. W. Getzels) of *Creativity and Intelligence*. Most recently he has co-authored (with Robert E. Boostrom and David T. Hansen) *The Moral Life of Schools*.

Hunter McEwan is associate professor of education at the University of Hawaii at Manoa. He has been closely involved recently with the development and implementation of a field-based teacher education program that places emphasis on teachers as researchers. His articles have appeared in *Educational Theory, Studies in Philosophy and Education*, and the *American Educational Research Journal*.

John Othus is a member of the English Department faculty at West Linn High School. John's story in this chapter was crafted during his participation in a graduate course in "Narrative and Voice" at Lewis and Clark College.

Vivian Gussin Paley teaches kindergarten at the University of Chicago laboratory Schools and makes storytelling and story acting the core of the curriculum. She is author of many books, including *You Can't Say You Can't Play* and *The Boy Who Would Be a Helicopter*. Mrs. Paley is a 1989 MacArthur Fellow.

Shirley Pendlebury is a senior lecturer in the Department of Education at the University of the Witwatersrand, Johannesburg, South Africa, where she teaches courses in Philosophy of Education, Curriculum, and Teacher Education. She served as a co-ordinator of the Teacher Education Research Group of the National Educational Policy Initiative which was responsible for analyzing policy options for democratic education in the new South Africa. Her articles have appeared in such journals as *Educational Theory, Studies in Philosophy and Education,* and *The Journal of Curriculum Studies.*

Brian Sutton-Smith is Professor Emeritus at the University of Pennsylvania in Philadelphia, with prior teaching appointments at Teachers College, Columbia University of New York and Bowling Green State University in Ohio with appointments in the Departments of Psychology, education and folklore. He is the author and editor of 30 books and 300 articles in the areas of child play, narrative, films and social development and a recipient of two Festchrifts from his colleagues for his research in play.

Hoan Tan Tran is a student in the Master of Arts in Teaching program at Lewis and Clark College and a teacher of art in a private school in Portland. Huan's contribution to the chapter is based on her participation in a course in "Moral Development, Ethics, and Education" at Lewis and Clark College.

Rob Walker is a professor of education at Deakin University in Australia. His current research interests include the evaluation of drug education programs, environmental education and the impact of information technologies in education. He is author of three widely used educational books *A Guide to Classroom Observation,* with Clem Adelman and Janine Wiedel; *Changing the Curriculum,* with Barry MacDonald; and *Doing Research.* He is currently writing a book with Michael Schratz, entitled *Doing Research as Social Change.*

Carol Witherell is an associate professor in education at Lewis and Clark College in Portland, Oregon. She is co-editor, with Nel Noddings, of *Stories Lives Tell: Narrative and Dialogue in Education* and the editor of a special issue of *The Journal of Moral Education* on "Narrative and the Moral Realm: Tales of Caring and Justice."

Nancy Zeller is an associate professor in the Department of Foundations and Research in the School of Education at East Carolina University. Her research interests include the rhetoric of research in the human sciences, qualitative research methodology, and higher education policy. Her article on writing qualitative research is published in a special issue on narrative of the *International Journal of Qualitative Studies in Education*. She has also written on distance education policy in the *Review of Higher Education*.

Index

Abrams, D., 80
Abstraction, in thinking of young children, 118
Actual Minds, Possible Worlds (Bruner), 70, 116
Agar, M., 212
Agency postures, of teachers
  perceptive equilibrium, 53, 54–55, 57, 63
  perceptive spontaneity, 53, 55, 56–57, 60–61
  reflective equilibrium, 53, 54, 55, 57, 60–61, 63
Alexander, T., 46, 48
Allport-Vernon-Lindzey scale, 31
Ambassadors, The (James), 58–59
Anderson, C., 212
Angels Fear (Bateson), 87
Anthropology, 86
APA Publication Manual, 211–212
Applebee, A. N., 119
Aristotle, 55, 57, 58, 60, 61, 171, 177–178
Atkinson, P., 212
Autobiography, teacher, 131–155, 197–202, 206–208
Ayers, W. C., 197

Bakhtin, Mikhail M., 71, 84–85
Balfour, I., 204
Ball, S., 132, 195
Baltes, P., 127
Barritt, L. S., 167
Barry, Lynda, 46
Bartlett, F. C., 116
Barzun, Jacques, 223–224
Bateson, Gregory, 87
Bateson, Mary Catherine, 87
Bazerman, C., 211, 212
Becker, H., 132
Beckett, Samuel, 75
Beloved (Morrison), 44, 45, 46, 47
Benjamin, Walter, xi–xii
Ben-Peretz, M., 25, 26, 27
Berger, J., 188–189

Bernstein, Richard, 178
Bettelheim, B., 117
Bhaskar, R., 141, 156
Bicameral mind, 85
Binary concepts, 118–122
  discrimination and mediation of, 120–122
  in fairy tales, 118–122
  and learning process, 120–122
  relevance of, to experience, 118–120
Biography, 10
  teacher, 197, 202–208
Black Elk Speaks (Niehardt), 46–48
Bloom, Allan, 46
BME (beginning, middle, end) form, 74
Boomer, Garth, 174
Botvin, Gilbert, 74
Bransford, J. D., 116
Brenner, M., 139
British Sociological Association, 188
Britton, James, x, xiv
Brooks, Ellen, 79
Brown, Dee, 46
Brown, R. M., 43, 138
Bruner, Jerome, xi, 27, 70, 71, 72, 73, 116, 129
Buchler, Justus, 17
Bull, B., 29, 175
Bury My Heart at Wounded Knee (Brown), 46
Butt, R., 140

Call of Stories, The (Coles), 44, 181
Carr, Wilfred, 177–178
Carter, C., 25, 27
Carter, K., 26, 28, 29
Case studies, 186–187
  defined, 186
  narrative techniques for, 212–217
  public versus personal meaning in, 187–189
  qualitative data in, 189–191
Caughey, John, 84
Characters, 80

Chatman, S., 25
"Chicago school" of sociology, 131–132, 159
Children's Riddling (McDowell), 75
Children Tell Stories (Pitcher & Prelinger), 80
Clandinin, D. J., 25, 26, 27–28, 30–31, 139, 140, 156, 196, 203, 211
Clark, D., 138
Clifford, G., 159
Clough, P., 155
Cochran-Smith, M., 128
Cognitive styles, 83
Cohen, L., 138
Coherence, of teachers' narratives, 137–138
Cohler, B., 138
Coles, Robert, vii, 40, 44, 181
Complications, 80–82
Confrey, Jere, 60
Connelly, F. M., 25, 26, 27–28, 30–31, 139, 140, 156, 196, 203, 211
Consciousness, ix, x
Consciousness-raising, and teacher narratives, 139–140
Conservatism, of teachers, 153–154
Consistency, of teachers' narratives, 137–138
Constructivist approach, 197
Creativity: Genius and Other Myths (Weisberg), 84
Cronbach, H. J., 83
Crow and Weasel (Lopez), 39–40, 44
Culler, J., 25
"Cultural literacy," 8
Culture, stereotypes concerning, 45–46
Curriculum, fantasy narrative in, 121–122

Dallmayr, F. R., 178
Danto, Arthur C., 11–12, 14
Darnton, R., 173
Death at an Early Age (Kozol), 197–202, 206–208
Decentering, 131
Dee, Ruby, 44
Defensive focusing, by teachers, 149
Dennett, D., 130
Denny, Terry, 186, 187
Derrida, Jacques, 85
Dewey, John, x, 28, 118
Dialogical other, 51, 52–55

Dialogic Imagination, The (Bakhtin), 84–85
Dialogue, in teaching, 42–48
Dillard, Annie, 40
Dilman, I., 14, 15
Discontinuity, in life cycles of teachers, 135
Discourse
  analysis of, 140–141, 142–145
  defined, 25
Discussion, narrative in, 100–114
Disenchantment, of teachers, 149–150
Disengagement, by teachers, 154–155
Displacement, 209 n. 2
Dollard, J., 128
Dorris, Michael, 44, 45, 47
Doyle, W., 28, 30
Dreams and daydreams, 83–84

Economy, defined, 32
Educational research
  ethnographic, 186–193, 212–213
  life-history narratives of teachers in, 127–161
  narrative in, 26–27
  narrative strategies for, 211–225
  in Swiss study of professional life cycle of teachers, 133–155
Egan, Kieran, 26, 28, 40, 100, 116–124, 118, 166, 211
Eisner, E., 137, 161, 187
Elbaz, F., 25, 26, 27, 28, 30–31
Elder, G., 135
Ellis, A. K., 119
Emic accounts, 187
Epistemology
  as function of stories, 5–9
  and teacher narrative, 155
  of teaching, 175–176
Erdrich, Louise, 45
Erikson, E. H., 73, 131
Erwanger, S., 27
Essentialism, in philosophy of teaching, 170–174
Ethnography, 186–191
  culture of research in, 191–193
  defined, 186
  narrative strategy for, 212–213
  public versus personal meaning in, 187–189
  qualitative data in, 189–191
Etic accounts, 187

Fables, 9, 12, 13–15
Fabric of Character, The (Sherman), 61
Fairy tales, 10, 117–122
  binary concepts in, 118–122
  structure of, 117–120
Familiarity, defined, 32
Faulkner, William, 74–75, 158
Featherman, D., 127
Fensham, Peter, 191
Fenstermacher, Gary, 50–53, 60, 64, 171
Fish, S., 32
Fitzgerald, J., 138
Flavell, J. H., 120
Fletcher, G., 137
Flocco, R., 138
Folkstories of Children, The (Sutton-Smith), 75
Foucault, Michel, 86
Fragility of Goodness, The (Nussbaum), 46
Frames of Mind (Gardner), 83
Freedman, Samuel G., 197, 202, 203, 204, 205–207, 208
Freud, Sigmund, 73, 82
Friedman, E., 154
Fry, N., 24–25
Frye, Northrop, 202–204, 209 n. 2
Fuhrman, R., 130

Gadamer, Hans-Georg, 103, 114, 176, 178, 179
Gardner, H., 83, 116
Gardner, John, 56–57
Garfinkel, H., 139
Garrison, J. W., 169, 171
Gee, J. P., 211
Geertz, Clifford, xi, 141, 159, 185
Gellner, E., ix, x
Gergen, K., 135
Gergen, M., 135
Giorgi, Amadeo, 141, 142, 155, 157
Goodman, N., 34
Goodson, Ivor F., 132, 184–194, 185, 195
Goodson, Y., 132
Good Times are Killing Me, The (Barry), 46
Gorgias (Plato), 12–18
Gough, P. B., 34
Graham, Robert J., 195–210, 196
Grant, G., 28, 30
Graubard, A., 200
Green, T. F., 171

Greene, Maxine, 40, 44, 195
Grossman, P. L., 27, 28, 29, 31
Gruendel, J., 130
Grumet, M. R., 140
Guba, E. G., 156, 212
Gudmundsdottir, Sigrun, 24–38, 26, 27, 28, 29, 30, 31, 33, 34

Habermas, Jurgen, 178
Hamilton, A. C., 205, 209 n. 2
Hammersley, M., 212
Handbook of Research on Teaching (Wittrock), 132
Hansel and Gretel, 118
Hardy, Barbara, vii, x, 130
Haroutunian-Gordon, Sophie, 100–115, 101–109, 111–113
Harré, R., 141
Harrell, J., 206
Harris, K., 156
Hart, F. R., 199
Hashweh, M., 28
Hauerwas, S., 9–10
Hawkins, P., 156
Hawpe, L., 32, 33, 129, 156
Heath, Shirley B., 72, 77
Hebb, D., 137
Hegel, G. W. F., ix
Hemingway, Ernest, 75
Hermeneutics, 176, 178–179
Herrenstein-Smith, B., 25
High school, interpretive discussion in, 100–114
Hirsch, E. D., 46
Hoan Tan Tran, 39–49
Hollowell, J., 213
House, E., 156–157
Howard, G., 138, 157
Hubbard, Ruth, 44
Huberman, Michael, 31, 127–165, 133, 135, 141, 147, 157, 160
Hughes, Langston, 200
Hurston, Zora Neale, 44

Ideology and Utopia (Mannheim), 207
Imaginary Social Worlds (Caughey), 84
Imagination, 39–42
Individual differences, 82–83
Informants, in life-span research, 128–129
Ingvarson, Lawrence, 191

Interpretation
  discussion based on, 100–114
  in philosophy of teaching, 175–177
Interpretation, and pedagogical content
    knowledge, 32–33
Interviews
  analyzing, 140–141
  in Swiss study of professional life cycle of
    teachers, 133–155

Jackson, Philip W., 3–23, 28
Jacobson, R., 142
Jacques, E., 150
Jalongo, M., 131
James, Henry, 58–59
James, William, 83
Jarolimek, J., 119
Jaynes, J., 85
Jordan, B., 30
Journal writing, 42, 43, 45
Jung, C., 154

Kerr, T. H., 170, 171
Kleiber, D., 154
Knowledge, pedagogical content, 27–35, 51,
    171
Knowledge disciplines, and multivocal minds
    of children, 85–86
Kozol, Jonathan, 197–202, 206–208
Krieger, S., 212
Kuczaj, S. A., 81
Kuhlen, R., 154
Kuhn, T., 85–86
Kuhns, Richard, 5
Kulik, J., 138
Kundera, Milan, xii

Labov, W., 190
Lakoff, G., 143, 158
Language, and multivocal minds of children,
    85
Learning to Labor (Willis), 188, 191
Lee, Joseph, 200
Leimar, U., 25–26
Leinhardt, G., 28
Lerner, R., 127
Leskow, Nikolai, xi–xii
Lévi-Strauss, C., 118, 120
Life-span research, 127–161
  informant role in, 128–129
  phases in, 134–135, 142–155

and professional life cycle of teachers,
    131–132
self-narrative in, 129–131
Swiss study, 133–155
validities of narrative inquiry in, 155–
    157
Lightfoot, S., 132
Lincoln, Y. S., 212
Lingkugel, W. A., 206
Literature. See also Stories
  and multivocal minds of children, 84–85
  philosophy versus, 11–12
Lives in Progress (White), 131
Lodge, David, viii
Loftus, E., 137
Lopez, Barry, 39–40, 41–42, 44, 48
Lorrigio, F., 157
Lortie, D., 132
Lytle, S., 128

MacDonald, B., 187
MacIntyre, Alasdair, viii, xi, xiii, 40, 166
Macmillan, C. J. B., 169, 171
Maehr, M., 154
Magee, Mary Ann, 71, 81
Mandler, J., 31–32, 74
Mannheim, Karl, 207
Markers, 79–80
Marshall, M. J., 167
Marshall, S., 25–26
McCabe, A., 74, 80–81
McCarthy, T. A., 178
McClellan, J., 170
McCloskey, D. N., 196
McDowell, John, 75
McEwan, Hunter, 29, 32, 33, 166–183,
    170–171, 172, 175, 178
McFarland, C., 137
McIntyre, A., 27
McLaren, O., 157
McNeill, William H., 10–11, 12
McPherson, G., 132
Mead, Margaret, 69
Measor, L., 132
Megill, A., 196
Michotte, A., 34
Miles, M., 127, 141, 157
Mind, conception of, 116–117
Mind and Nature (Bateson), 87
Mindfulness, of teachers, 136–137
Mishler, E., 139, 142

Moger, Angela S., 19–22
Moral imagination (Coles), 40, 181
Morality of perception (Nussbaum), 61
Morals, 79–80
Morgan, Barbara, 50, 52–55, 58, 62, 63
Morrison, Toni, 44–45, 46, 47
Mulkay, M., 212
Multi-metaphoric mind, 87
Multivocal mind of the child, 69–88
    scaffolding and, 69, 70–73
    and schools of multivocal consciousness,
        83–86
    structuralism and, 69–70, 73–82
Myths, 10, 74–75

Narrative. *See also* Stories
    in accounts of history of human conscious-
        ness, ix
    action-based approach to, 25–26
    autobiography, 131–155, 197–202, 206–
        208
    case studies, 186–191, 212–217
    defined, x, 24–27
    dialogue in, 42–48, 51, 52–55
    in education, viii–xiii
    educational value of, 3–5
    fables, 9, 12, 13–15
    fairy tales, 10, 117–122
    interpretive discussion as, 100–114
    interviews, 133–155
    life-history of teachers, 127–161
    myths, 10, 74–75
    nature of, vii–viii
    in pedagogical content knowledge (Shul-
        man), 27–35, 51, 171
    in philosophy of teaching, 26, 166–173
    relationship between teacher and, 19–
        22
    religious, 9–10, 12
    role of, 114
    self-, 129–131, 197–202, 206–208
    structuralist approach to, 25, 69–70, 73–
        82
    types of, 26
    validity of, 155–157
Narrative strategies, 211–225
    for case studies, 212–217
    in new journalism, 212–213, 217–223
Neihardt, John, 47
Nelson, J. S., 196
Nelson, K., 130

New journalism, narrative strategy for, 212–
    213, 217–223
Nias, J., 132
Night (Wiesel), 43–44, 46
Ninio, A., 70, 72, 73
Noddings, N., 132, 174, 195
Nonpositivist research, 212–213
Nonsense, 77–78
Norris, N., 187
Nussbaum, Martha C., 46, 53, 55, 57, 58,
    59, 61, 62–63, 64

Of Grammatology (Derrida), 85
Olsen, Tillie, 44–45
Order, from experience, 31–32
Orientations, 79–80
Orr, J., 30
Othus, John, 39–49
Ozick, Cynthia, 41

Pagano, J., 196
Paley, Vivian Gussin, 25–26, 91–92, 91–99,
    118, 121–122
Palmer, R., 32, 178
Pathetic fallacy, 208
Pedagogical content knowledge (Shulman),
    27–35, 51, 171
    components of, 28–29
    interpretation in, 32–33
    practical experience in, 30–32
    reflection in, 33–34
    transformation in, 34–35
    and values, 29, 31
Pedagogical interpretation (McEwan), 32
Pedagogically-seeking-eyes (Gudmundsdot-
    tir), 32–33
Pedagogy, relationship between text and,
    19–22
Pendlebury, Shirley, 33–34, 50–65, 51, 52,
    59, 63, 171
Perceptive equilibrium, 53, 54–55, 57, 63
Perceptive spontaneity, 53, 55, 56–57, 60–
    61
Perverse content, 80
Peter Rabbit, 119–121
Peterson, C., 74, 80–81
Peterson, W., 132
Philosophy of teaching, 26, 166–173
    and concept of practice, 177–180
    and critical approach by teacher, 174–175
    epistemology in, 175–176

Philosophy of teaching (*continued*)
  essentialist program in, 170–174
  evolution of practice in, 168, 169–
    173
  hermeneutics in, 176, 178–179
  interpretive approach in, 175–177
  literature versus, 11–12
  and multivocal minds of children, 85
  and new directions, 180–182
  and structure versus process, 172
  and teaching practices, 174
  themes of, 168–173
Phonology, 76–77
Photographs, 188–189, 224
Piaget, J., 73, 87, 118
Pitcher, E., 80
Plato, ix, x, 5, 12–18
Play, 72, 92–94
Plot, 74, 75–76
Polkinghorne, Donald, 33, 130, 136, 140–
  141, 156, 195
Polymorphous perversity, 82
"Portrayal" (Stake), 185
Positive focusing, by teachers, 149
Positivist research, 211–212
Powdermaker, Hortense, 190
Practical experience
  and binary concepts of children, 118–
    120
  and pedagogical content knowledge, 30–
    32
  and philosophy of teaching, 168, 169–
    173, 174
Practical reasoning, 50–52, 171
  argument appraisal standards for, 51
  dialogical other in, 51, 52–55
  types of premises in, 51–52
Prelinger, E., 80
Professional life cycle of teachers, 131–155
  described, 131–132
  Swiss study of, 133–155
Prophetic Worlds (Miller), 46–47
Propp, Vladimir, 74

Qualitative data, 189–191
Quest myth, in teacher narratives, 197, 202–
  208

Rabelais and his World (Bakhtin), 71
Raphael, R., 132
Ravitch, Diane, 197–198

Rawls, John, 53, 57, 58, 61
Raymond, D., 140
Reason, P., 156
Reassessment stage, of teacher life cycle,
  147–148
Ree, Jonathan, 167, 175
Reflection
  and life cycle of teachers, 131
  and pedagogical content knowledge, 33–
    34
  and teacher narratives, 139–140
Reflective equilibrium, 53, 54, 55, 57, 60–
  61, 63
Refuge (Williams), 40
Religious narratives, 9–10, 12
Renewal stage, of teacher life cycle, 148–
  150
Report of the Commission on the Humani-
  ties, 7
Research. *See* Educational research
Reynolds, A., 28
Rhetorical theory, 197, 211–212
Rhyming, 76–77
Richardson, L., 157
Richardson, Virginia, 50, 51–52, 53, 64
Richert, A. E., 28
Ricouer, Paul, viii, xiii, 138, 140, 141, 167,
  168, 176, 178, 181
Riddles, 75
Riley, M., 154
Riseborough, G., 159–160
Robinson, J., 32, 33, 129, 156
Roesch, E., 158–159
Romance, teacher narratives as, 197, 202–
  208
Romeo and Juliet (Shakespeare), 100–114
  focus on text of, 108–114
  misinterpretation of text of, 104–108
  revenge stories of students, 101–104
Rorty, Richard, 127, 169, 174, 175–176,
  178, 182
Rosaldo, Renato, 224
Rosen, H., x
Rosenbaum, J., 145
Ross, M., 137, 138
Rumelhart, D. E., 116
Ryle, Gilbert, 171

Safire, William, 85
St. John, Primus, 39
Sanford, N., 154

Sarbin, T., 128
Sartre, Jean-Paul, 3–4
Scaffolding, 31, 135
  and narrative, 69, 70–73
Scholes, R., 25
Schon, D., 30
Schubert, W. H., 197, 209 n. 1
Schwab, J., 28
Scollon, L., 72
Scollon, N., 72
Secord, P. F., 141
Selectivity, defined, 32
Self-narrative, 129–131, 197–202, 206–
  208
Serenity, of teachers, 153
Shabatay, V., 40
Sherman, Nancy, 61
Shulman, Lee S., 27, 28, 29, 30, 51, 171
Siegal, Jessica, 197, 202–208
Siegler, R. S., 120
Sikes, P., 132
Simons, H. W., 196, 197
Simple weighing, 62–63
Situational distance, 54
Situational immersion, 54
Small Victories (Freedman), 197, 202–
  208
Smith, D., 28
Smyth, J., 131
Social Science Research Council, 184
Sockett, Hugh, 51, 172
Sommer, R., 213
Son of the Morning Star (Connell), 46
Spence, D., 26, 156
Spender, Humphrey, 190–191
Spradley, J., 134
Stabilization stage, of teacher life cycle, 152–
  153
Stake, Robert E., 185, 212
Standardized testing, 7
Standing commitments, 56–57, 63–64
States of character, 53
Stories, 3–22, 186–187. See also Narrative
  as culture builders, 93–95
  Death at an Early Age (Kozol), 197–202,
    206–208
  defined, 25, 186
  educational value of, 3–5
  epistemological function of, 5–9
  imagination and, 39–42
  moral call of, 39–42

as natural method of learning, 92–93, 95–
  98
and other educational objectives, 6–7
in presenting narrative, 129
public versus personal meaning in, 187–
  189
qualitative data in, 189–191
selection of, 6
shared knowledge of, 5
skill-oriented subjects versus, 7
Small Victories (Freedman), 197, 202–
  208
of teachers, 195–209
transformative function of, 9–22
types of, 129
Strawson, P. F., 173
Strong evaluation, 62, 63
Structuralism, 25, 69–70, 73–82
  characters in, 80
  complications in, 80–82
  of fairy tales, 117–120
  markers in, 79–80
  morals in, 79–80
  nonsense in, 77–78
  orientations in, 79–80
  perverse content in, 80
  phonology in, 76–77
  plot in, 74, 75–76
  titles in, 80
Super, D., 132
Sutton-Smith, Brian, 69–90, 71, 72, 74, 75,
  77, 80, 81, 86, 116
Swearingen, C. J., 180
Swiss study of teacher life cycles, 133–155
  analysis of interviews in, 140–141
  coherence of narratives in, 137–138
  key hypothesis of, 160
  methodology of, 133–134
  mindfulness of informants in, 136–137
  modal sequences in, 146–150
  phases in, 134–135, 142–155
  presentation of autobiographical self in,
    138–139
  progressive condensation in, 142–145,
    150–155
  reflectiveness in, 139–140
  sampling in, 133–134

Taylor, Charles, xiii, 62, 170, 176, 178,
  179, 196
Teacher lore, 197

Teachers
    agency postures of, 53–57, 60–61, 63
    autobiography of, 131–155, 197–202,
        206–208
    biography of, 197, 202–208
    "conditional alliance" with chance, 17, 22
    conflicting signals of, 19
    and philosophy of teaching, 166–173
    planning by, 21–22
    practical reasoning by, 50–52, 171
    professional life cycle of, 131–155
    relationship between text and, 19–22
Teasdale, J., 138
Tell Me a Riddle (Olsen), 44–45
Terkel, Studs, 159
"Thick description" (Geertz), xi, 185
Thinking
    binary concepts in, 118–122
    and conception of mind, 116–117
Thinking Creatively (Tyler), 84
Three Ways of Looking at Children's Narra-
        tives (Peterson & McCabe), 80–81
Titles, 80
Towbes, L., 138
Toynbee, Arnold J., 10–11, 12
Toys, 86–87
Tragedy, teacher narratives as, 197–202,
        206–208
Transformative function
    Gorgias (Plato), 12–18
    of pedagogical content knowledge, 34–35
    of stories, 9–22
    types of transformation, 9–12
Turning the Soul: Teaching through Conver-
        sations in the High School (Haroutun-
        ian-Gordon), 100–114
Tyler, Leona E., 84

Values, and pedagogical content knowledge,
        29, 31
Van Maanen, J., 212
Veenman, S., 152
Vygotsky, L. S., 70, 72, 86–87

Waiting for Godot (Beckett), 75
Walker, Robert, 184–194, 185–186, 187
Warner, Sylvia Ashton, 25–26, 91
Warren, D., 159
Weisberg, Robert W., 84
Werner, Heinz, 73, 82
Wertsch, J., 72
White, H., 196, 198, 201, 207
White, Robert, 131, 152
Whyte, H., 24, 25, 26, 27, 29, 31
Wiesel, Elie, 43–44, 46
Wiggins, D., 52, 59
Williams, Terry Tempest, 40
Willis, Paul E., 27, 188, 191
Wilson, S. M., 28
Wineburg, S., 28
Winnicott, Donald W., 87
Witherell, Carol S., 39–49, 132, 195
Wittgenstein, L., 100, 142
Wittrock, M., 132
Wolf, D., 211
Wolfe, Tom, 213, 217
Woods, P., 132
Wyer, R., 130

Yellow Raft in Blue Water (Dorris), 44,
        47

Zeller, Nancy, 211–225, 212
Zone of proximal development (Vygotsky),
        70, 72